American and Chinese Energy Security

American and Chinese Energy Security

A Grand Strategic Approach

Ryan Opsal

LEXINGTON BOOKS
Lanham • Boulder • New York • London

Published by Lexington Books
An imprint of The Rowman & Littlefield Publishing Group, Inc.
4501 Forbes Boulevard, Suite 200, Lanham, Maryland 20706
www.rowman.com

6 Tinworth Street, London SE11 5AL, United Kingdom

British Library Cataloguing in Publication Information Available

Library of Congress Cataloging-in-Publication Data

Names: Opsal, Ryan, author.
Title: American and Chinese energy security : a grand strategic approach /
  Ryan Opsal.
Description: Lanham : Lexington Books, [2019] | Includes bibliographical
  references and index.
Identifiers: LCCN 2018056260 (print) | LCCN 2018060099 (ebook) | ISBN
  9781498580793 (Electronic) | ISBN 9781498580786 (cloth) |
  ISBN 9781498580809 (pbk)
Subjects: LCSH: Energy security. | Energy security—United States. | Energy
  policy—United States. | Energy security—China. | Energy policy—China.
Classification: LCC HD9502.A2 (ebook) | LCC HD9502.A2 O67 2019 (print) | DDC
  333.790951—dc23
LC record available at https://lccn.loc.gov/2018056260

Contents

List of Tables

List of Figures

Abbreviations and Acronyms

/d	Per Day
/yr	Per Year
A2/AD	Anti-Access and Area Denial
AAR	Availability, Affordability, and Reliability
APAC	Asia-Pacific
ASCI	Argus Sour Crude Index
Bbbl	Billion Barrels
bbl	Barrel
BP	British Petroleum
BTU	British Thermal Units
CCP	Chinese Communist Party
CDB	China Development Bank
CENTCOM	United States Central Command
CNOOC	China National Offshore Oil Corporation
CNP	Comprehensive National Power
CNPC	China National Petroleum Corporation
EBIT	Earnings Before Interest and Taxes
ECI	Economic Complexity Index
EIA	Energy Information Administration
EXIM	Export-Import Bank
GDP	Gross Domestic Product
HDI	Human Development Index
HHI	Herfindahl-Hirschmann Index
IEA	International Energy Agency
IMF	International Monetary Fund
IOC	International Oil Company
LNG	Liquefied Natural Gas
LOOP	Louisiana Offshore Oil Port

Mbbl	Thousand Barrels
MCI	Ministry of Chemical Industry
MMbbl	Million Barrels
MPI	Ministry of Petroleum Industry
MPT	Modern Portfolio Theory
MRBM	Medium Range Ballistic Missile
MTOE	Metric Tons of Oil Equivalent
NATO	North Atlantic Treaty Organization
NOC	National Oil Company
NPC	National People's Congress
NSS	National Security Strategy
OIP	Oil-in-Place
OECD	Organization for Economic Cooperation and Development
OPEC	Organization of the Petroleum Exporting Countries
OSR	Oil Security Rating
PCA	Principal Components Analysis
PLA	People's Liberation Army
PLAN	People's Liberation Army Navy
PRC	People's Republic of China
PSC	Politburo Standing Committee
RDJTF	Rapid Deployment Joint Task Force
ROACE	Return on Average Capital Employed
SINOPEC	China National Petrochemical Corporation
SLOCs	Sea Lines of Communication
Socal	Standard Oil of California
SOE	State-Owned Enterprise
SPR	Strategic Petroleum Reserve
SSN	Nuclear Powered Attack Submarine
SWI	Shannon-Weiner Index
TPEC	Total Primary Energy Consumption
TPES	Total Primary Energy Supply
ULCC	Ultra Large Crude Carrier
UN	United Nations
USAID	United States Agency for International Development
USD	United States Dollar
VLCC	Very Large Crude Carrier
VSTOL	Vertical Short Take-Off and Landing
WTI	West Texas Intermediate
WTO	World Trade Organization

Chapter One

Introduction

As is the case with the study of all social phenomena, the future of the oil market is inherently difficult to predict, prone to volatility, and subject to political whim. This makes determining supply, demand, price, booms, and busts a hazardous proposition even a few years ahead. For over two decades since the end of the Cold War, oil markets have witnessed bouts of business and investment cyclicality, political interruption, and technological change, resulting in sometimes radical shifts in supply, demand, and price. However, during this period, there was a broad array of factors and conditions constraining the global supply of energy resources. The combination of expensive, capital-intensive production techniques required for extraction,[1] higher reliance on heavier crudes, and increased demand placed on all sources of primary energy from China, Brazil, India, Eastern Europe, and other emerging economies strained remaining global supplies of energy. Oil, of course, was no exception, and this cacophony of demand caused a worrisome level of reserve depletion, resulting in higher overall prices and increasing volatility in the market. These issues were especially acute during the latter half of the period under review in this text. This work begins its examination in 1993, when China became a net importer of oil and marks the beginning of the Middle Kingdom's necessity to move security of energy supplies to the top of their agenda; energy demand became a larger issue due to rapid economic growth, placing the same constraints on China as those placed on the United States, and these constraints have only grown over time as Chinese dependence on foreign sources of oil has increased. The timeframe under review then ends in 2012.

Since this study focuses on the post–Cold War period up through 2012, it does not fully account for the recent shale oil and gas revolution that is taking place at the time of this writing, in early 2017. Since shale development only started to become a noticeable source of energy beginning in 2010, it has only an extremely marginal impact on the study. It's also important to reiterate, over the period under review, there were real increases in the supply of crude oil available on the global market, albeit at higher prices, but global reserve growth had slowed and stagnated, and there was substantial concern as to whether there would be enough oil to meet global demand at reasonable prices in the future. This confluence of events culminated in the extremely high price levels witnessed in 2008, when demand increases in the global oil market had even debilitated the ability of Saudi Arabia to play the role of surplus producer and price balancer, denying the market an effective swing producer. This situation was highly problematic as it reinforced a focus on energy security over the 20-year period, and pressured states to fundamentally reexamine how they perceive and pursue their energy security strategies. Of notable concern is the way one of the reigning global giants of energy consumption, the United States, adapted and adjusted to the rise of China over this 20-year period. In addition, understanding how China, starting at a distinct strategic and supply disadvantage relative to the United States, has chosen to pursue its energy security strategy, concomitantly with its growing power and global clout, is worthy of examination.

The approach these two colossal consumers, China and the United States, pursue in their respective strategies for energy security and supply is a highly complex and multifaceted approach that is rooted in their respective national grand strategies. And, even though the development of responses took place in a high-price environment, before the recent tight oil and gas boom in North America, followed closely by demand growth stagnation in Asia and the subsequent drop in oil prices in 2014, it still has strong implications for the behavior of both states in their future pursuit of energy supply security. These strategies have not changed as the result of low prices, primarily due to the reality of the oil market as noted in the opening lines of this introduction. Long-term constraints and market cyclicality ensure a return to higher prices and volatility. There are already warnings regarding medium-term supply constraints,[2] and oil supplies cannot escape long-term demographic trends, increasing global economic growth, and multiple projections of long-term oil demand growth.[3] In addition, market supply and demand remains notably silent regarding the strategic considerations of competing consumers. An uncertain future means the energy security frameworks developed are the templates moving forward, for both great powers. Understanding each state's pursuit of this strategic commodity can potentially be applied to analyses of other commodities as well. In any case, the shadow of the future looms large.

Competition over secure access to energy supplies, whether under current market conditions, or orientation for future conditions, is a sensitive and volatile combination that deeply affects the global economy, especially since energy supplies are generally deemed strategic, vital resources by a state's national security policy. The emergent, and competitive, energy relationship between China, a comprehensively growing power, and the United States, the preponderant global military, economic, and political power, is consequential and impacts the entire international system. Accordingly, their approaches to energy security developed in the 1990s and 2000s will remain and intensify given the evolving security competition between these two states, and it is this condition that motivates this analysis. In order to foment such an understanding, these countries will primarily be examined using the comparative method, and will generate a statistical analysis to reinforce the comparison. Primarily, the monograph examines the following guiding questions: *how do the United States and China approach the issue of oil security; where have they converged or diverged in their approaches; and have their respective pursuits have posed a threat to each other's oil security need? Ultimately, this research aims at gauging if and how their respective approaches created an atmosphere whereby they affect or even prevent each other's energy security. If so, what would this imply for greater management of international life?*

Energy security is a complex topic, normally consisting of domestic and international dimensions. When it comes to foreign policy, utilization of a state's armed forces does seem to play a prominent role since this greatly impacts the physical availability of supplies and affects international markets by reducing threats from hostile forces. For instance, a cursory glance at the historical record and continued U.S. engagement overseas makes a cogent case that American energy security policy has a strong military component.[4] Continued U.S. political involvement and military engagements in the Middle East and persistent dominance of the Sea Lines of Communication (SLOCs), where a significant amount of global oil is transported, would seem to validate this appraisal of the U.S. approach, and would be indicative of the high priority attached to securing energy supplies. However, the approach taken by the United States is much more complex than the mere strategic deployment and application of armed force. Not only are there multiple dimensions to the approach, but the United States has even dramatically reduced energy imports from the global energy focal point, the Middle East, raising the following questions: Why does the United States continue to remain so militarily and politically active in this region? How does this approach fit into the greater security paradigm of America?[5] As for China, a typical approach to energy security has been non-militaristic "oil diplomacy" and a series of bilateral deals with resource-rich states, many times in the form of equity oil contracts,[6] political relationships, and other economic interdependencies.

This coincides with the development of a limited ability to counter aggressive acts in surrounding waters, with growing naval assertiveness towards territorial claims, especially in the South China Sea. But, as with the United States, this misses the complexity and an understanding of key components of the Chinese approach. It does not even begin to engage their approach to security of long-range supply lines in the current environment. While these two approaches do demonstrate a more aggressive tone for energy security in the 21st century, they also miss the broader and more intricate approaches taken by each state, and the various shrewd strategies taken to safeguard their energy supplies. China, for instance, has clearly elevated the security of energy resources and energy supply routes to the highest level of its security considerations. Chinese force procurement and military posture indicate a growing desire to secure the critical sea lanes feeding into the South China Sea, with particular attention paid to the Malacca Straits, where the majority of its imported oil flows. Furthermore, even the highest levels of decision-making in China indicate some emphasis on energy. Among the highest-ranking members in the Chinese Communist Party (CCP), where energy-related decisions are ultimately made, there is a continual presence of former and active members of the Chinese energy industry. For example, Zhou Yongkang, until recently a member of the Politburo Standing Committee (PSC), the highest organ of power in the party, is the former head of the China National Petroleum Corporation (CNPC) from 1996 to 1998, served at the CNPC and the Ministry of the Petroleum Industry in various high ranking capacities from 1985 to 1996, and has been in the oil industry since the late 1960s.[7] In fact, every five years, with the formation of each new Politburo Standing Committee (PSC), there are always one or two members connected to the energy industry in China, whether oil, power, or chemicals.[8] The 18th Central Party Committee, with its new PSC members, has Zhang Gaoli, who spent a great deal of time with SINOPEC and in the broader petrochemicals industry.[9] It is widely suspected that current heads of the respective national oil companies (NOCs) maintain active ties with members of the Politburo Standing Committee (PSC) and utilize it as an avenue for career progression.[10] The companies are deeply connected to top party officials and many see progression in these key state-owned enterprises (SOEs) as a way to advance their political careers in the CCP.

With similar levels of consumption, strong oil interests in the Middle East, and security stakes in Asia, the possibility of both countries entering into a more conflict prone relationship over energy supplies is a growing concern. How the United States and China have chosen to pursue their energy policies may have a direct impact on the security of one another. The international system has experienced conflict and war over energy resources in the past, and the potential of this occurring again should not be underestimated.

Both states had very different starting points and learning processes in terms of energy security in the 20th century. The United States began dealing with energy security after its shift from exporter to importer in the mid-20th century, and as a dominant, global military power after World War Two. China, on the other hand, was a constrained, autarkic, and contained power for much of the century, learning to cope in a world with the United States as the dominant global power and increasingly scarce energy supplies. China retains this same problem in the post–Cold War era as it continues to cope with U.S. hegemonic power. The different starting points of both states, as each shifted from exporter to importer, and their different geopolitical constraints, have given rise to a diverse set of approaches to energy security; approaches developed by both in accordance with their own specific constraints. However, despite the differences, there are similarities between the two in certain aspects. Furthermore, both states may even be converging in their approaches to energy security as they both "learn" and adapt over time. China has also "learned" a great deal about how best to approach energy security during the past decade, and is clearly altering its approach, in some cases modeling behavior more on American methods, which in this case includes greater reliance on the global marketplace, increasing its military capabilities, and enhancing its regional and global political clout. The inherent complexity of the issue of energy security is further convoluted by the dearth of knowledge on the topic and poor understanding of the issue in policy circles, academia, and the media, both in the United States and China. In America, there are constant reports of the need for energy independence, while at the same time decrying China's overseas expansion of its national oil companies (NOCs) as an attempt to "lock up" energy resources, supposedly in a bid to keep such resources from others.[11] On the Chinese side, the issues tend to be those of nationalism, sovereignty, and self-sufficiency as their firms scramble to lay claim to whatever global resources they can.

This monograph focuses on a single primary energy source: oil. This is due to the tremendous importance oil has played in the global economy and in global politics over the past 150 years, and its direct, extensive relationship to international politics. Furthermore, the energy stories of the United States and China over the past two decades have been primarily related to oil, and the exclusion of other energy sources will be needed in order to maintain an intensive focus on this relationship and to keep the analytical scope of this monograph manageable. However, it should be noted other sources are extremely important and interconnected. Many states have various sources of energy available and when one source is lacking, it can many times be made up with the others, especially in the case of electricity generation. For instance, states that use more coal-fired plants may have more petroleum and natural gas to use for transportation, space heating, and cooking. Other sources could easily be included in the energy security nexus as well. Renewable sources of energy have the capacity to make a state more self-reliant while satisfying certain environmental objectives. Nuclear power is another source that is directly relatable not just to energy security, but to other security issues such as nuclear proliferation.

Other reasons for the focus on oil is its place as the key form of primary energy that has been in high demand in both countries and is the most susceptible to foreign pressure resulting in a direct impact on security. Oil plays an incredibly prominent role in both countries. For instance, a brief look at petroleum statistics for 2011 will show the United States consumed 18.9 million barrels per day (MMbbl/d) and imported 8.8 MMbbl/d, which means approximately 47 percent of petroleum consumed in the United States was from overseas sources.[12] With imports that high, a state becomes very susceptible to price and supply volatility. China was in a similar situation in 2011, consuming 9.8 MMbbl/d and importing 5.5 MMbbl, resulting in importation of 56 percent of China's daily consumption.[13] However, the revolution in shale oil and gas will have a profound effect on global energy security, impacting the dependencies of both states on overseas sources of fossil fuels. These recent technological advancements have made it possible to extract vast amounts of fossil fuel resources that have been otherwise commercially unrecoverable, fundamentally impacting global supply. Commercial viability of shale resources has enhanced available reserves in both states and added to global supplies. The impact of commercially available shale is just beginning to be felt, and as production increases in the United States, and the technology is diffused globally, the effect will be increasing supplies and less dependence by both states on some overseas sources of energy. Once again, however, the extent of this impact is relatively weak during the 2000s, and the full future impact remains uncertain.

It may also be necessary to reference other sources of energy from time to time as their fluctuations possess the capacity to affect oil security. In these cases, it may be necessary to understand oil security in a broader energy context. For instance, it is difficult to understand China's domestic energy concerns without a consideration of coal, which has remained of the utmost importance in China, and will continue to be their dominant form of energy for domestic power for several decades. Of the 8.14 billion short tons of coal consumed in the world in 2011, China consumed 3.83 billion short tons, accounting for approximately 47 percent of global demand for coal.[14] This is a staggering amount, and accounts for approximately 70 percent of China's overall energy consumption.[15] Coal imports to China are low, given an abundance of domestic supply and matching production; however, emerging constraints over the last decade will be an important consideration for their internal security and cohesion, as well as for their energy security. China depends heavily on coal for power generation and heating; switching from coal to higher-cost alternatives will be difficult, but necessary, and this will place additional strain on other energy imports, including oil.[16] Many coal plants have been built as the result of *ad hoc* policies on the part of the CCP, some of which have been frantic responses to electricity shocks as happened with the severe power supply disruptions that occurred in China in the mid-2000s. Events like this are not quickly forgotten by the leadership and can impact attitudes and approaches to the security of oil supplies.

Another Sino-American energy relationship to consider for future research is the emerging business structure of new energy technology development, where emerging technical knowledge is developed and researched in the U.S. and then co-developed and scaled up in China. This has direct implications not just on energy security and oil consumption but can be a point of cooperation or a source of friction in the Sino-American relationship. Cooperative development on projects of importance to both states may provide necessary common ground to tackle energy security; however, to some this may look like a transfer of U.S. technology to China, which could result in growing resentment and increased conflict. Both states at times appear myopic in their approach to energy security, focused only on physical products of oil and gas, but both have in recent years made important steps to approach energy security in the same way Japan did after the Second World War. When Japan lost its military option to secure energy supplies, the country instead embarked on a campaign to advance their level of energy technology in all sectors and made incredible gains in energy efficiency; this approach allowed for the peaceful pursuit of Japanese energy security over the past 60 years. This is yet another key factor for a state looking to enhance its security, and the development of this approach in the United States and China is a major contributing factor to their levels of oil consumption.

In determining the points of comparison each state takes in their approach to oil security, the full range of issues pertaining to oil supply security will be examined, including: energy efficiency, diversity of supply, the reciprocal impact of the international oil companies (IOCs) and national oil companies (NOCs), advancements in technology, and price volatility, among others. An exploration of these key points of oil security, which takes place in the literature review, indicates how each state's approaches developed and evolved over time, why they share certain similarities and differences in their approaches, how they impact each other, and greater implications for the international management of global energy supplies.

PROBLEMS WITH EXISTING APPROACHES
TO ENERGY AND OIL SECURITY

The primary focus of this monograph is to determine Sino-American approaches to oil security, and why these approaches are different or similar despite the comparatively analogous situation of distinctly high consumption and pronounced reliance on foreign supplies. These differences are derived from grand strategic variance, and a closer look at energy security in general and how it fits in the grand strategies of both states will be crucial. This is required since energy acquisition is a core concern for any state, more so for global or systemic players like the United States and China. Energy is fundamental to the security and economic well-being of the state, and further understanding of each state's grand strategy will help to understand their approaches within broader grand strategic and international political economic understanding. This is important, since many current approaches to this topic use piecemeal analyses, missing crucial points of their energy security strategies, and usually utilize narrow definitions. These approaches are faulty, and energy security would be better understood as part of a state's grand strategy. Only at the level of grand strategy can one fully comprehend how states, particularly great powers, fit this crucial aspect of security into their broader strategic approach. By utilizing grand strategy as a theoretical anchor in this study, one can fully appreciate the political, economic, and security goals that are connected to the secure supply of energy resources, particularly oil.

Most sources, whether scholars, journalists, policymakers, or pundits, take a simplistic approach to energy security and merely categorize states as either producer or consumer, and then identify their energy security requirements based on a narrow or broad definition. Even the broad definitions do not place their arguments as part of a state's grand strategy, which is an important failing, or gap, this study aims to resolve and to fill satisfactorily. Analyzing American and Chinese approaches under this framework will generate a more robust approach to recognizing their own unique energy security requirements. The approaches taken by each are also highly dependent on the Sino-American relationship itself. All these peculiarities are contrary to the view taken by most sources, to treat all international political conditions as similar, assess certain countries and their respective approaches to energy security as categorically simple (*e.g.*, producer or consumer), and generate assumptions and approaches based on those simplistic categories; almost as though speaking of an energy security "black box" where all states operate in a typical fashion according to the features they exhibit. Then, the critical question is: How does one account for apparent divergences in the oil security approaches of the two largest energy-consuming states in the world, both with unique oil-demand and geopolitical conditions? Additionally, how does their strategic competition for energy resources impact their security? According to the "black box" approach, their approaches should be similar, and predictable. However, they are not similar in many ways and this is due to significant differences in their approaches to their respective grand strategies. This research brings grand strategy into the analysis, recognizing that both the United States and China are categorically different from other states in the international system and cannot be treated as "typical cases" in their approaches to energy security. This research will ultimately argue that in important aspects, Chinese and American approaches to energy security are different, and to understand these differences, an understanding of their respective grand strategies must be taken into account. The United States views energy security as part of its broader grand strategy of reliance on economic liberalism, which directly clashes with the Chinese approach that cannot rely heavily on the market due to historical unease and internal politics. These different worldviews generate different grand strategies, and by extension, different views of energy security. When accounting for grand strategy, the oil security approaches pursued by each state are more understandable.

The linkage between energy security and grand strategy is fundamental. Without a sufficient supply of primary energy in the modern era, especially oil, a state is unable to develop economically and critically, from a security perspective, cannot field a modern, effective military. Modern society relies on petroleum for cars, delivery trucks, power plants, asphalt, tanks, and fighter planes. These are all vital for a state to function. Without energy powering human activity, there isn't an economy or a military. This is such a fundamental resource, it must be accounted for in the grand strategy of a state and treated as a vital security interest that affects not only the economy, but the short and long-term security of the state as well. This threat is particularly acute for great powers with systemic interests, like the United States and China. Analyzing energy security in the context of the grand strategies of two systemically significant powers with the capacity to affect one another's energy supplies is a far more fruitful approach for examining energy. It is also important to note that for the majority of the history of mass oil consumption, a single dominant political and military power has formed the core of that system. The power of oil was realized during World War Two, and from that point forward, the United States pursued major sources of oil globally by any means, sometimes alongside European allies.

But, we are now entering an era where the United States and its allies will not be entirely dominant in their management of global supplies, agitating the broader political situation. Grand strategy is transcended at all levels by energy, cannot be ignored by any state, and provides the necessary approaches to take in securing energy supplies.

METHODOLOGY

The United States and China are the only two states similar in their levels of consumption and obligation to pursue energy supplies globally. This leaves a very limited number of cases available for examination, resulting in the use of the comparative case study method for this monograph. A key purpose of this examination is to understand the reasoning behind the various approaches and motivations to secure oil supplies by the United States and China. This research will demonstrate that Chinese and U.S. approaches to energy security are integrally rooted within their grand strategies, and are, thus, the result of their worldviews and relative power in the international system. China and the United States are also categorically different from other states, accounting for their respective national demands, systemic political-economic influence, central roles in managing international and regional politics, and their similarly enormous energy requirements. Paradoxically, though, they exhibit some divergent approaches and policies. Accordingly, in-depth comparative case study is the most useful and appropriate approach to understand and explain the reasons behind the similarities and differences in their respective approaches. The preliminary argument of this work is U.S. reliance on economic liberalism has been a cornerstone of its greater grand strategy and perceives energy security more in terms of markets and the free flow of supplies. China, on the other hand, cannot rely solely on the marketplace because of its dominance by the U.S. and the West, and it has been forced to find alternative means to secure its supply. As a component of grand strategy, their common and divergent approaches can be clearly explained.

As for the commonality that distinguishes the U.S. and China from most other states, it is their level energy consumption, which is massive. The total primary energy consumption of the United States was approximately 95 quadrillion BTU in 2009.[17] In the same year, China's consumption was approximately 90 quadrillion BTU, a 6 percent rise from the previous year.[18] As a matter of perspective, India's consumption was 22 quadrillion BTU, Japan's was 21 quadrillion BTU, and Russia's was 27 quadrillion BTU. All of Europe (European Union) was 81 quadrillion Btu.[19] Both the U.S. and China face many of the same constraints and threats to their respective supplies, as consumption on that magnitude forces heavy reliance on overseas sources of primary energy, most notably oil.

Not only will the comparative case study method be used, since these are the only two states in the international system with such high requirements for energy resources, but this examination will also employ a focused method of comparison given the existence of only two states that fit these parameters. As a result, this research will also have aspects of the intensive case study approach given the in-depth of examination for each case, much in a similar fashion to the methodological classic on deterrence by George and Smoke.[20] Each case will be handled by analyzing the various economic, military, and political approaches each state takes to ensure their security over their petroleum sources. This will allow for both similarities to surface, giving way to certain generalizations, as well as differences.[21] The differences will be especially important in this study, since detailing the differing circumstances for each case will allow for a deeper and structured examination into the multifaceted approaches states take to achieve energy security, possibly leading to "contingent generalizations."[22] These generalizations will allow a proper "fitting" within grand strategy, and will aid in our understanding of how grand strategy directs the security of energy supplies for larger consuming states.

Furthermore, this book follows a more developed approach to the structured, focused comparison drawn from more recent work on the subject.[23] Each case is drawn from the same class, or type, a well-defined research objective is established, and variables are used of theoretical interest for the purpose of explanation.[24] Standardized, structured questions are then asked reflective of the research objective and theoretical focus appropriate for that objective.[25]

Understanding approaches to energy security can be difficult since it is an interconnected issue that may be linked to many others. Without the ability to approach the issue through experimentation or large-N case studies, a comparative rationale exists to determine common themes of energy security between the two states. These common themes or differences between the two states will contribute towards understanding how and why they approach energy security within their respective grand strategies in the way they do. For instance, great powers, operating in the international state system, are forced to rely more on overseas sources, from insecure countries, along vulnerable trade routes, and as a result rely more heavily on military force as a method to ensure secure supply. Engaging these themes can provide useful information to understand how these states secure their supplies and how the modern conception of energy security has evolved over time. These common themes will also tell us typical approaches taken by large energy consuming states in order to secure their energy supplies, validating or discounting some prescribed approaches explored in the literature review. There are inherent limitations in the analysis of single cases, where current energy security generalizations are taken and used to analyze U.S. approaches to energy security and Chinese approaches to energy security individually. This simply does not provide a useful guide or general approach that states may use when their energy requirements are significantly high, at the levels of the U.S. and China. While single case studies "provide interesting insights, they do not by themselves provide clear guidance for generalization to other cases."[26]

Further rationale exists for this approach, as outlined by Lijphart, where he cites Stein Rokkan as writing that for cross-national analyses one typically pursues "macro hypotheses," being the "interrelations of structural elements of total systems," where there are a small number of cases available.[27] This focus on two states leads to the use of the comparative method, and the many similarities shared between the United States and China adds greatly to this reasoning. This case also requires the inherent flexibility afforded to the comparative method where explanations of both similarities and differences will be examined.[28]

Despite the similar massive energy requirements of both states, the U.S. and China have in some respects approached energy security in different ways. The American reliance on the market and the Chinese approach of exercising greater control over the entire supply chain are by-products of their grand strategies. Furthermore, the political and military capabilities and geographic location of each state provide further constraints or enhancements to security. Mentioned above, a key difference between the two has been an almost mercantilist approach by China to ensuring secure sources of energy overseas. For example, the Chinese engagement in overseas equity contracts to supposedly "lock up" energy sources for its sole use, and bilateral deals, has been in direct contrast to the United States' market-based approach relying on energy markets and a multilateral approach through the International Energy Agency (IEA) and the Organization for Economic Cooperation and Development (OECD).

The comparative analysis in this research will be conducted by examining the political, military, and economic approaches of both states to energy security, and by accounting for their similarities and differences in a systematic manner, in an attempt to draw out generalizations or contingent generalizations, as mentioned earlier, with data derived from several governmental, inter-governmental, and private-sector databases. Furthermore, as elaborated below, the United States and China will be rank-ordered and compared to other countries, in order to provide greater perspective. These other states are mostly from Europe, due to data availability and levels of development, but other large consumers are included as well. Several variables will be used, including material military capability involved, access to the sea lines of communication (SLOCs), total primary energy supply (TPES) available to the state, energy demand, efficiency, and the technological capability to extract oil, among others. The features for examination here are not exhaustive, but representative of some of the areas where approaches to security will be similar, and areas that will vary between the two states. In order to complete this focused comparison, an examination will be made of the literature pertaining to the transactions and deals of both states and their energy policies, congressional and government records on the subject, and various business and financial databases for specific industry information.

HOW DO WE SYSTEMATICALLY MEASURE OIL SECURITY?

How do we systematically gauge and measure oil security? While this is an inherently unique proposition for any given state, there are still a number of overlapping variables that provide evidence on the level of supply security for any one country. Just as a state's grand strategy is an inherently tailored blueprint for survival and security, there are certain features that can be measured that allow a determination of the overall view of the security situation for a given state. But, concepts like security are difficult to quantify, since there does not exist a direct way to measure such unobservable indicators. This is the same for other abstract measures like development, power, or political risk. These measures are unobserved, or indirectly measured, by mathematical modeling of observable, or directly measured, variables. The product indicators derived through this process are referred to as "latent" variables. These measurements of such latent variables have always been a challenge but can be of great importance not just in academia for theory building, but also in business or policy circles where critical decisions and comparisons must be made.

It is for this reason, many in academia[29] and government,[30] especially in the European Union,[31] have made attempts at creating a strong model for use in informing broad energy security policy, with some companies utilizing these techniques to inform business decisions.[32] These broader types of latent indicators are prevalent not only in academia and policy circles, but in business and finance as well. Take for instance the corporate or sovereign credit ratings generated by Standard & Poor's, Moody's, or Fitch. These are all multiple, amalgamated indicators subjectively weighted into a new latent variable, producing a "rating" or "score" for each corporation or sovereign state.

This is also true in other areas of credit analysis, and especially in the areas of country risk, which rely on mathematical modelling of areas including sovereign, political, and transfer risk. Various banks and consultancies such as the Eurasia Group and the Economist Intelligence Unit generate similar latent variables, published as numerical ratings for individual countries. This is a widely used practice; however, it is always a challenge to decide which variables to use as inputs in these models and then how to give proper weight to the individual variables so as to produce an accurate and robust result, with minimal subjectivity. In these cases, the utilization of a quantitatively derived variable is able to eliminate as much subjectivity as possible. Hence, that is in essence the point of creating latent variables such as these: to generate a less subjective quantitative indicator that can be used to inform theory, business, and policy. It is important to note these indicators are not meant to be used to make definitive decisions on their own but are meant to be mixed with a qualitative analysis, at least in optimal circumstances. Essentially, they are used to aid decision-making and provide condensed, comparatively less sub- jective, information to the decision maker, and to quantify the unobservable.

It still remains a difficult process to determine which variables to use as in- puts to the model, and then how to weight, or transform, the variables into the final latent variable used for scoring, ranking, and comparison. Much work has been completed on this in the financial industry, especially pertaining to credit risk, and many methods have been utilized within the country risk in- dustry. Additionally, although in its nascent stages, this approach has recently been used to generate latent variables for energy security in organizations ranging from the International Energy Agency (IEA) to European Union's Joint Research Center Commission on Energy Security, both mentioned ear- lier.[33] However, more advanced approaches to generating latent variables for energy security have emerged in recent years. These new approaches gener- ated in academia are more technically robust, but that is part of their flaw, in that these scholars have spent more time on technical skill, and less on policy and political implications for the inputs. This is simply because many in this new way of research have different backgrounds, and therefore many of these models have not been created with sound policy or political science components, which weakens many of these same models.

THE APPROACH USED IN THIS MONOGRAPH

The primary source and methodology that will be used to generate the an- nual latent variables in this research is that of Gupta's Oil Vulnerability Index, developed in 2008.[34] Aside from generating a list of new variables for his index, Gupta utilized a different statistical technique,[35] for weighting the variables in an attempt to standardize the process and further remove subjectivity from the results. This has always been a weak point in these analyses; an area of high subjectivity as it is completely left to the user to determine the best weights attributed to each variable, or each category of variables. Gupta attempts to overcome this by using the statistical approach called principal components analysis, which is an advanced technique used in multivariate statistics, where the variables tend to be highly correlated, creating new variables in the process.

This is a factor analysis, dimension reduction technique and not one typically applied in the social sciences. For instance, this technique is one of the primary approaches used in facial recognition software.[36] There are a high number of data points on the human face and this data as a whole is reduced and transformed, from a 2-dimensional matrix to a 1-dimensional vector, essentially creating a lesser number of new variables in the process. The object, however, of this research, as with Gupta's, is not necessarily data reduction and the creation of new "principal component" variables, but to use instead the weightings derived by the technique to determine the relative importance of each input variable. Through this process of dimension reduction, it is determined mathematically, which input variables account for the highest degree of variance in the entire dataset, entitling them to higher weightings according to their relative importance to the data as a whole. This has been a very successful technique and is used in other areas. It has even been proposed that better-known social science indices, such as the Human Development Index (HDI), utilize a PCA to determine the final composite score for each country in the index, which currently takes the geometric mean of the three normalized indicators, life expectancy, education, and income.[37]

Gupta derives his approach from an engineering-based infrastructure study conducted by Nagar and Basu[38] and while using Gupta's research as a primary source for developing the techniques used in this research, several important points were gleaned from Nagar and Basu's other work on human development,[39] given its more direct social science leanings.

THE VARIABLES REPRESENTING THE OBSERVABLE COMPONENTS OF ENERGY SECURITY

The full model, populated with the observable variables, is termed the Oil Security Rating (OSR), and generates a final OSR score, which includes ten key variables used as inputs. Unless otherwise noted, all data is derived from EIA[40] and IEA[41] databases. The indicators used follow.

Oil Intensity:

The first variable is oil intensity, which is a calculation that represents the amount of oil required to produce one unit of economic output. In order to arrive at this figure, we convert oil consumption in the economy to metric tons of oil equivalent (MTOE), and then divide by the country's gross domestic product (GDP) at market exchange rates, in constant 2005 dollars. For ease of access, this research drew from The Shift Project, an independent energy think tank based in Paris, which draws its data for this figure from the EIA and UN.[42]

Production to Reserves:

This is an annualized ratio that demonstrates the potential amount of time left, usually indicated in years, to deplete a country's oil reserves at current production levels, and at economically viable levels. This is determined by dividing the reserve amounts by the level of production for the same year, both measured in barrels. The author completed the calculations with the data drawn from the EIA and IEA.

Import Dependence:

This is a frequently used metric for energy security, demonstrating the shortfall of domestic sources of petroleum to domestic consumption. This measures dependence on external, overseas sources of oil, increasing the ratio with higher levels of external dependence. There are two ways to measure this amount, represented by the EIA and IEA. The EIA simply takes net oil imports divided by consumption, while the IEA calculates this ratio by taking the difference domestic consumption and domestic production. These allow arrival at nearly the same figures, but this research utilizes the EIA approach, simply dividing net imports of petroleum by overall oil consumption in the economy.

Oil in Total Primary Energy Consumption (TPEC):

This looks at energy consumption as a whole throughout the country, cataloging all primary sources, including fossil fuels (petroleum, natural gas, coal), renewables (solar, wind, hydroelectric), and nuclear. This measures all energy utilized in a country in given year, and the variable takes as a ratio the percentage that oil makes up of the whole economy's consumption. Oil consumption is simply divided by the amount of total consumption. This informs the level of structural dependence on oil as an individual source of energy in the target country. The author completed the calculations.

Oil Price Volatility:

For long-term security and economic interests, stability in the price of oil is essential. This variable is a normalized indicator accounting for the small variation in pricing between the WTI crudes and Dubai crudes, used for pricing exports to the United States and Asia, respectively. This indicator is a proxy for oil price volatility and uses the standard deviations of the previously annualized monthly averages for each type of crude, creating a range-bound variable. The author using data drawn from the BP Statistical Database completed these calculations.[43]

Supply Diversity:

Using an approach mentioned heavily in previous sections, to measure the level of supply diversity, meaning the national and geographic level of import concentration for each country, this research will use a modified Herfindahl-Hirschmann Index (HHI). The HHI is in wide use for multiple purposes, however, its most notable use is by the Department of Justice for determining the level of market concentration in a given sector of the economy.[44] Just as in the same way the Department of Justice uses this method to determine which one single firm has gained too much market share and control in a sector or industry, this research uses the measure to determine when too much oil is coming from too few sources, meaning the individual supplier countries. Higher levels of concentration result in negative scores for the indicator. The following formula is used, with variables provided in more detail in chapter 3:

$$HHI = \sum_{a=1}^{n} c_a^2$$

In this formula, a indicates the number of each country from the first to the open-ended last, represented by n, and c represents the actual country being analyzed. Each state's share of exports to the country under analysis is squared and added to all other export countries, originally resulting in scores ranging from 0 (the best theoretical score representing a purely competitive, atomized market) to 10,000 (representing a pure monopoly). These scores are then rescaled for this research on a 0 to 1 scale and used for the input variables. These calculations were completed by the author using data derived from the United Nations Comtrade Database using HS Commodity Code 2709 (petroleum oils, oils from bituminous minerals, crude).[45]

Consumption to Proved Reserves:

This is a variable used to measure the amount of domestic sources available to the state, based on current pricing and consumption levels, for a given year. This is meant to simulate an extreme scenario and to understand how long a state can survive cut off from overseas markets, without any decreases in consumption. It is calculated by dividing annual consumption over the overall proved reserves of the state.

Net Oil Imports to GDP:

This indicator tests the overall sensitivity of the economy to oil price and supply shocks. The larger the proportion of oil in the economy, the greater sensitivity the direct economy will have to any shocks. Energy touches all aspects of the economy indirectly, but this measure is meant to gauge the direct impact in terms of pricing to the overall economy. Net oil imports are derived from the EIA database while the GDP figures are at market exchange rate from the International Monetary Fund.[46]

National Power:

A power measurement is also incredibly important and one of the more notable features lacking in other energy security models. This is more representative of the capacity of a state to sufficiently respond to security issues involving the oil supply chain. This is the ability to rapidly respond to threats, and the resources to sustain those efforts over time. National power is perhaps the most thoroughly explored quantitative indicator in international relations, and as such, there are multiple studies regarding this measure, one which, in one way or another, has been studied for several thousand years.[47] There is a diverse array of measures, ranging from the classics,[48] to the new and innovative,[49] but since this is an indicator being used as an input to another model, parsimony was given preference for the measure.[50] This research will use the preferred model by Chin-Lung Chang.[51] The following formula is remarkably indicative of existing power relationships despite its parsimonious presentation, and the data is readily available.

$$power = \frac{critical\ mass + economic\ strength + military\ strength}{3}$$

Again, power in this case is primarily referring to hard power, including its latent potential. The individual components are calculated as follows:

$$critical\ mass = \left(\frac{country\ population}{world\ population}\right) \times 100 + \left(\frac{country\ area}{world\ area}\right) \times 100$$

$$economic\ strength = \left(\frac{country\ GNP}{global\ GNP}\right) \times 200$$

$$military\ strength = \left(\frac{country\ military\ spending}{global\ military\ spending}\right) \times 200$$

The author performed these calculations by using the IMF data for population, area, and GNP (Gross National Product) measures while the measure for military strength was derived using data from the Stockholm International Peace Research Institute (SIPRI).[52]

Massachusetts Institute of Technology Economic Complexity Ratings:
This is a fascinating indicator drawn directly from a special project and database supported by MIT which gauges the level of economic "complexity" in a given country. This project will rely on this indicator as a general measure, or proxy, of the overall level of economic advancement in the country, with special regard to the knowledge economy and entrepreneurship. This is a necessary measure since technological advancements have ushered in extraordinary change in the energy sector, the recent tight oil boom only the most recent. These types of advancements can be most closely gauged by demonstrating a dynamic and flexible economy. These ECI ratings are meant to be an indicator of the capacity of meaningful technological advancement available to the entire state. This also adds a certain level of dynamism to the model, accounting for the possibility that advances in the broader economy and the energy sector can significantly, and positively, impact oil security. Furthermore, many new indicators that attempt to gauge this might be sufficient, but only utilize data going back a few years or tend to be highly indirect at best. The economic complexity scores from MIT are much more direct, and they have generated these scores going back to the 1980s in many cases, with very few gaps. This represents the most complete way to measure these impacts with a sufficient time horizon. According to the information provided with the datasets, the conceptual reasoning behind the scores is based on Adam Smith's concept of the division of labor and the availability of the "multiplicity of useful knowledge embedded in it."[53] Additionally, they state that more advanced products "embed large amounts of knowledge and are the results of very large networks of people and organizations . . . [and] these products cannot be made in simpler economies that are missing parts of this network's capability set."[54] Finally, they express economic complexity as the "composition of a country's productive output and reflects the structures that emerge to hold and combine knowledge."[55] Utilizing a time-series measure of this nature is unique and adds increased robustness to the study, measuring the capacity for technological innovation that is otherwise absent from other studies on oil security. The scores generally range from 0 to 2 but for the model these are normalized on a 0 to 1 scale using all countries included in the study.

CONCLUDING REMARKS

Ultimately, this focused comparative monograph allows for generalization of certain oil security approaches by states in similar large-consumption, and competitive, scenarios. This provides a blueprint for understanding strategic interaction in a competitive environment, and in a potentially high-price, low-reserve environment. Furthermore, using data and a quantitative approach reinforces and enhances the primary qualitative approach taken in this work. The composite scores, acting as the overall score, will provide a broad indicator for overall security, and the individual indicators can be examined to understand their resulting impacts on the overall score, aiding in our understanding of how these two states have shifted their approaches over time. All the calculations described in this section provide this single composite rating, allowing for a more direct and objective qualitative comparison between both the United States and China on an annualized basis. This informs and enriches the work, giving further empirical substance for debate and theory building. The scoring, coupled with the primarily qualitative comparison, in this volume provides a rich overview of these two states' approaches to oil security.

NOTES

1. For instance, oil sands in Canada and global deepwater production.

2. Andrew Ward, "Saudi Aramco Warns Investment Cuts Risk Long-term Oil Crunch: Crude Producer Says Overall Demand for Fossil Fuels Will Continue to Rise," *Financial Times*, October 11, 2016, https://www.ft.com/content/14ec741a-8f94-11e6-8df8-d3778b55a923 (accessed January 15, 2017); Matt Clinch, "Oil CEO Sees 'Significant' Impact on Capacity in the Coming Years," Consumer News and Business Channel (CNBC), January 20, 2017, http://www.cnbc.com/2017/01/20/oil-ceo-sees-significant-impact-on-capacity-in-the-coming-years.html (accessed January 15, 2017).

3. A good point of reference is the International Energy Agency's World Energy Outlook for 2016, found here: http://www.iea.org/newsroom/news/2016/november/world-energy-outlook-2016.html.

4. For instance, U.S. guarantees to Saudi Arabia beginning with President Roosevelt, the inception of the Carter Doctrine declaring the Persian Gulf a "vital interest" paired with the establishment of the Rapid Deployment Force (RDF), and continued dominance by the U.S. Navy of the global commons.

5. As will be explained later in the research, this is primarily due to the U.S. stake in not only physical and regional supplies, but in the entire global energy market, which is dependent on Persian Gulf oil.

6. Joseph Y. S. Cheng, "A Chinese View of China's Energy Security," *Journal of Contemporary China* 17:55 (2008): 297–317.

7. "Zhou Yongkang," *China Vitae*, http://www.chinavitae.com/biography/Zhou _Yongkang (accessed July 5, 2015); Zhou Yongkang has been part of the oil industry for over 40 years beginning in 1961 as a student at the Beijing Petroleum Institute. He held numerous posts over the course of his career including with the Liaohe Oil Exploration Bureau, the Petroleum Administration, Tarim Oil Exploration Campaign Headquarters, the Ministry of Petroleum Industry, and China National Petroleum Corporation. He was involved in politics much of that time before leaving in 1998 to focus solely on politics.

8. Author survey of Politburo Standing Committee members starting in 1992 with the 14th CPC Central Committee using information from: *China Vitae*, Reference Library, www.chinavitae.com/library. *China Vitae* is an excellent broad source on CCP personnel and is affiliated with the Wilson Center's Kissinger Institute on China and the United States.

9. "Zhang Gaoli," *China Vitae*, http://www.chinavitae.com/biography/Zhang _Gaoli (accessed July 5, 2015): Zhang Gaoli was with SINOPEC from 1970 to 1984, and then Maoming Petrochemical Company from 1984 to 1985, before moving strictly into politics.

10. Eric Downs and Michal Meidan, Business and Politics in China: The Oil Executive Reshuffle of 2011, *China Security* Issue 19 (2011): 3–21.

11. Christopher Swann and Wei Gu, "With Oil Deals, Merger Advisors Rejoice," *New York Times*, http://www.nytimes.com/2010/04/15/business/15views.html ?dbk&_r=0 (accessed February 23, 2015).

12. International Energy Statistics, Energy Information Administration, http://www.eia.gov/cfapps/ipdbproject/IEDIndex3.cfm (accessed March 23, 2015).

13. Ibid.

14. Author's calculations using previously referenced EIA data.

15. International Energy Statistics, Energy Information Administration (accessed March 23, 2015).

16. Ibid.

17. International Energy Statistics, Energy Information Administration (accessed March 23, 2015).

18. Ibid.

19. Ibid.

20. Alexander L. George and Richard Smoke, *Deterrence in American Foreign Policy: Theory and Practice* (New York: Columbia University Press, 1974), 95–103; Alexander L. George, "Case Studies and Theory Development: The Method of Structured, Focused Comparison," in *Diplomacy: New Approaches in History, Theory and Policy*, ed. Paul G. Lauren, 43–68 (Free Press, 1979).

21. George and Smoke, *Deterrence in American Foreign Policy: Theory and Practice*, 95.

22. Ibid., 96.

23. Alexander L. George and Andrew Bennett, *Case Studies and Theory Development in the Social Sciences* (Cambridge, MA: MIT Press, 2005), 67–124.

24. Ibid., 67–69.

25. Ibid.

26. Christopher H. Achen and Duncan Snidal, "Rational Deterrence Theory and Comparative Case Studies," *World Politics* 41:2 (1989): 146.

27. Arend Lijphart, "Comparative Politics and the Comparative Method," *The American Political Science Review* 65:3 (1971): 682–693.

28. Robert A. Segal, "In Defense of the Comparative Method," *Numen* 48, no. 3 (2001): 339–373.

29. Edgard Gnansounou, "Assessing the Energy Vulnerability: Case of Industrialized Countries," *Energy Policy* 36 (2008) 3734–3744.

30. Gail Cohen, Frederick Joutz, and Prakash Loungani, "Measuring Energy Security: Trends in the Diversification of Oil and Natural Gas Supplies" (Working Paper, International Monetary Fund Research Department, 2011); Jessica Jewell, "The IEA Model of Short-term Energy Security (MOSES) Primary Energy Sources and Secondary Fuels" (International Energy Agency 2011).

31. Anca Costescu Badea, "Energy Security Indicators" (European Commission Joint Research Centre, Institute for Energy Security Unit 2010), http://www.jrc.ec.europa.eu/.

32. "Oil Security Index," *Quarterly Update* (Securing America's Energy Future in partnership with Roubini Global Economics 2014).

33. Jessica Jewell, "The IEA Model of Short-term Energy Security (MOSES) Primary Energy Sources and Secondary Fuels" (International Energy Agency 2011); Anca Costescu Badea, "Energy Security Indicators" (European Commission Joint Research Centre, Institute for Energy Security Unit 2010), http://www.jrc.ec.europa.eu/.

34. Eshita Gupta, "Oil Vulnerability Index of Oil-Importing Countries," *Energy Policy* 36 (2008): 1195–1211.

35. This is one of the first times this technique was used to measure energy security.

36. Kyungnam Kim, "Face Recognition using Principal Components Analysis," Department of Computer Science, University of Maryland College Park, http://www.umiacs.umd.edu/~knkim/KG_VISA/PCA/FaceRecog_PCA_Kim.pdf; Federal Bureau of Investigation, https://www.fbi.gov/about-us/cjis/fingerprints_biometrics/biometric-center-of-excellence/files/face-recognition.pdf

37. A. L. Nagar and Sudip R. Basu, "Weighting Socio-Economic Indicators of Human Development: A Latent Variable Approach," in *Handbook of Applied Econometrics and Statistical Inference* eds. A. Ullah, Alan T. K. Wan, and Anoop Chaturvedi (New York: Marcel Dekker, Inc., 2002); United Nations Development Program, Human Development Report 2013, http://hdr.undp.org/sites/default/files/hdr_2013_en_technotes.pdf.

38. A. L. Nagar and Sudip R. Basu, "Infrastructure development index: an analysis for 17 major Indian states," *Journal of Combinatorics, Information and System Science* 27 (2002): 185–203.

39. Ullah and Wan, "Weighting," *Handbook of Applied Econometrics and Statistical Inference*.

40. International Energy Statistics, Energy Information Administration (accessed March 29, 2015).

41. Statistics, International Energy Agency, http://www.iea.org/statistics/ (accessed March 26, 2015).

42. Energy Intensity of GDP, The Shift Project Data Portal (Paris, France: The Shift Project) http://www.tsp-data-portal.org/Energy-Intensity-of-GDP#tspQvChart (accessed March 26, 2015).

43. "Statistical Review 2014: Data Workbook," BP, http://www.bp.com/en/global/corporate/energy-economics/statistical-review-of-world-energy/downloads.html (accessed July 23, 2015).

44. "Herfindahl-Hirschmann Index," The United States Department of Justice, https://www.justice.gov/atr/herfindahl-hirschman-index (accessed June 14, 2015).

45. United Nations Comtrade Database, United Nations (New York: United Nations Statistics Division), http://comtrade.un.org/ (accessed July 17, 2015).

46. "IMF Data" (New York: International Monetary Fund), http://www.imf.org/en/Data (accessed July 15, 2015).

47. Karl H. Höhn, "Geopolitics and the Measurement of National Power" (PhD Dissertation, Universität Hamburg, 2011): 53–58.

48. Ray S. Cline, "The Power of Nations in the 1990s: A Strategic Assessment" (Lanham: University Press of America, 1994); Wilhelm Fucks, "Mächte von Morgen: Kraftfelder, Tendenzen, Konsequenzen" (Stuttgart: Deutsche Verlags-Anstalt, 1978); F. C. German, "A Tentative Evaluation of World Power," *Journal of Conflict Resolution* 4:1 (1960); David J. Singer and Melvin Small, "The Diplomatic Importance of States, 1816–1970: An Extension and Refinement of the Indicator," *World Politics* 24:4 (1973).

49. Karl Höhn, "New Thinking in Measuring National Power" (paper presented at the 2nd Global International Studies Conference by the World International Studies Committee (WISC) at the University of Ljubljana, Ljubljana, Slovenia, July 23–26, 2008) (for instance, this particular work focuses on the overall balance of the national economy using the concentric mean); Gregory Treverton and Seth G. Jones, "Measuring Power: How to Predict Future Balances," *Harvard International Review* 27:2 (2005) (this model was built for long-term projections, and the models and data are maintained through the University of Denver).

50. For an exhaustive, recent study on attempts at modeling national power, reference Höhn 2008.

51. Chin-Lung Chang, "A Measure of National Power," Fo-guang University, Taiwan.

52. Military Expenditure Database (Stockholm: Stockholm International Peace Research Institute) http://www.sipri.org/research/armaments/milex/milex_database (accessed March 11, 2015).

53. AJG Simoes and CA Hidalgo, "The Economic Complexity Observatory: An Analytical Tool for Understanding the Dynamics of Economic Development," Workshops at the Twenty-Fifth AAAI Conference on Artificial Intelligence (2011); References in this study are made specifically concerning data derived from the Economic Complexity website and database: *The Observatory of Economic Complexity*, http://atlas.media.mit.edu/en/resources/economic_complexity/ (accessed August 21, 2016).

54. Ibid.

55. Ibid.

Chapter Two

Grand Strategy

INTRODUCTION

A thorough understanding of grand strategy is required in order to appreciate how critical energy is to a state's long-term security requirements, and how energy policies are generated and altered by domestic actors, external diplomatic initiatives, and the short and long-term economic and security environment. After consideration of the many aspects of grand strategy, a review of energy security will be conducted in the following chapter. It is important to think of these two areas as inextricably linked, and how constraints that act on grand strategy have similar impacts on energy security as well. These are complex, interrelated issues, especially when dealing with great powers.

Policy constraints exist both internally and externally and must be fully accounted for in order to catalogue the changes and shifts in policy over time. For the domestic environment, interest groups, public policy, environmental costs, industry, and technology have significant impact on policy. The other more external aspects, such as diplomacy and the geopolitical environment of oil, will form the cornerstone of the research, and are of the utmost importance. Each state has its own advantages and disadvantages when managing their supply security; however, this volume does make the argument that the United States has the clear advantage in this facet of energy security despite some high levels of domestic alarmism. This point, it will be contended, also has greater implications for the conclusions drawn later in the text, pertaining to direct Sino-American energy relations and the broader strategic relationship. It is also argued that China is following a similar path as was followed by the United States in its attempts to secure overseas sources of energy, although the path may at times be cautious and tepid.

Grand strategy is ultimately understood as a cost-benefit analysis in a world of scarce resources and hard-fought security. Carl von Clausewitz sums it up best by famously stating, "war is not an exercise of the will directed at inanimate matter, as is the case with the mechanical arts, or at matter which is animate but passive and yielding, as is the case with the human mind and emotions in the fine arts. In war, the will is directed at an animate object that reacts."[1] This cost-benefit analysis and "animate objects that react," under the umbrella of scarcity, result in strategic interaction. This strategic interaction involves the interrelationship of several high-level categories of security, to which this research elevates energy security. Permeating these high levels is also a complex set of objectives, threats, and capabilities that will ultimately determine grand strategic outcomes. All of this comes together to form a coherent and more encompassing approach to energy security that will be utilized by analyzing the approach between China and the United States in chapters 3 and 4. At the level of grand strategy, the major components are so interrelated that a weakness in one will prevent the successful fruition of the strategy in general. In this sense, all the components are completely reliable, and interrelated to one another, whereby the security of the state is in peril without proper consideration of each component individually and its relationship to the other components. The following section will begin with a more in-depth understanding of grand strategy and why the intricacies of this approach more fully account for energy security approaches by states.

What Is Grand Strategy?

In this work, the notion of grand strategy will serve as a theoretical referent, or context, to anchor the examination of energy security policy approaches by the U.S. and China. Accordingly, in order to demonstrate each state's respective energy security approaches, there must be a clear understanding of grand strategy. Grand strategy has generated many variances, with some scholars denying that grand strategy is even separate from other areas of research.[2] So, what is grand strategy? What is it not? Why is it so important?

Referencing the brief discussion of grand strategy in chapter 1, it concludes by stating broadly that grand strategy is the national reconciliation of means and ends; the feasible objectives given the limited resources available to the state. It is the long-term approach to survival and security of a particular state, accounting for specific threats, utilizing all forms of statecraft at its disposal, whether it is military, economic, or political. Grand strategy essentially provides the "political" ends which guide Clausewitz's "war," or strategy. Despite this rather inclusive conceptualization, there is by no means a universally accepted approach or definition to grand strategy, making it at times difficult to compare. However, all states have one, even if not explicitly stated or in full cognizance, "because grand strategy is simply the level at which knowledge and persuasion, or in modern terms intelligence and diplomacy, interact with military strength to determine outcomes in a world of other states with their own 'grand strategies.'"[3] Whether accidental, concerted, planned, or confused, a grand strategy is present at the very least as the aggregate of state function and as bureaucratic reaction to other states' strategies. And, these should over time create a "coherent body of thought and action geared toward the accomplishment of important long-term aims."[4]

States cannot do without grand strategy because it is critically important and vital, which in the words of Edward Meade Earl is "the highest type of strategy,"[5] and as Christopher Layne points out beginning with his own explanation of grand strategy as "the most crucial task of statecraft."[6] Indeed, grand strategy is at its very core concerned with the enduring survival of the state; it is crucial, and central to all other considerations.

And, just as Posen points out that military doctrinal mismatch with the threat or political environment can end with poor results, it is the position of this research that blatant mismatch in any of the major categories of grand strategy can prove catastrophic, and failings at the grand strategic level are often the most difficult to overcome. Grand strategic calculations are made with "conflict unfold[ing] at separate levels—grand strategic, theater-strategic, operational, tactical—which interpenetrate downward much more easily than upward."[7] Just in the way Hitler's gross grand strategic miscalculation of allies and enemies couldn't be countered by the brilliant theater-, operational-, and tactical-level victories of the German military,[8] no amount of multi-level successes and victories by General Lee and the Confederate Army could have overcome the weaknesses in all other areas of statecraft, eventually succumbing to the Union's superior supply lines, industry, and numbers, in a conflict essentially lost before it started.

Additionally, it's not just blatant mismatches in grand strategy that states must be concerned with, but other seemingly smaller issues that over time can begin to decrease security, as with the conflation of capabilities and objectives. As Christopher Fettweis points out, "influence, presence, credibility—even alliances have all too often become the ends of policy in themselves, raising the possibility of conflict in the process."[9] This conflation of means and ends can have a deleterious long-term impact on state security, committing resources where they are not needed, sapping strength, and potentially creating new frictions and enemies along the way. This concept is not new to statecraft. It is perhaps espoused most succinctly by Frederick the Great's dictum that "Generals with little experience wish to save everything: those who are wise consider only the principal point, seeking to ward off large blows and patiently suffering minor misfortunes in order to avoid large ones. He who attempts to defend too much defends nothing."[10] Simply put, scarcity requires the thoughtful application of state resources.

And, in the clear majority of cases, a state typically does not have the luxury to choose most components of its grand strategy, simply because there may be many fixed components to the threat environment of a state, out of which a state's strategy is derived, and in which it will become necessarily defined. For instance, the state of Israel cannot simply pick up and move elsewhere, and thus will have a grand strategy significantly defined by that particular threat environment. The same is true of, for instance, the Baltic states, with comparatively small populations, resources, and who cannot divorce themselves from their Cold War past and the imposed strategic reality of their close proximity to the Soviet successor state of Russia. Fettweis refers to this useful concept as strategic flexibility[11] and as will be seen in later chapters, the United States does exist in a privileged environment given its inherent strategic flexibility following the end of the Cold War, directly dichotomous to China, which has several, severe constraints on its grand strategic formulations. So, how does statecraft produce an effective plan for survival?

Before tackling these questions, it should be noted there is an issue with a theoretical understanding of grand strategy: the rather fluid nature of the concept. A theory implies some universality that can be applied to related events or objects of study, under different circumstances. This means some degree of commonality must be identified; some causal logic that connects the seemingly unconnected. For example, one can examine the dominant theoretical strand in international relations, Realism, and note a key underlying premise, which is the distribution of material power, and then make causal predictions from that premise, ultimately utilizing its explanatory power to understand all states that fall under that rubric, which is at the very least, great powers. Alternatively, with the democratic peace theory, it is understood that this theoretical approach is meant to explain outcomes pertaining to war and peace among, specifically, democratic states. Grand strategy, and strategy in general, is much more problematic given the greater variance in actions and outcomes from one state to another. Security and survival are taken as the ultimate objectives, but the capabilities, threats, and lesser objectives that "cause" security will be distinctive. In fact, John Gaddis ponders this point in one of his many writings on grand strategy. The fact that grand strategy is different and unique to every state, based on threat and capability, makes one wonder if a universal strategic logic exists; as Gaddis explains:

> Much of the confusion over whether strategic "logic" exists or not stems from the fact that we have never made the criteria for "success" in strategy—and particularly in "grand strategy"—very clear. [Grand strategy] . . . requires the

integration of military strategy with such non-military considerations as politics, economics, and psychology, law, and morality, and it involves doing so over indeterminate periods of time. Specifying what constitutes success under those conditions is indeed no easy task.[12]

Problems mount when accounting for what Edward Luttwak describes as the persistent "paradoxical logic of strategy," whereby frequently the "poor" option is the "best" and vice versa, all in order to gain surprise, or minimize risk and friction.[13] He typically begins with the oft quoted Roman proverb *si vis pacem, para bellum* (if you want peace, prepare for war), and gives numerous examples of these paradoxes. For instance, one of his cases involves nuclear deterrence, where in order to defend one must be ready to attack at all times, and in order to be effective, one must not use the very costly nuclear weapons acquired.[14] The true, and indeed only, strategic impact of acquiring the most destructive weapons humanity has yet to conceive resides in their utter disuse. Thankfully, we have yet to arrive at Oppenheimer's "destroyer of worlds." To Luttwak, strategy lacks any degree of linearity, especially when one rises to the level of grand strategy and in a way echoes Liddell Hart's "indirect approach" with the application of energy where the enemy least expects. He ultimately draws on an approach to strategy as "the art of the dialectics of wills that use force to resolve their conflict,"[15] which seems to pervade much of his work on the subject.

Some criticize Luttwak's paradox by pointing out that to proceed logically, one must take context into account. For instance, he often utilizes the analogy of an army marching on the long, unpaved road, which is preferred to the shorter, paved road since that one will be guarded and its use expected by an adversary, whereas the former (unpaved) road will not. However, with context considered, logically an armed force should not expect, during wartime, that the short, paved road would be the best road, but that the long, unpaved road would be preferable.[16] However, this isn't necessarily true, as the distinction between various contexts is often blurred in international politics and grand strategy, along with state perceptions of which "roads" are actually preferred or less preferred. In a sense, that is the point of strategic interaction: understanding the best approach to a given problem while being conscious of the competitor's reactions in a murky context.

Not only that, but if per "context," the less preferred road is always the preferable route to take, as Gregory Johnson suggests, then there isn't any strategic logic since the choice is automatically made *ex ante* and the competitor will react accordingly, and predictably. This is reducing the process down to simple, deterministic, linear decision-making, something that cannot be done in order to achieve optimal strategic outcomes. Luttwak promotes an approach far more cognizant of the inherent temporal fluidity and fluctuating nature of strategy where a scheme one day is surprising, while the next it is commonplace. Indeed, if an army takes the same road all the time, no matter what road it is, it can no longer be considered a surprise.

John Gaddis, while elucidating his own opinion of grand strategy, suggests it as an enduring concept, more theoretical in nature, and in the same vein as Clausewitz's distinction between theory and practice; something meant to stimulate thought, rather than be "carried into the field." But in a more direct sense, his core recurring theme for grand strategy is the fundamental difficulty in "balancing the risks against the costs of securing vital interests."[17] Gaddis goes on to state, with perhaps some of his own "paradoxical logic," that "Destruction, after all, can come either from the actions of adversaries or from what you do to yourself. These two priorities compete, because the things you do to minimize risks tend to drive up costs; but the things you do to minimize costs tend to drive up risks."[18] It's almost as if the logic of grand strategy carries with it an intrinsic equilibrium or balance that must be maintained per specific circumstance.

In Gaddis' conception, risk-minimizing actions entail attrition campaigns, large military presences, reliance on technology, industry, an open-ended timeframe, and most importantly, "unlimited resources" and "steady political support."[19] On the other hand, cost minimizing focuses on tactics, maneuver, surprise, technology to rapidly move conflict forward, urgency, and crucially, the constraining forces of "limited resources" and "limited political support."[20] At the level of grand strategy, these trade-offs certainly still exist.

However, while Gaddis is correct in characterizing grand strategic decision-making as consistent with an inherent tension between risk and cost, this may not always be the case, nor will they always be mutually exclusive. Take the unambiguous instance of a state engaged in imperial overreach. In Gaddis's conception, this is a strategy of risk minimization, which results in more engagement, resulting in decreased risk, but at the price of increased costs. But, in the case of overreach, there's no tension; there is both increased risk and increased cost. If the overreaching political unit withdraws to maintain manageable boundaries, there will be less risk and reduced cost. The opposite would be low risk and low cost, clearly optimal as opposed to the other. But, perhaps aside from more extreme examples, this approach is instructive. For instance, as Gaddis would apply this tension to grand strategy, with the utilization of containment, there is typically symmetrical and asymmetrical containment. This is conceptualized in much the same way of risks and costs, where the former "strategy expends resources in order to play it safe; the [latter] takes chances to avoid expending resources."[21] Containment of the Soviet Union followed much the same process with George Kennan's approach emphasizing psychological aspects over the physical, but with the final NSC-68 document emphasizing physical, kinetic approaches over other asymmetric approaches.[22]

So, if each state is required to pursue a unique grand strategy, determined by the inherent capabilities, threats, and objectives present, and there are inherent tensions and paradoxes, how does one approach this as a unifying concept towards the ultimate objective of state survival?

In a sense, there is no perfect answer. Just as there is yet to be a perfect theoretical understanding of war and conflict in the interstate system, grand strategy itself, unsurprisingly, rests in an indeterminate existence, with waters further muddied by "outcomes depend[ent] not only upon the quality of one's thought, or the efficiency of one's actions, but upon circumstances not wholly under one's control, most notably the actions of adversaries and the role of the unforeseen."[23] Perhaps this variance gives cause to reason that in order to grapple with grand strategic thinking, one must view it as an "ecological discipline,"[24] disregarding any pull towards "theateritis,"[25] and approach the study as a "generalist"[26] and interdisciplinarian.[27] Grand strategy, simply put, requires a high degree of versatility and flexibility.

Another important point to consider is whether conflict or direct confrontation is worth engaging in at all. This is a very common strand of thought throughout Liddell Hart's seminal text, *Strategy*, where he has a very strong focus on the costs of war and his particular aversion to such costs. When attempting to find balance between ends and means, one must give serious thought to inaction or restraint as a serious course of action, especially if the aftermath of such actions do not result in a "better peace" for the state in question,[28] and in terms of strategy, the perfection of which "would be, therefore, to produce a decision without any serious fighting."[29]

While Liddell Hart did tend to focus on holistic grand strategy only under the auspices of conflict, he is one of the earliest to delve into the idea of grand strategy by stating:

> Grand strategy should both calculate and develop the economic resources and manpower of nations in order to sustain the fighting services. Also the moral resources to foster the people's willing spirit is often as important as to possess the more concreter forms of power. Grand strategy, too, should regulate the distribution of power between the several services and between the service and industry. Moreover, fighting power is but one of the instruments of grand strategy which should take account of and apply the power of financial pressure, of diplomatic pressure, of commercial pressure, and, not least of ethical pressure, to weaken the opponent's will. Furthermore, while the horizon of strategy is bounded by the war, grand strategy looks beyond the war to the subsequent peace.[30]

A host of other scholars focus on more concrete aspects of grand strategy, always cognizant to privilege security interests above all else. For example, Hal Brands believes grand strategy to be the "intellectual architecture that gives form and structure to foreign policy," a "purposeful and coherent set of ideas about what a nation seeks to accomplish in the world, and how it should go about doing so," and is the "theory, or logic, that guides leaders seeking security in a complex and insecure world."[31]

William Martel finds grand strategy to be

> a coherent statement of the state's highest political ends to be pursued globally over the long term. Its proper function is to prioritize among different domestic and foreign policy choices and to coordinate, balance, and integrate all types of national means—including diplomatic, economic, technological, and military power—to achieve the articulated ends.[32]

Note in this definition, he is very inclusive of technological elements, perhaps more than other scholars. Martel even includes these elements in his lower tiers of foreign policy analysis, where grand strategy is, necessarily, in the top tier.[33]

In a recent work on grand strategy, *The Challenge of Grand Strategy*, Lobell, Ripsman, and Taliaferro use another John Lewis Gaddis definition as a starting point, asserting grand strategy is "the process by which a state relates long-term strategic ends to means under the rubric of an overarching and enduring vision to advance the national interest."[34] This is also a good starting definition for grand strategy, but some clarity is required, as the definition has become a little more detailed. What processes are included? Who calculates the strategic ends and means? How are the state's enduring vision and national interest generated? While broad, grand strategy can of course be quite detailed. Lobell et al. then end with defining grand strategy as "the organizing principle or conceptual blueprint that animates all of a state's relations with the outside world, for the purpose of securing itself and maximizing its interests. It shapes the parameters of the specific foreign, military, and economic strategies states pursue toward particular states, toward specific regions, and toward other actors on the world stage,"[35] which is key to understanding both the broad nature of grand strategy, but also that it is an inherently unique approach that must be tailored to each individual state.

Of all the approaches to grand strategy, Gaddis's approach is perhaps conceived of most broadly with "the calculated relationship of means to large ends" and how "one uses whatever one has to get to wherever it wants to go" with knowledge derivative of "war and statecraft, because the fighting of wars and the management of states have demanded the calculation of relationships between means and ends for a longer stretch of time than any other documented area of collective human activity."[36] However, he extends that even further when he states grand strategy is "potentially applicable to any endeavor in which means must be deployed in the pursuit of important ends" which can include anything from "surviving a summer internship" to "achieving success in soccer, football, [and] rowing."[37] This research, however, will stick to politics. He narrows this a bit seeing strategy as "the calculated relations of ends and means" and grand strategy as the "application of 'strategy,' . . . by states acting within the international state system, to secure their interests: it is what leads, if all goes well, to 'statecraft.'"[38]

While primarily a piece on military doctrine, Barry Posen's *The Sources of Military Doctrine* has an influential definition of grand strategy, and an applied follow-up discussion regarding the finer points of how a state's grand strategy must operate in concert with a state's military doctrine. Posen's approach to military doctrine, and his subsequent discussion of grand strategy, retains a preeminent position in the literature, and some of his framework and categories derived for military doctrine are relied upon in this work. Significantly, he draws on a definition of grand strategy as "A political-military, means-end chain, a state's theory about how it can best 'cause' security for itself."[39] He elaborates further by mentioning, "A grand strategy must identify likely threats to the state's security and it must devise political, economic, military, and other remedies for those threats."[40] Posen further discusses the need to prioritize under anarchy given scarce resources.[41] And, specifically, he mentions the devising of, "political, economic, military, and other remedies for [. . .] threats," with this research conceiving of energy security as an additional tool at this level. In addition, the identification of threats is mentioned in his approach, and elucidated throughout the work.[42] All these points add some greater, and more robust, dimensionality to the definition. This lifts security as the primary purpose, and crucially recognizes the use of non-military means in achieving the goals of a state's grand strategy. In fact, Posen goes to great lengths in his first chapter to describe the importance of integration of grand strategy, military doctrine, and political ends, along with a subsequent discussion on how they operate together, much the way this work conceptualizes energy security in relation to grand strategy.[43]

Taliaferro, Lobell, and Ripsman echo this approach later in their work when they write, "A grand strategy, in essence, is the organizing principle or conceptual blueprint that animates all of a state's relations with the outside world, for the purpose of securing itself and maximizing its interests. It shapes the parameters of the specific foreign, military, and economic strategies states pursue toward particular states, towards specific regions, and toward other actors on the world stage."[44] In this approach, it is also important to note their inclusion of "other actors," which would include non-state actors. And finally, they state that grand strategy "is a future-oriented enterprise involving considerations of external threats and opportunities, as well as the specific material, political, and ideological objectives of the state." Crucially here, they include an internal, domestic dimension as well as the conscious inclusion of temporal considerations, and further echo an emphasis on specific threats.[45]

As Christopher Layne further describes grand strategy, it is, in "its essence [. . .] about determining a state's vital interests—those important enough to fight over—and its role in the world. From that determination springs a state's alliances, overseas military commitments, conception of its stake in the prevailing international order, and the size and structure of its armed forces."[46] Grand strategy is inherently based on the threat of another state or group of states and rank-ordering those capabilities and interests in relation to those threats.

It should also be noted that this preferred use of grand strategy in the provision of long-term security is an expansive approach, utilizing all available tools of statecraft. This means military power is not conceived as the only means to preferred grand strategic outcomes. While used as the preferred approach in this book, it should be noted other strategic scholars do give primacy to hard power and the military balance in their conceptions of grand strategy. For example, while Robert Art concludes, correctly, that the purpose of grand strategy is security, he tends to focus on the means to that security purely through military force, distribution, and posture, as the only means to attain that security within a grand strategic framework.[47] For Art, this is due primarily to the "fungibility" of military power, and its spillover effects into other areas of strategy.

However, this research does not find Robert Art's view of grand strategy compelling, because it breeds reliance on a single avenue of statecraft when others might be more effectively used to meet objectives. Art purely views military power as shaping the entire strategic environment, in a manner that is quite top-down, without accounting for the other components of statecraft that feed upward, impacting the military situation. Politics, geography, alliance formation, historical context, and economic growth or malaise can all impact the formulation of military strategy and help or hinder the overall security of the state. A good example of this would be the structuring and timing of the Trans-Pacific Partnership (TPP), a trade deal the United States ultimately decided not to pursue in early 2017. On the surface, this is merely a trade deal meant to remove barriers to trade, harmonize exchange among multiple trading partners, and establish rules, but it is also widely understood to have a strong geopolitical element concerning China. The strategic implications of firmly embedding the United States in a codified, multilateral trading structure that also excluded China would have afforded the United States greater influence and the ability to shape events in Asia. This is a far cheaper, and effective, approach to competition in the Asia-Pacific, in contrast to the exclusively military conception of Art, which might instead advocate the additional deployment or reorientation of military forces to the region.

Just as Clausewitz sharpened the mind of the military strategist by emphasizing that war doesn't exist in a vacuum simply to tally wins and losses, but is ultimately a blunt political instrument, a grand strategist must recognize all the various elements of statecraft available towards the political ends of security. Security attainment should not be concerned with how it is attained; the ends in this case justify the expansion of means from material power to anything that can reinforce and secure the state. This leads to the utilization of all forms of statecraft. *A grand strategy requires uniformity of purpose and coordination and calibration, so all parts of statecraft are working together toward this singular end.* Luttwak reminds one that synergistic grand strategies make optimal grand strategies:

> All states must have a grand strategy, but not all grand strategies are equal. There is coherence and effectiveness when persuasion and force are each well guided by accurate intelligence, then combine synergistically to generate maximum power from the available resources. More often, perhaps, there is incoherence so that the fruits of persuasion are undone by misguided force, or the hard-won results of force are spoiled by clumsy diplomacy that antagonizes neutrals, emboldens enemies, and disheartens allies.[48]

In a sense, that is an indicator of good versus poor grand strategy. To think of grand strategy as the ultimate conception, or blueprint to pursue security in global politics, and to only pursue this strategy with military power, relegating other components of statecraft to the area of relatively aimless foreign policy, is a bit like fighting a boxing match with one hand tied behind your back and a leg strapped down with weights. Sure, that one arm is important, but so is everything else. All devices of statecraft matter in the pursuit of security, and therefore all should be pursued uniformly in order to achieve and retain security and survival. States with predominant military power in the interstate system can sometimes get away with pursuing the military-only approach, masked by overwhelming power, but eventually this lack of an overarching or continuity-inducing approach fails, especially as power shifts occur.

Luttwak is instructive in flexible and expansive use of grand strategy in his works on the Roman and Byzantine Empires. For instance, "In the imperial period at least, military force was clearly recognized for what it is, an essentially limited instrument of power, costly and brittle. Much better to conserve force and use military power indirectly, as an instrument of political coercion."[49]

Statecraft is meant to utilize all instruments at a state's disposal, as he goes on to explain that for Rome, "the dominant dimension of power was not physical but psychological—the product of others' perceptions of Roman strength rather than the use of that strength," displaying what was an incredibly sophisticated approach to grand strategy, ensuring the survival of Rome as a political entity for a millennium.[50] As for the Byzantines, even less traditional and indirect methods of statecraft were employed to great success. For example, the use of the growing popularity of Christianity by the Byzantine Empire is a well-documented case of grand strategic asymmetry. When the city of Constantinople was founded in 330 A.D., it certainly didn't hold any special position within the world of Christendom, but that soon changed. Lineages of emperors and patriarchs purposefully pursued a strategy whereby the city was established and maintained as a preeminent site of Orthodox Christianity, with the construction of the Hagia Sophia in 537 A.D., along with hundreds of other churches, the acquisition of famous saintly relics and religious icons, and the active use of missionaries in surrounding areas.[51] All this effort, particularly the construction of the spectacular Hagia Sophia, made Constantinople into a "Christian city par excellence" and major pilgrimage destination for the faithful, establishing the city as a center in the world of Christendom, ultimately "widening the cultural sphere of the Byzantines."[52] It was no longer a lone city to the east, but a central component of a larger world through the intense pursuit of prestige within Christendom. On its own, this might not matter much, but as part of a larger package of statecraft, it mattered greatly.

More recent examples of comprehensive approaches to grand strategy exist as well. For instance, diplomat George Kennan, the author of the prominent "X" article and generally considered the main architect of U.S. containment during the Cold War, conceived of containment in more expansive terms where he focused on repelling Soviet subversion and "psychological"[53] pressures with "measures short of war"[54] since the true danger is the "people of Western Europe and Japan, two of five vital centers of industrial power, might become so demoralized . . . by war and reconstruction . . . to communist-led coups, or even to communist victories in free elections."[55] Kennan firmly believed much could be confronted on the psychological front, since to him "the communist threat lies largely in certain subjective deficiencies and vulnerabilities of Western society itself. War would not remedy those deficiencies and liabilities."[56] As Gaddis states, paraphrasing Kennan, "It was against this contingency that the strategy of containment was primarily aimed—not Soviet military attack, not international communism, but rather the psychological malaise in countries bordering on Moscow's sphere of influence that made them, and hence the overall balance of power, vulnerable to Soviet expansive tendencies."[57]

Ultimately, the purpose of grand strategy is to secure the state from foreign powers and maintain national sovereignty. The security, or survival function, of grand strategy is essential to this definition, since without the possibility of compromised state security, or even the elimination of the state, there is no need for strategic interaction or the need to trade essential interests for those that are less essential. This understanding is extremely important to make an analytical distinction between grand strategy and foreign policy, two concepts that are often confused or used interchangeably. Generally, foreign policy governs all interactions between states. It can be directed towards anything and utilized for any purpose. Grand strategy is separate from this, in that a state may use many of the same tools available in foreign policy, but it is for the sole, ultimate purpose of providing long-term security for the state. Grand strategy is foreign policy, but foreign policy is not necessarily grand strategy. Foreign policy encompasses all interstate interactions, but only if these interactions involve some type of security consideration can they be considered part of a state's overall grand strategy.[58] Grand strategy gives specific purpose to foreign policy. Kazakhstan has a foreign policy towards Guatemala, but grand strategy does not factor into the approach, because of the lack of security concerns. Grand strategy exists with the real threat of force or ultimately the survival of the state. Kazakhstan would have a grand strategy for Central Asia and its survival as an independent political entity. In that sense, grand strategy entails continuity and longer-term goals, like national security and survival, that are, in turn, directly or indirectly pursued by achieving specific shorter-term and context-dependent foreign policy objectives—some of these more pressing than others, but, ultimately, these are cogently contained in the grand strategy projection of the state. Grand strategy provides the boundaries or context for the pursuit of foreign policy goals from means to ends.

This research argues that grand strategy generally establishes present and long-term state goals. It links immediate and future means, calculations, and decisions with enduring and longer-term state goals with respect to the rest of the world. In other words, grand strategy is the state's continuous position vis-à-vis the world and other states. Foreign policies effectuate the grand strategic purpose on a shorter-term basis. The latter is often affected by the historical context and the governing style or decision-making approaches of present executives, reflecting the decision-making processes, agendas, and objectives of different administrations and bureaucracies. A degree of continuity in grand strategy is key for a state's long-term survival, even if foreign policy varies over time. Foreign policy is ultimately in need of guidance, which would come from the grand strategy put in place by a state. Ultimately,

Grand strategy involves the prioritization of foreign policy goals, the identification of existing and potential resources, and the selection of a plan or road map that uses those resources to meet those goals. Whenever foreign policy officials are faced with the task of reconciling foreign policy goals with limited resources, under the prospect of potential armed conflict, they are engaging in grand strategy. Levels of defense spending, foreign aid, alliance behavior, troop deployments, and diplomatic activity are all influenced by grand strategic assumptions.[59]

These authors in combination touch on important aspects of the combination of the constituents of grand strategy and the imperative inclusion of threats and interests. It is because of the importance of this level, this research finds it necessary to ultimately include energy security.

Taking the previous passages into consideration, we can gain a fairly clear picture of grand strategy: *it is the national reconciliation of security-related means and ends, consistent with all available resources to the state, under the constraints of an indeterminate future.* It is the state's overall approach to long-term survival and security, accounting for specific threats to the state, utilizing all available forms of statecraft. Furthermore, when considering the components of grand strategy, it is important for the purpose of this examination to understand the role energy plays. It is the position of this research that energy plays an integral role in the formation and execution of each state's grand strategy. Without the necessary energy supplies, modern states would not have the ability to field a military, or the capability to grow an economy and provide for its population. Energy is a foundational element of national power, and as such, a critical component of grand strategy. Given the enormous energy requirements of both the U.S. and China, their placement in the world, and global reach, these energy considerations are magnified, and their respective approaches and policies directly affect one another.

Energy is integral to all state's grand strategies, including of course those of the United States and China, because without sufficient supplies, their economies and militaries simply do not exist in a contemporary format. With that level of importance attached to secure energy supplies, significant portions of their grand strategies are forced to revolve in many ways around the security of overseas energy supplies. Not only is energy important enough itself, but it also tends to intertwine with security pursuits in other areas of grand strategy as well. For instance, during the Cold War, China was forced to source a large amount of its energy supplies from the Soviet Union in order to meet minimum levels of domestic utilization.[60] One could argue this forced China into a security arrangement with the Soviets to meet energy needs, even though the Soviet Union was a large, proximate, potentially threatening power to China during the Cold War. When China became self-sufficient in oil production, it was free to hold a more contentious relationship with the Soviets, and then even a new security arrangement with the United States in the early 1970s. Oil supplies were integral to security decision-making for the PRC throughout the Cold War and served to both hamper and restrict policy actions vis-à-vis the Soviets. Indeed, this research will also argue that energy has been a large, looming foreign policy factor for the PRC since its establishment, far more so than to the United States since its inception. Since oil became a vital commodity, the U.S. has been far more blessed by geology in its secure sources than the PRC. As a result, China has had to elevate its energy security to extremely high levels in its grand strategy in order to maintain its security at a satisfactory level. The United States, given its comparatively secure energy position for a great power, has had to pay less direct attention to this over the decades, opting for a more hands-off approach, even as its importance has remained high. Additionally, it is also crucial to note, the *United States has the direct ability to interdict Chinese overseas energy supplies, whereas China does not have similar recourse, putting it at a significant disadvantage.* This may be one of the most important factors shaping foreign policy and international security in this century and will certainly provide a cornerstone of U.S.-Chinese relations. Over the course of this review, it is important to recognize that China "knows" its inherent weakness to control its energy supplies overseas and that the U.S. at any point could have interdicted these in a security crisis with China.

With these points in mind, we should be drawn to the point that when it comes to grand strategy and energy security, we do not necessarily have any "black boxes" nor does one approach fit all. Just as Poland's grand strategy and energy security approaches will be a specific fit to Poland, the United States and China will have their own grand strategies and energy security approaches for their own specific needs. It is particularly instructive to point to Posen's work on military doctrine, mentioned earlier in the chapter, in order to illustrate how a particular state, or strategic situation, will require specific considerations in order to attain security. As Posen explains, in 1973, Israel's military doctrine was "dangerously loose" with that of the state's grand strategy and resulted in some of the negative outcomes in that year's conflict.[61] When Israel engaged in an arms race with surrounding Arab states leading up to 1973, it was in dire need of a patron power to compete, since Soviet arms provision to Egypt was giving Israel's competitors both a qualitative and quantitative advantage in military hardware. The natural Israeli partner became the United States. This need for direct supplies and support from an outside power would cause a misalignment between existing doctrine and grand strategy, which would prove near catastrophic for Israel.[62] Israel's military doctrine was largely based on a defensive strategy reliant on a 48-hour advance notice. However, failing the full 48-hour notice, it appears Israel was to rely on preemptive attacks by the air force against its Arab neighbors.[63] This was all meant only to occur in the event concrete intelligence was received of an impending attack. This intelligence was received (and was accurate, albeit off by a few hours), and gave less than 48 hours for an impending Arab attack. However, the orders for a preemptive Israeli attack by the air force were never given. This was due to the tenuous partnership Israel had with the United States, and the realization they may not receive any further support against Arab attack if they waged a preemptive campaign against their neighbors. The United States would only allow Israel to respond after they had been attacked, eliminating the Israeli Defense Force's (IDF) preemptive failsafe in the event of an impending attack. As Posen states:

> Just as important as the absence of warning was the inability to use the air force effectively once it was known that war was imminent. The air force, as a capital-intensive rather than labor-intensive fighting force, was Israel's ever-ready ace-in-the-hole. It was the insurance policy against the possibility of surprise, the cutting edge of any preemptive strike. Yet at this moment of crisis, a hidden obstacle suddenly emerged. There was apparently no way to use the air force that was consistent with the major political change in Israel's grand strategy, the increased dependence on the United States. Thus, on the morning of October 6, Israeli military doctrine could not provide an answer to the state's predicament.[64]

Political and grand strategic disconnect can prove catastrophic. And, just as a faulty military doctrine can prove disastrous for a state, so can a faulty energy security strategy that fails to take all elements of grand strategy into account. Energy security strategy is a highly bespoke proposition for a state, as is military doctrine, and grand strategy in general. Just look at the stark differences between a net energy consuming state, and a net producer state. A consumer state will have an unambiguously different energy security strategy from a producer state, with both of their objectives being resolutely opposite, aside from energy market stability. A smaller state like Iceland will have a very different strategy and requirements as compared to a larger, great power like China or Russia. State size and capability play a significant role in these formulations. A small city-state, like Singapore, with a relatively small, albeit advanced, military, imports all its energy needs from overseas suppliers. Singapore certainly does not have the capability to secure overseas supplies of energy with its military, and therefore has to rely on global energy markets and good diplomatic relations with an array of oil-producers. It is also beneficial for Singapore to take measures to support the global commons and the global energy market, on which it is heavily reliant. The United States, on the other hand, has the military capability to protect overseas sources of energy militarily, and has acted to protect these sources in the past. This has garnered a direct and indirect benefit to the United States in support of the greater market, and in turn, its own supplies of overseas petroleum. These states have similar objectives, but will employ explicitly different means for attaining those objectives based on their capability and capacity to act, and their role in the international system.

What Are the Components of Grand Strategy?

This research conceives of the organization of grand strategy in a somewhat traditional way but gives prominence to energy security as an individual component, instead of subsuming it within the economic component, because of its vital importance to every country. Looking back at Posen, a state will "cause" security for itself by identifying the best military, economic, and political approaches to satisfy that security requirement.[65] There is something striking about the high level of importance given to these components: without a satisfactory approach to one, the others will simply fail. Without a proper system to distribute and utilize scarce policy resources, there aren't the hardware, materials, or resources available to field a military, nor is there the ability to grow a developed, advanced economy, where the needs of the population are met and the political situation is stable. Similarly, without the necessary protection in place by the military, trade routes are not protected, and the people and the government are not secure. And without a stable political system, it becomes difficult to project power abroad or in some cases even field a modern military, and instability and weak institutions stunt economic growth, preventing sustainable advancement wealth, technology, and increasing standards of living. They succeed or fail together when it comes to securing the state.

This research takes a similar approach, but expands on the political aspect and, of course, adds in energy security. The political aspect should be expanded to account for both domestic politics and diplomacy; this is important for both grand strategy and energy security. Accounting for the domestic situation will impact how easily a state is able to engage its military resources, or how much energy is required for the state to function properly. For instance, increasing a fuel tax in Europe will be much easier politically than in the United States, and this is important because it directly affects how much energy is consumed and the manner in which it is consumed. It is also indicative of constraints on political elites and may eventually restrict actions. In a similar fashion, diplomacy will affect a state's security for more obvious reasons, since diplomatic efforts are considered a state's first line of defense in international matters. And finally, energy security needs to be at this level because of its vital importance to the functioning of the state. This will be elaborated further in the section on energy security. All these elements are highly interdependent and come together to impact the highest levels of statecraft.

A question may arise after reviewing the necessary placement of energy security, on par with issues such as how a state wields its hard power. Why not include energy security as a part of economic policy? Simply put, states do not treat it this way. It clearly holds a special place in policy, especially for great powers. Even the United States, through its ideological adherence to the market, will ultimately wage war in order to protect vital sources of energy. The United States, China, any great power, or any state for that matter, cannot go for too long without keeping up the flow of energy. Energy is a necessity for everything in the state, society, and economy to function at even a minimum. Economic transactions serve as a coordinating mechanism for the broader economy, allocating resources and products to where it makes the most sense. These transactions include millions of products, on top of commodities, currencies, the financial and banking infrastructure, investments; essentially everything that keeps the economy liquid and growing. If any one of these components suffers, the resulting "shock" can usually even be absorbed. Even in the case of a major shock, such as the global financial crisis in 2008, the broader economy was able to adapt, sustain necessary function, and did not result in an existential threat to the state. Taken collectively, the economy as a whole can pose a threat to state security, as was the case with the failure of the Soviet economy during the Cold War. But, there typically isn't a single component of the "normal" economy that can be eliminated, resulting in an existential security crisis to the state, within a relatively short amount of time.

Essential State-Specific Dimensions of Grand Strategy

This discussion has thus far excluded another essential component of grand strategy alluded to earlier: state-specific approaches. All states will essentially have a grand strategy, with the components mentioned above. They will have the appropriate military, economic, political, diplomatic, and energy policies in place for long-term security. But what else do states need to consider in formulating their grand strategies?

To begin with, a state must identify its vital, or core, interests. These are the inherent, core interests of the state, their *sine qua non*, without which their very existence would be put at stake. This privileged state of the existential existence of the state is something most of the previously mentioned scholars and authors emphasized. Most grand strategic writings will have interests ranked in order, demonstrating their relative importance to one another. Typically, with these rank-ordered lists, when a state's core interests are threatened, it is a signal that a state will risk open warfare, or engage in open warfare, in order to defend them. Every state must identify these interests, and while there will be considerable overlap amongst states, many will have unique core interests not shared with others. Too many interests will lead to overreach and the exhaustion of resources, while not protecting enough interests may leave the state essentially vulnerable. At times, a state can achieve clarity in core interests, and at other times it can be relatively hazy. Other times, some core interests may be a political question, determined by domestic politics or some other reason, instead of purely security related considerations. China, in its determination to secure the entirety of the East and South China Seas, may even fall into this category.[66] Some core interests are given, but some are chosen by the state, just as core energy interests will result in similar choices. For instance, the need to secure overseas sources of petroleum seems a relatively easy determination; however, the long-term shift to renewable sources of energy, which could be considered a security imperative, would be a political choice.

The next calculation in a state's grand strategy is to assess the specific threats to the state. This will, of course, affect the state's considerations of core interests as well, making these two considerations highly dependent. These threats will also change over time, as core interests change, or as the state grows or shrinks. As Great Britain's power shrank considerably in the early 20th century, their government's calculations of threats and interests had to adjust in order to accommodate the new reality of their capabilities. In the 19th century, encroachment by foreign powers on India may have constituted a threat to Great Britain, but in the 20th century (after independence), it did not. This process was not easy and involved ceding many interests, and in turn, threats, to the United States. This was starkly demonstrated as the United States used economic warfare against the French and British governments during the Suez crisis in the 1950s.[67] Properly identifying threats to the state is vital in a state's assessment of a grand strategy as it allows the proper allocation of military and other economic resources and a realistic assessment of core interests that the state is actually capable of protecting.

A final assessment of the means and resources capable of meeting these threats and protecting interests is required as well. The means assessment is an obvious assumption to make, and determines, realistically, what a state can and cannot do. A state the size of Jamaica, for instance, is hardly going to be able to project power outside of its region to protect energy and economic interests; it must meet these security goals in another way. An accurate assessment of capabilities is required and will negatively affect the assessment of threats and interests if not reviewed correctly. This can be difficult, as states at times have an inherent interest in capability inflation, either purposeful or unintentional, which can potentially mislead an assessment of capabilities, resulting in negative grand strategic outcomes.[68]

CONCLUSION

Grand strategy is a difficult concept to understand, and perhaps even more difficult to properly implement given the complexity of the security environment. It has been determined grand strategy can be robustly understood to be the national reconciliation of security-related means and ends, consistent with all available resources to the state, under the constraints of an indeterminate future. The temporal constraints are particularly notable, especially in a shifting security environment. All of this is accounted for by understanding the specific threats to the state and mitigating these threats by utilizing all resources available. And, in a more pragmatic sense, any assessment of grand strategy will involve an honest appraisal of a state's core interests, threats, and their means and capabilities. All these aspects together characterize the operationalized aspects of grand strategy, and when these components are then deployed for use in energy security, it provides for a more robust analytical framework.

NOTES

1. Carl von Clausewitz, eds. and trans. Michael Howard, and Peter Paret, *On War* (Princeton, New Jersey: Princeton University Press, 1984), 149.

2. Referring primarily to Robert Art's conception of grand strategy, explained later in the chapter.

3. Edward N. Luttwak, *The Grand Strategy of the Byzantine Empire* (Cambridge, MA: Harvard University Press, 2009), 409.

4. Hal Brands, *What Good is Grand Strategy? Power and Purpose in American Statecraft from Harry S. Truman to George W. Bush* (Ithaca, NY: Cornell University Press, 2014), 6.

5. Edward M. Earl, ed., *Makers of Modern Strategy* (Princeton: Princeton University Press, 1971), viii.

6. Christopher Layne, *The Peace of Illusions: American Grand Strategy from 1940 to the Present* (Ithaca, NY: Cornell University Press, 2006), 13.

7. Luttwak, *The Grand Strategy of the Byzantine Empire*, 414.

8. Ibid., 414.

9. Christopher J. Fettweis, "Threatlessness and US Grand Strategy," *Survival* 56, no. 5 (2014): 56.

10. Frederick II of Prussia and ed. and trans. Jay Luvaas, *Frederick the Great on the Art of War* (New York: Da Capo Press, 1999), 120.

11. Christopher J. Fettweis, "Free Riding or Restraint? Examining European Grand Strategy," *Comparative Strategy* 30, no. 4 (2011): 317.

12. John L. Gaddis, "Containment and the Logic of Strategy," in Benjamin Frankel, ed., *In the National Interest: A National Interest Reader* (New York: University Press of America, 1990), 20.

13. Edward N. Luttwak, *Strategy: The Logic of War and Peace* (Cambridge, MA: Harvard University Press, 2003).

14. Ibid., 1–15.

15. André Beaufre, *Introduction à la Stratégie* (Paris: Armand Colin, 1963), 16, in Edward Luttwak, *Strategy: The Logic of War and Peace* (Cambridge, MA: Harvard University Press, 2003), 269.

16. Gregory R. Johnson, "Luttwak Takes a Bath," *Reason Papers* 20 (1995): 121–124.

17. Frankel, "Containment," 23.

18. Ibid.

19. Ibid., 24.

20. Ibid., 24.

21. Ibid., 26.

22. John L. Gaddis, *Strategies of Containment: A Critical Appraisal of American National Security Policy During the Cold War* (New York: Oxford University Press, 2005).

23. Ibid., 21.

24. John L. Gaddis, "What is Grand Strategy" (Yale University, New Haven, CT, February 26, 2009), 16.

25. Ibid., 3.

26. Ibid., 9.

27. Ibid., 15.

28. B. H. Liddell Hart, *Strategy: Second Revised Edition* (New York, NY: Praeger Publishers, 1991), 259–263.

29. Ibid., 237.

30. Ibid., 236.

31. Brands, *What Good is Grand Strategy? Power and Purpose in American Statecraft from Harry S. Truman to George W. Bush*, 3.

32. William C. Martel, *Grand Strategy in Theory and Practice: The Need for an Effective American Foreign Policy* (New York, NY: Cambridge University Press, 2015), 32–33.

33. Ibid., 30.

34. Steven E. Lobell, Jeffrey W. Taliaferro, and Norrin M. Ripsman, "Grand Strategy between the World Wars," in *The Challenge of Grand Strategy: The Great Powers and the Broken Balance between the World Wars*, eds., Jeffrey W. Taliaferro, Norrin M. Ripsman, and Steven E. Lobell (New York, NY: Cambridge University Press, 2012), 14.

35. Ibid., 15.

36. Gaddis, "What is Grand Strategy," 7.

37. Ibid.

38. Ibid., 22.

39. Barry R. Posen, *The Sources of Military Doctrine: France, Britain, and Germany between the World Wars* (Ithaca, NY: Cornell University Press, 1986), 13.

40. Ibid.

41. Ibid.

42. Ibid.

43. Ibid., 24–25.

44. Lobell, Ripsman, Taliaferro, "Introduction: Neoclassical Realism," 15.

45. Ibid.

46. Layne, *The Peace of Illusions: American Grand Strategy from 1940 to the Present,* 13.

47. Robert J. Art, *America's Grand Strategy and World Politics* (New York, NY: Routledge, 2009), 7–32.

48. Luttwak, *The Grand Strategy of the Byzantine Empire,* 409.

49. Edward N. Luttwak, *The Grand Strategy of the Roman Empire: From the First Century CE to the Third,* Revised and Updated Edition (Baltimore, MD: Johns Hopkins University Press, 2016), 2.

50. Ibid., 3.

51. Luttwak, *The Grand Strategy of the Byzantine Empire,* 114–123.

52. Ibid., 114–123.

53. "Measures Short of War (Diplomatic)," National War College; 1946 September 16; George F. Kennan Papers, Box 298, Folder 12; Public Policy Papers, Department of Rare Books and Special Collections, Princeton University Library; also see classics like *On War* and *Strategy* by Liddell Hart on the importance of psychology in strategy.

54. Ibid.; "Basic Factors in American Foreign Policy," Dartmouth College; 1949 February 14; George F. Kennan Papers, Box 299, Folder 23; Public Policy Papers, Department of Rare Books and Special Collections, Princeton University Library.

55. John L. Gaddis, *Strategies of Containment: A Critical Appraisal of American National Security Policy During the Cold War* (New York: Oxford University Press, 2005), 34.

56. "Basic Factors in American Foreign Policy," Dartmouth College; 1949 February 14; George F. Kennan Papers, Box 299, Folder 23; Public Policy Papers, Department of Rare Books and Special Collections, Princeton University Library.

57. Gaddis, *Strategies of Containment: A Critical Appraisal of American National Security Policy During the Cold War,* 34.

58. In this sense, the United States is more likely to adopt a foreign policy initiative towards a state like Mozambique, since this country isn't integral to any security interests. However, the United States would implement policy in accordance with its grand strategic interests when dealing with a state like Russia or Vietnam, given its close proximity to China.

59. Colin Dueck, *Reluctant Crusaders: Power, Culture, and Change in American Grand Strategy* (Princeton, NJ: Princeton University Press, 2006), 9–13.

60. Tatsu Kambara and Christopher Howe, *China and the Global Energy Crisis: Development and Prospects for China's Oil and Natural Gas* (Northampton, MA: Edward Elgar Publishing, 2007), 23–24.

61. Posen, *The Sources of Military Doctrine: France, Britain, and Germany between the World Wars*, 27.

62. Ibid., 28.

63. Ibid., 29.

64. Ibid., 29.

65. Posen, *The Sources of Military Doctrine: France, Britain, and Germany between the World Wars*, 13.

66. Leszek Buszynski, "The South China Sea: Oil, Maritime Claims, and U.S.-China Strategic Rivalry," *Washington Quarterly* 35, no. 2 (2012): 139–156.

67. David S. Painter, "Oil and the American Century," *Journal of American History* 99, no. 1 (2012): 31.

68. Posen, *The Sources of Military Doctrine: France, Britain, and Germany between the World Wars*, 27–29.

Chapter Three

Energy Security

INTRODUCTION

Energy security is an enigmatic concept, frequently used across media, government, academic, and policy debates, often without any real meaning or purpose. This chapter will attempt to shed light on the concept of energy security, allowing a certain degree of structure, and will attempt to avoid overly narrow or broad definitions, a trap many security concepts fall into within the international relations discipline. Part of the discussion will concern the connection between energy security and grand strategy, allowing for further justification of this linkage of security goals. The concept will also be narrowed to include a single energy source, petroleum, and an examination of various avenues of security threats will take place.

What Is Energy Security?

It is not surprising that most scholars and analysts miss crucial components of states' approaches to energy security, given the inherent difficulty in defining "energy security," and a lack of understanding of the interconnected nature of energy security to the broader security goals of a state, which is connected to a state's grand strategy. Daniel Yergin sums up the complexity of defining energy security when he asserts:

> Energy security may seem like an abstract concern—certainly important, yet vague, a little hard to pin down. But disruption and turmoil—and the evident risks—demonstrate both its tangibility and how fundamental it is to modern life. Without oil, there is virtually no mobility, and without electricity—and energy to generate that electricity—there would be no Internet age. But the dependence

on energy systems, and their growing complexity and reach, all underline the needs to understand the risks and requirements of energy security in the twenty-first century. Increasingly, energy trade traverses national borders. Moreover, energy security is not just about countering the wide variety of threats; it is also about the relations among nations, how they interact with each other, and how energy impacts their overall national security.[1]

In the passage above, Yergin not only provides a helpful overview of the difficulty of defining energy security, but in the last sentence, he also brings up the importance of state-to-state relations and their respective security situations. In a sense, he is alluding to energy security nestled within grand strategy when he refers to national security. So, what is energy security and how do states go about achieving energy security? Above, Yergin mentions, "countering a wide variety of threats" before his point on state-to-state relations. The former component consists of much of what many scholars, analysts, and policymakers think of when they talk or write about energy security. Nearly everyone has a different notion of what should be included when talking about "energy security." This can result in wildly different ideas and approaches to energy security depending on the state and its structure, along with its location, security situation, technological status, the proficiency of its energy industry, access to supplies, whether a producer or consumer state, size of population and industry, composition of domestic consumption, energy intensity, and so on. It tends to be defined and examined in focused, narrow terms, which does a disservice to the wide variety of approaches taken by various states that have adapted to their specific energy situations, and usually do not include these focused areas as part of a broader grand strategy. Furthermore, it is necessary to understand the variety of approaches available, since the United States and China employ many of these.

Most scholars tend to give primacy to their own respective narrow viewpoints in many cases. Many fail to recognize the full range of energy vulnerabilities states experience and in far too many instances believe there are threats where none exist. This variance in "energy security" lends itself to weaknesses in academic understanding, and in the policy environment, for that matter, of a proper understanding of states' various approaches to energy security. Much of our understanding is dated as well, and does not address new, specific threats to energy infrastructure such as cyber-attacks, aimed not at the retrieval of industry data and trade secrets, but the slowing or halting of production altogether. Politically motivated cyber-attacks affecting the security of supply are new to the industry, and have yet to be addressed. The relatively recent cyber-attack on Saudi Aramco, and subsequent attack on RasGas, in Qatar, has brought cyber security to the forefront of the energy industry, in a way not yet explored.[2] This discussion will attempt to mitigate some of these weaknesses in our understanding, taking into account all aspects of energy security in this research, and building it into a grand strategy for each state, in order to determine what constitutes true energy security for each respective state.

Further, energy security is a difficult concept to define, as it falls into a familiar trap in the social sciences where a lack of strict definition allows some to narrow it to the point where its specificity among a complex topic becomes a shortcoming, or broaden it to the point where the definition lacks discipline and standards to set it apart from other concepts. Energy, however, is different and unique. It transcends, deeply, all aspects of grand strategy, since without reliable sources of energy, all the important pillars of grand strategy would crumble.

Most authors and scholars tend to approach energy security in very broad, undefined terms, or focus on narrower aspects of energy security. Deutch and Schlesinger, in their CFR report on U.S. oil dependency, give perhaps one of the most widely used and succinct definitions of energy security: the reliable and affordable supply of energy.[3] Such broad definitions tend to be useful, since they afford a high degree of flexibility to understand how a given state pursues its respective energy security policy, within its own grand strategy or foreign policy. But, key questions are left unanswered. How do states pursue their affordable and reliable supplies? What do they consider affordable and reliable? To whom is the supply being delivered? Why do individual states choose to pursue supply security in the manner they do? In short, more specificity is required for a proper analysis.

Michael Klare finds most analysts tend to view energy security "as the assured delivery of adequate supplies of affordable energy to meet a state's vital requirements, even in times of international crisis or conflict."[4] This is a narrowing of the definition, but problematic since "vital requirements" will be viewed very differently depending on the state's goals in the international system. That is, the foreign policy objectives of Argentina, Bolivia, and Burundi are narrower and evidently distinct from those of states like the U.S., Russia, and China. Ignoring this difference is problematic. Further, Klare's definition also connotes that the state will be running on just the essentials, or the bare minimum required to operate the economy. But, the political elites in both states are forced to respond to domestic demands; consumer requirements in the U.S. and energy required for continued development in China. For these simple domestic reasons, the bare minimum amount of energy required is simply not feasible over the long term. However, the inclusion of international crisis or conflict does add a useful dimension to the debate. In a sense, that is the reasoning behind the strategic petroleum stockpiles held by International Energy Agency (IEA) members and many other countries.

Michael Klare also views energy security as a very state-centric proposition, where the government has a strong role. Many countries operate national oil companies (NOCs), where the state's involvement is obvious. But, the state also plays a large role in Western countries relying on private firms, albeit the role is not as overt as with NOCs. While a hands-off approach is taken, governments tend have an active role due to the importance of energy.[5] In this sense, Klare finds the state's role to be making sure the correct inducements are in place for private energy firms to provide suitable supplies of energy, and when the private sector is unable to fulfill this role, the state inevitably must intervene.[6] Klare does begin to clue readers into the how and why of energy security. He makes a distinction between national oil companies and privately owned oil companies and cites their different approaches as a result. But, since examination carried out in this volume involves two net oil-importing states, it doesn't make any actual distinction over the respective company approaches.

Another workable definition of energy security is the "assurance of the ability to access the energy resources required for the continued development of national power. In more specific terms, it is the provision of affordable, reliable, diverse, and ample supplies of oil and gas (and their future equivalents)—to the United States, its allies, and its partners—and adequate infrastructure to deliver these supplies to market."[7] This is an all-encompassing approach, yet narrower in some key areas. The development of national power, assuming the inclusion of sustainable economic growth in line with Realist thought, is a good approach, since this would be the end goal. Another interesting aspect is the inclusion of not just the United States, but also its allies and partners. China does not need to worry about this as much given its absence of official military allies, but the United States certainly has commitments and stakes involved with its global network of allies. It is important not to forget the impact of alliance commitments, as most energy analysts do. Additionally, the inclusion of proper infrastructure is important as well. For instance, China may soon have new sources of natural gas available, but without the proper pipeline network to get the supplies to where they need to be, they may as well not have those sources in the first place. However, there is no framework in place in order to understand how this is accomplished and why states would choose separate paths in achieving these goals.

It's also important to understand that the majority of "everyday" threats to the supply of oil come from "revolution, civil unrest, economic collapse, and acts of terror . . . [and] these threats can only be addressed by conflict prevention and diplomacy, not by deterrence."[8] Furthermore, the U.S. is specifically engaged in the task of preventing major impacts or shocks on the global economy as the result of considerable supply disruptions or price volatility.[9]

This is helpful, since it should be kept in mind that primary threats to the energy security of states may not be the result of state-to-state interactions, but more frequently the result of economics or terrorism. All of this must be included in the approach. This helps to broaden the concept of energy security and to understand it exists on multiple levels of analysis. But, why do states choose to develop resources in such tenuous parts of the world? Why does China do this in some cases, but not in others? What causes the United States to make similar choices?

With the core definition of energy security in mind—reliable supply at affordable cost—a more practical approach comes from Daniel Yergin, describing energy security as something that cannot be attained without proper global engagement. Developing robust security and economic programs and responses to a state's energy supplies overseas are essential to the security of those supplies. Developed as a reaction to the 1973 oil shock, he describes the current energy security "system" as designed to coordinate and inform the efforts of OECD countries to secure supplies and deter any future use of the "oil weapon," centered around the International Energy Agency, petroleum stockpiles, and emergency sharing.[10] Within this framework, diversity of supply, buffers against shocks, integration with the global oil market, information sharing, acceptance of oil market globalization, and full supply chain protection.[11] This is, and has been, a robust approach to energy security, especially for the OECD countries, but fails to take into account bilateral or unilateral efforts to secure energy supplies. This is especially important in the case of China since they do not fully integrate their energy security policies with the IEA and OECD, mainly due to their tepid multilateral engagement in energy matters and lack of trust of Western states. Furthermore, energy security with that approach was designed to counter the use of the "oil weapon," which is of considerably less threat to the energy security of states today as compared to myriad other threats. It also does not account for the full spectrum of U.S. energy security policies and leaves out responses made by China to secure their supplies. In that vein, why is China not integrated in the IEA as such a major energy consumer?

It is also important to note the interaction between China and the United States in terms of energy security. Yergin mentions that "some in the United States see a Chinese grand strategy to preempt the United States and the West when it comes to new oil and gas supplies, and some strategists in Beijing fear that the United States may someday try to interdict China's foreign energy supplies."[12] This will be explored in depth later in this research; not only are both striving to find ample energy at low enough prices for their respective economies, but their size and suspicion towards one another puts them in direct competition for global supplies, regardless of the state of the oil market. As with any strategic interaction, "each actor's ability to further its ends depends on how other actors behave, and therefore each actor must take their actions into account."[13] Energy will be a pillar of Sino-American relations for the next several decades, with the possibility of causing conflict. However remote that may seem, it is important to keep in mind that competition for energy will likely serve as an exacerbating feature in an already existing issue between the two consumer giants. This has the greater probably to draw these states into diplomatic or even military conflict, making energy security exceedingly important. A principal point is drawn from this: when two disproportionately large energy-consuming states exist at the systemic level, they will be put into direct competition with one another for energy supplies, threatening the energy security of each other.

Among the many ways to view energy security, or insecurity, is to examine political effectiveness or ineffectiveness and the resultant lack of a sustained policy approach. This is especially true in the case of the U.S., where "the lack of sustained attention to energy issues is undercutting U.S. foreign policy and U.S. national security."[14] Since 1973, the U.S. has approached energy policy in a very disjointed, *ad hoc* manner, whereas China has had a more concerted, steady approach to certain parts of its energy policy since 1993. This certainly affects the respective security of the two states. The Council on Foreign Relations piece, however, does not begin to approach the underlying issues that contribute to the different policy approaches by the two states.

Other approaches to energy security may even seem to be good, effective solutions; however, they are not. For instance, energy "independence" and equity deals made with producer states are also seen as a way by many, especially in the policy circles, to ensure energy security by analysts on each side. But as mentioned above, many approaches to energy security are poorly supported by the facts and are ineffectual. Phillip Andrews-Speed finds great fault with the idea of energy independence as a viable way to secure a state's energy future. He writes, "China's ignorance of the nature of international oil markets and its feeling that they were dominated by Western, especially U.S., interests resulted in a reluctance to be dependent on these markets and a preference to seek a high degree of control over the full supply chain."[15]

In a similar vein, Yergin finds that for increased energy security, the entire global system must be viewed as a whole, and not just as individual states. Protection of the global infrastructure and supply will realize secure supplies for consuming nations far better than individual, mercantilist approaches.[16] On the U.S. side, per one of the earlier definitions, we have already pointed to weaknesses for U.S. energy "independence" for simple reasons such as global commitments and alliances. But other, lesser-known reasons crop up as well. In 2005, after Hurricanes Katrina and Rita hit the Gulf Coast of the

U.S., damage was widespread to the electric grid, shutting down refining capacity all along the coast, crippling the ability of the U.S. to refine and process petroleum, disrupting supply from domestic sources for a significant period of time.[17] Restricting sources of energy to the U.S. Southeast in this case reduced flexibility and diversity of supply in the face of a major disaster and prolonged energy shortages in the region. This situation illustrates the interdependence of energy infrastructure and turns energy independence on its head by demonstrating a weakness of that independence. Relative independence in this case meant a decrease in the diversity of supplies and energy sources available. While these scholars have rightly pointed out critical errors in approaches to energy security, many states still continue to pursue these somewhat futile paths to securing energy supplies, without offering any detailed reason as to why.

The meaning of energy security may also shift somewhat over time due to international politics and the evolution of energy markets. The pre-1990s system of cheap energy,[18] excess Saudi and OPEC capacity, lack of environmental concern, and a dearth of interest in oil efficiency, alternate sources of primary energy, and reductions in nationwide oil intensity, has gradually given way to markets subjected to extreme price volatility, increasing capital requirements, environmental concern, all underpinned by the dramatic rise of consumption in Asia, along with the global growth and dominance of state-run national oil companies (NOCs) over global reserves.[19] There are more NOCs out there in control of more oil and gas than the independent, Western international oil companies (IOCs). Global warming and its calamitous potential have caused a great push towards efficiency and renewables. Importantly, "energy consumers, and many producers, now realize that the days when enhancing energy security was simply a matter of increasing the size and diversity of supplies are over: now energy security also means implementing policies designed to reduce the demand for energy."[20] These are not minor changes to the global energy landscape, and have altered approaches to security. And if, for instance, new issues like demand reduction are so important, why has the United States had such a lackluster response to demand, and why has Chinese demand continued to grow at such a high rate? These are questions left unanswered.

Aside from fundamental changes to the structure of global energy, short- and long-term impacts of actions must be examined as well. For instance, in 1973, the oil weapon was able to extract short-term concessions, but OPEC oil producers in general suffered over the long run as a result. The shock led to a rapid rise in oil prices and caused immense economic strain in Western economies; but overproduction and the drop in global demand brought down the price in the long run.[21] Any power gained by OPEC was illusory and short-lived, and ultimately the producers sacrificed their own energy security as a result. The system did not favor the producers over the next decade; they were too dependent on the West as an export market and for ensuring the security of maritime trade routes for oil supplies.[22] After the shocks of the 1970s, the oil market settled into a system whereby the U.S. provides security and Saudi Arabia has to ship oil to market and maintain spare capacity.[23] Energy security for Saudi Arabia meant a military alliance with the United States in order to secure the safe transit of oil supplies and for overall demand security. "The Middle East was interested in preserving the Western market for its oil. In return, the West took increasing control over economic and military security in the Middle East region."[24] These efforts stabilized the global supply of energy and Europe leaned more on Russia for diversification. This favorable, consumer-dominated situation persisted until a short time after the Asian Financial Crisis and put the issue of energy very low on the agenda of the West. This period witnessed dependence on the part of producers towards their Western consumers: these customers were so secure that they would even apply energy sanctions and deny investment in many producing states.[25] And, given this narrative of the security situation in oil over the past 40 years, why is China consistently increasing reliance on Middle East oil during a time when power has adjusted more in favor of the producing states? Why is China not doing more to integrate in the global energy system to balance against possible negative outcomes? And, why does China seem to be so generous to many of these producing states as opposed to others?

The approaches to energy security discussed here are not exhaustive and mainly explore security from the consumer state's point of view. But, they tend to be representative of the typical approaches mentioned earlier. Some are quite broad and all-inclusive, which at times lacks the ability to fully understand the full spectrum of possibilities, consequences, and trade-offs to certain approaches to energy security. Some other approaches are narrow and focused, but lacking in a way that would be appropriate for state policy on a national scale, and certainly not in a comparative approach between the United States and China. However, a common thread throughout these analyses is a dearth of understanding of the underlying dynamics of both states that drive them to take, and forgo, certain actions in pursuit of energy security. There are many different avenues to pursue in order to secure the supply of energy, but specific approaches are tailored to the specific situation of the state, and their resulting strategy for maintaining the overall security of the state. A broad approach must be taken with the necessary inclusion of grand strategy in these analyses.

And, should we care where our energy comes from? As Levi and Clayton note, there are essentially two camps approaching this issue: the economist that says no, oil is a single market with a more or less unified global price, and the strategist that says yes, it is a point of vulnerability.[26] It is the position of this research that the view of economists dominate under normal market and political conditions, however, the view of the strategist will ultimately prevail in times of political turmoil. In addition, states must prepare for future international political difficulties even if they are not experiencing them currently.

The Connection Between Energy Security and Grand Strategic Elements

The components and assessments used to determine a proper grand strategy for a state permeate the levels of grand strategy horizontally and vertically, making all highly interconnected to one another. As such, energy security, as a branch of grand strategy, has many of the same required calculations that must be made in order to properly assess and secure the state's energy supplies. Here, an appraisal of the military, economic, political, and diplomatic dimensions must be completed, along with a proper review of core interests, threats, and capabilities.

Much of the analysis of this research will be focusing on the heavily discussed availability, affordability, and reliability (AAR) components of energy security, since these tend to have measurable data available over the time period under review. However, before getting to AAR's measurable constituents, there are a few more steps for understanding the energy security of the state. First, look to the interests, threats, and capabilities (ITC) of the state. Any good grand strategist knows ITC must be kept in mind at all times, and at all levels of consideration. Wavering from these core concerns jeopardizes energy security and national security.

Referring once again to Posen's work, he made reference to the different tools available to policymakers in order to meet their grand strategic objectives. These components rely on energy in the following ways:

Military Interest of Energy

The direct interest in energy of the military, and hard power assets of a state, is quite obvious. As General Patton put it, "My men can eat their belts, but my tanks have gotta [*sic.*] have gas."[27] A modern military runs on fuel. Without fuel, the air force would not exist. The navy would not exist. Support and supply vehicles, responsible for keeping service members on the ground in fighting condition, would not exist. Since the use of combustible fuels was put to widespread use beginning in the late 19th century with coal, fuel has been a major requirement for a military. Before the use of mechanized and industrial level warfare, the hi-tech predecessor in warfare was the horse, which reigned supreme as the premier battlefield combatant for nearly 6,000 years, since their domestication and widespread use. It was only little over a mere century ago that we made the jump from horseback to tanks, and sails on naval vessels to steam engines, and the combustion engine on warships. Without proper supplies of fuel in place, the military takes a century's step backward, placing it squarely in an antiquated, past generation of war fighting capability. Clearly, the military has direct, and myriad indirect reasons to support the secure acquisition of fuels.

Economic Interest of Energy

Energy as a national security interest is quite clear, given the state's direct interest in economic growth, which supports the overall resources and technological development of the state. This is the most proximate requirement for energy security: supporting the state through economic growth and advancement. Without energy for power plants, there is no power not just to keep people warm in their homes during a cold winter, and cook their food, but also to power the myriad industrial plants and manufacturing centers that support a modern economy. Additionally, the temperature control to keep normal working conditions, the lights so a worker may see, and a power outlet to plug in a laptop are all necessary components of an information age knowledge economy on the micro level. These same power sources power transportation throughout a city, whether by automobile or public transport in the form of a metro or dense bus network. These same fuels also power cargo transport, giving rise to an industry where thousands of trucks crisscross the roads of every country picking up and delivering all types of goods. Transport by rail is widely used, requiring yet more power, and this all does not even include the global shipping industry, which accounts for the vast majority of world trade, where massive vessels cross the oceans and traverse the waterways of the world supporting an incredibly dense and flexible international trade network. Without energy, this all grinds to a halt; and, in particular this all is not possible without petroleum. Fuel used to underpin the global trade fleet is reason enough for petroleum to have a massive global impact, but it even goes beyond that. There are a staggering number of everyday and industrial products that require petroleum, or petrochemicals, either as part of the production process or as a necessary component, or ingredient.

Political (Domestic and International)

The population and political elite have an interest in energy as well. It's simple for the elites: the people need energy, and they need to deliver. Whether in a democracy, where a politician can be voted from office, or a dictatorship where if discontent becomes widespread enough, is able to overwhelm the state's security services, the elites need to be concerned about delivering the necessary fuels to the population at an acceptable price level. The population requires access to affordable fuels as part of their daily routines and commutes, and for many other purposes. Not only is fuel required for automobiles, but it also is required for cooking and space heating. Transportation is integral to the economy and cooking and heating in some situations can be a matter of living and dying. As this is being written, the new president of Ukraine is engaged in a dispute with Russia over deliveries of natural gas. This affects not only Ukraine, but several European states as well. This is because it is a threat to the lives of the population when the gas does not arrive, and many people end up freezing to death.

The international component varies mainly along producer and consumer state lines, where the former is going to be concerned with maximizing not only profit from resource sales, but also political and even coercive power, and the latter is concerned not only with cheaper resources but also minimizing political entanglements and coercive power of producing states. In fact, the current structure of the global energy market is a direct consequence of the 1973 oil shock and the countermeasures employed by the Organization for Economic Cooperation and Development (OECD) states in the aftermath.

International Political Climate

Perhaps one of the most detrimental failures of current and previous energy security scholarship is the lack of differentiation between variations in the political climate, which fundamentally alters a state's approach to energy security. Take China as an example. China recognizes the efficiency and effectiveness of the global oil market, but does not rely on it completely because of security considerations. Under normal political conditions, China has no problem accessing and profiting from these markets. However, if global politics were to shift, China would most likely need to rely on these markets far less than it has in the past 30 years if its principal adversary is the United States, which dominates global energy markets. In an extreme political scenario, China may be locked out of these markets, and will need to pursue energy security by falling back on bilateral agreements with resource suppliers around the globe. This does not even broach the subject of energy security in a completely hostile environment, constituting open warfare. These differing conditions need to be included in any analysis of energy security, for a full understanding of the energy security situation of a specific state. Many scholars and analysts, as seen in the section on energy security, do not take the "energy security" argument to its logical end, which is open warfare. The same goes for quantitative studies on energy security, which typically lack even a minor conversation on the military component of energy security. That is, however, what is referred to when discussing the "security" of a state; steadfast preparation for war is crucial to state security, and most arguments for energy security do not consider the "war" aspect in their conceptions. The following description gives a full understanding of this relationship:

Political Scenarios for Oil Security

Normal political conditions: Rely on market and typical ES mechanisms to provide energy security. Under this scenario, the global oil market is the most efficient means of oil security for both states.

Politically adverse/antagonistic conditions with the U.S./West: This is a scenario that includes an abnormal political climate, up to and including sanctions and other forms of economic warfare. This is the scenario that China has been preparing for over the past 20 years—a way to resist the first level of oil scarcity from the market. This is where more politically risky suppliers come in, continuing to provide oil to China, regardless of pressure applied by Western powers.

Open warfare: While China has been able to attain oil security in the previous areas, it is still woefully unable to compete in this zone, and will be for some time, since at this level there is direct military competition. China's comparatively weak military in terms of personnel, technology, doctrine, and joint operations capabilities, among others, simply do not allow meaningful competition outside its own littoral environment, putting at risk any overseas supplies within the reach of U.S. naval power.

Depending on the current operating environment, the states in question will require different approaches to securing energy supplies. A proposed comparative model of the United States and China follows in table 3.1. Please note that this model could also be applied to numerous bilateral energy relationships.

Table 3.1.   Political Scenarios and Supply Reliance

Political Climate	United States	China
Normal Political Conditions	Market	Market, Bilateral Deals
Politically Adverse Conditions	Market	Restricted Market Reliance, Bilateral Deals, Political Clout, Economic Influence
Open Warfare	Market, Military	Military, Bilateral Deals, Political Relationships

After accounting for the ITC of a state, and the operating political climate, we can begin to see the end results of these approaches as outputs in a state's energy availability, affordability, and reliability (AAR). Now a closer look at the AAR of a state is required to further analyze and compare. It is the outputs of these specific components that will be analyzed in the following chapters. While many of the indicators may not be directly related to these items, they will typically be connected in some way. For instance, the "sufficiently current extractable reserves" category listed below will have outputs measuring oil imports and domestic reserves, as well as the production of those reserves. It should also be noted many of these items do not fit neatly into single categories, and can be used interchangeably.

A Note on Specific Energy Security Components

Most scholars tend to stop at availability and affordability when assessing energy security approaches, followed by a few issue areas, like the security of the Hormuz Strait, but this simply does not allow one to grasp the complexity of attaining energy security for the state, nor is it at the proper depth for an accurate analysis. In order to appropriately formulate policy approaches to energy, this research takes on a modified framework akin to that presented by Jonathan Elkind.[28] Utilizing that framework will allow a better grasp of the full range of objectives, threats, and capabilities afforded to various states in the system, and in particular, to the United States and China. The framework adopted here is reliant on Elkind's categorization; however, for the purposes of this research, it was modified to include some new components, and in other cases, some of the original components, especially those that constituted significant enough overlap, were eliminated. Notably, Elkind's entire section on sustainability was removed, because this was much more of an environmental discussion, something this research concluded does not belong in the security deliberations for energy supplies.

In this conception, we see the inclusion of a third branch, reliability, in addition to the typically discussed availability and affordability. This is preferred because separating this allows us to create a further distinct section apart from the politics and economics that are more dominant in the availability and affordability section. Breaking this third piece off allows a section that is more in tune to the military and security interruptions that can take place, ultimate thwarting a state's supply security. This is an important distinction to make, since these are clearly different issue areas, requiring vastly different assessments and responses by the state. It also makes more sense viewing the category as separate in light of its inclusion in grand strategy. A reliable, or resilient, energy security apparatus is clearly distinct from availability and affordability, as it is attempting to gauge how well the apparatus holds up against actual shocks, and how well it is prepared for such shocks in the future, without grossly affecting the availability and affordability of the source. Conceptually, this is important in order to consider the importance of time and adverse, unaccounted shocks to the energy market.

Essential Components for Energy Security

Availability

Sufficient physical infrastructure:

This includes both domestic and cross-border energy-related infrastructure. Oil doesn't do much good for a country if it does not have the requisite pipeline network to complement petroleum inflows. The United States has a dense, highly developed pipeline network for oil, centered on Cushing, Oklahoma, which in turn reaches out all over the country. Most states do not typically have such a comprehensively developed internal oil infrastructure, and as such, is an important measure to gauge. Additionally, the United States continues to develop and attempt to develop this network internally and across state borders.[29]

Sufficient currently extractable reserves:

In this context, this includes both reserves from supplier states as well as domestically held extractable reserves. While reserves in supplier states can be important, this research only considers extractable reserves which are domestically held proved reserves (1P or P90), meaning the reserves have a 90 percent probability of being developed at current technological and price levels.[30]

The ability of consumers, producers, and intermediate countries to agree on transit and price:

This is a highly political matter. Economics provide a base platform for negotiations, but many times the politics surrounding this area are quite volatile. Take the European Union, Ukraine, and Russia as a stark case in point. In 2014, the new Ukrainian administration was refusing to pay Russia the higher cost of gas supplies sourced from Russia's state-owned natural gas company, Gazprom. These costs were mainly in the form of past debts and accumulated natural gas consumption that Russia is attempting to recoup, or extract, from Ukraine for political purposes.[31] At the time, Ukraine wasn't even allowing natural gas to flow through their network and into the European Union network, which relies on Russian gas for the majority of its externally sourced domestic energy consumption. To compound issues, as with this case, these disputes usually flare up as winter approaches, increasing the bargaining power of the exporting country. A drastic political shift in Ukraine sparked this situation, and it only settled in an unstable state, with the constant possibility of renewed outbreak in hostilities between Ukraine and Russia. Europe needs gas and so does Ukraine. The transit state is the key, and can make or break supplies for an entire region.

Technological solutions and advancements throughout entire supply chain:
While Elkind includes this component only in the availability section, it can be used all throughout the energy utilization process, from exploration all the way to consumption. For instance, vessel support and refining capacity are two other areas that can be important and are related to technological advancement.

Capital investment:
There must be a dense financial network available to support oil and gas operations, which can include everything from exploration and drilling to financing for research and development in smaller and midsize firms. Capital availability is crucial to these operations as is the efficiency of the use of capital itself. This can be skewed more towards capital provided by the state or by financial markets and other sources of private capital.

Strong legal and regulatory framework:
Ensuring a level playing field and a strong institutional structure is important not only to energy, but to the overall functioning of the state and economic development.[32] Perhaps more important is the competitive advantage this provides to foreign energy companies that require a stable environment in order to make investments that may last several decades.

Affordability

Low price volatility:
Stable energy pricing, for both the long and short term, is imperative for economies to run efficiently and effectively. If the price for a barrel of oil is $50 one week, and next week it shoots up to $90 a barrel, this can throw an inordinate amount of domestic consumers, industries, and companies into complete disarray.[33] Any companies involving transportation, or relying on transportation for pickup and delivery of products—which is nearly the entire economy—would have to radically alter their estimates of profit and loss, not mention readjust pricing for all their products. Prices would be revised upward, affecting inflation, and myriad sectors. This is a far bigger issue than simply driving up to the pump and finding the fuel you put in your car has risen in cost by a significant amount. Without proper, stable, predictable pricing, there

cannot be future planning, which would drastically impact investment and finance.[34] Having the huge price swings in oil witnessed in 2008, resulting in the
commodity's record high of $147 a barrel on July 11, is simply not feasible to
have on a regular basis, while expecting a stable economy.[35]

Realistic expectations of future price:
   This accounts for the long-term pricing of oil. Whereas the previous pricing item dealt with short-term impacts on pricing, usually unforeseen, or political events, this deals with long-term expectations. Whatever would impact
the cost 20 or 30 years from now needs to be reasonably accounted for and
factored into economic and financial considerations.

Transparent pricing:
   Readily available pricing information, which is not always necessarily accurate and available, is important to maintaining competitively priced imports
and maintaining steady costs over time. Much of this market relies on price
reporting agencies (PRAs) like Argus and Platts, but even their methodology
can be clouded at times, and there are significant areas of the energy market
that do not have readily available pricing, or simply rely on reports from the
companies and shipping agencies.[36]

Prices that reflect full costs:
   Primarily, this is in reference to states that spend large sums to subsidize oil
and gas consumption among their population. This is very frequently found
in states with energy abundance, since they can easily provide fuel at a lower
price compared to market rates. This can be problematic, in that it has the
tendency to drive up consumption and distort the overall energy market and
pricing throughout the economy.

Reliability

Diversified sources along supply chain:
   This is perhaps one of the most important, and readily recognized, aspects
of energy security. Churchill said it best when he stated, "On no one quality, on no one process, on no one country, on no one route, and on no one
field must we be dependent." He went on to succinctly state, "Safety and
certainty in oil lie in variety and variety alone." Diversification is one of the
most important concepts with energy security, and was pursued early in the
20th century after Churchill recognized the inherent vulnerability in relying
on overseas sources of oil, after converting the British fleet to use petroleum
instead of coal. This should be diversity of source and fuel type.[37]

Reserve capacity for entire supply chain:

Without proper reserve capacity throughout the entire value chain, from source to gas pump, any small shock to the system will be unnecessarily magnified and will result in price shocks. This can be national emergency capacity, as with a country's strategic petroleum reserve, or spare production capacity as with Saudi Arabia's typical role as swing producer, maintaining a stable level of global spare capacity.[38]

Short- and long-term protection from political interruptions and terrorist attacks:

Nearly all countries must deal with these issues and their impacts on energy either directly or indirectly. For instance, the threat of an attack on Saudi oil infrastructure from domestic elements is a relatively frequent occurrence. The Saudis have developed many countermeasures for this, and these effective countermeasures serve to reduce Saudi risk as an exporter, but these threats can be potentially significant and should be taken seriously. If an attack occurs, decommissioning a pipeline in eastern Saudi Arabia, which brings petroleum from their mammoth Ghawar field to port in the Persian Gulf for transit, it has the capability to take millions of oil off the market daily.[39] Interruptions along the entire supply chain can impact supply and pricing.

How Can We Properly Conceptualize Energy Security Within Grand Strategy?

All of the categories listed in the previous section are important components that come together to form the intricate and complex web that is energy security. They are highly interconnected, and transcend the military, economic, political, and diplomatic levels of grand strategy. Energy security in the context of grand strategy is something elevated to the utmost height of a state's security, meaning, access to adequate supplies (in the case of consumer states such as China and the United States) is a vital national security interest, ultimately resulting in a situation where these states will go to war over access to these supplies, and will treat significant supply interdiction as a primary threat to national security. Energy, oil in particular, is something that will, in and of itself, force states to go to war, and as such, states go to great lengths to secure their energy supplies, taking multiple steps towards security, just as they secure themselves militarily, economically, and politically.

A grand strategy requires an understanding of state interests, threats, and capabilities to meet current and future threats, and for each of these, the state utilizes all political, diplomatic, and military resources at its disposal to meet these objectives. With the first, state interests, it should also be noted that energy security of some sort is considered a vital interest for all states in the international system, although how much and in what way will be determined on a case-by-case basis. For the purpose of this study, it is important to clarify that energy security, broadly speaking, is a vital national interest to both the United States and China. Additionally, their immense domestic energy needs and military, economic, and political capabilities oblige and allow both states to have aggressive and evolving energy security agendas designed to provide as much security as possible to each state. With this consideration in mind, viewing energy security on par with the other components of grand strategy is essential, and is viewed as such in this work. The same process applied to understand grand strategy is applied to understand energy security.

Again, many of these concepts are interrelated and constitute grey areas that can easily have them found in other components of this model. So, this represents a best-fit, conceptual model of the process of energy security as a component of grand strategy. Energy is essentially on the same level as military and economic considerations when determining grand strategy. A state's ITC guides strategy at every level and constitutes many unique components for each state. Further constraining a state's pursuit of energy security is the operating political climate, which can dramatically alter a state's pursuit of energy security. Finally, the output of the preceding components of the model can be seen and measured in the AAR after accounting for the political climate. However, since this study focuses on the 1993–2012 period, the analysis will focus on the "normal" political relationship, given this has been the state of affairs over the research period. It should be noted, however, that each state continually prepares for potential deterioration in the political climate, hence China's strong bilateral relationships and military buildup.

CHAPTER SUMMARY

This discussion provides not only an understanding of energy, but also its importance and why it is to be elevated to the level of grand strategy in this research. It should not escape the reader that energy security is extremely vital to any state in question, a component without which the state as a viable actor would perish. This means states are constantly shifting and posturing for potential future security or supply disruptions of any kind, attempting to meet and mitigate any potential threats to their supply infrastructure.. This posturing is not just military posturing since that is not the only threat to energy security, nor the only avenue to secure and adequate supplies. Posturing can also include economic policy and political engagement, both domestic and international. For instance, a change in economic or domestic policy impacting the level of taxation of companies may affect their incentives or capabilities to retrieve oil. International politics may devolve into a less cordial atmosphere, resulting in sanctions, or a Cold War–style containment policy affecting the economic dimension of grand strategy as well. Internally, political order may deteriorate, making extraction and export of strategic materials unfeasible. Energy security considerations are inextricably integrated into all facets of state power and as such it is preferable to integrate energy security as its own domain within a grand strategic framework for any state, accounting for the specific energy-related interests, threats, and capabilities appropriate for that state's specific national security profile. The following chapter will introduce indicators and measures of energy security as applied to the United States, following a short historical overview of U.S. specific grand strategy and energy security.

NOTES

1. Daniel Yergin, *The Quest: Energy, Security, and the Remaking of the Modern World* (New York, NY: The Penguin Press, 2011), 293.

2. Camilla Hall and Javier Blas, "Qatar Group Falls Victim to Virus Attack," *Financial Times*, August 30, 2012, https://www.ft.com/content/17b9b016-f2bf-11e1-8577-00144feabdc0 .

3. Chairs: John Deutch, James Schlesinger, David Victor, Council on Foreign Relations National Security Consequences of U.S. Oil Dependency Independent Task Force Report No. 58 3 2006.

4. Michael T. Klare, "Energy Security," in *Security Studies: An Introduction,* ed. Paul D. Williams (New York, NY: Routledge, 2008), 484.

5. Ibid.

6. Ibid.

7. Jan H. Kalicki and David L. Goldwyn, "Introduction: The Need to Integrate Energy and Foreign Policy" in *Energy and Security: Toward New Foreign Policy Strategy*, eds., Jan H. Kalicki and David L. Goldwyn (Washington, DC: Woodrow Wilson Center Press, 2005), 9.

8. Ibid.

9. Ibid., 10.

10. Daniel Yergin, "Ensuring Energy Security," *Foreign Affairs* 85, no. 2 (2006): 75.

11. Ibid., 75–77.

12. Ibid., 77.

13. David A. Lake and Robert Powell, "International Relations: A Strategic Choice Approach," in *Strategic Choice and International Relations*, eds., David A. Lake and Robert Powell (Princeton, NJ: Princeton University Press, 1999), 3.

14. John Deutch and James R. Schlesinger, National Security Consequences of U.S. Oil Dependency, Independent Task Force Report No. 58, Council on Foreign Relations, 2006, 3.

15. Philip Andrews-Speed, "Do Overseas Investments by National Oil Companies Enhance Energy Security at Home? A View from Asia," in Oil and Gas for Asia: Geopolitical Implications of Asia's Rising Demand, eds., Philip Andrews-Speed et al. (NBR Special Report no. 41, 2012), 38.

16. Yergin, "Ensuring Energy Security," *Foreign Affairs*, 78.

17. Ibid.

18. Referring primarily to the oil supply glut in the 1980s.

19. Andreas Wenger, Robert W. Orttung, and Jeronim Perovic, *Energy and the Transformation of International Relations: Toward a New Producer-Consumer Framework* (New York, NY: Oxford University Press, 2009), 4.

20. Ibid.

21. Ibid., 29.

22. Ibid.

23. Ibid., 31.

24. Ibid.

25. Ibid., 32.

26. Blake Clayton and Michael Levi, "The Surprising Sources of Oil's Influence," *Survival* 54, no. 6 (2012): 107–108.

27. Chester Wilmot, *The Struggle for Europe* (Westport, CT: Greenwood Press, 1972), 473.

28. Jonathan Elkind, "Energy Security: Call for a Broader Agenda," in *Energy Security: Economics, Politics, Strategies, and Implications*, ed., Carlos Pascual and Jonathan Elkind (Washington D.C.: Brookings Institution Press, 2010), 121–130.

29. Steven Mufson and Juliet Eilperin, "Trump Seeks to Revive Dakota Access, Keystone XL Oil Pipelines," *Washington Post*, January 24, 2017, https://www.wash ingtonpost.com/news/energy-environment/wp/2017/01/24/trump-gives-green-light -to-dakota-access-keystone-xl-oil-pipelines/?utm_term=.dfa96bf804e1 (accessed February 15, 2017).

30. Joseph F. Hilyard, *The Oil and Gas Industry: A Nontechnical Guide* (Tulsa, OK: PennWell Publishing, 2012), 15.

31. Paul Kirby, "Russia's Gas Fight with Ukraine," British Broadcasting Corporation, October 31, 2014, http://www.bbc.com/news/world-europe-29521564.

32. Daron Acemoglu and James A. Robinson, *Why Nations Fail: The Origins of Power, Prosperity, and Poverty* (New York, NY: Crown Publishing, 2012), 70–95.

33. Robert McNally and Michael Levi, "A Crude Predicament: The Era of Volatile Oil Prices," *Foreign Affairs* 90, no. 4 (2011).

34. Bassam Fattouh, *Oil Market Dynamics Through the Lens of the 2002–2009 Price Cycle* (Oxford Institute for Energy Studies: WPM 39, 2010), 18.

35. Catherine Clifford, "Oil's Record High, One Year Later," Cable News Network, July 2, 2009, http://money.cnn.com/2009/07/02/markets/year_oil/index.htm.

36. Bassam Fattouh, *An Anatomy of the Crude Oil Pricing System* (Oxford Institute for Energy Studies: WPM 40, 2011), 30–35.

37. For an analysis of diversification for oil-importing countries, see: Vlado Vivoda, "Diversification of Oil Import Sources and Energy Security: A Key Strategy or an Elusive Objective?" *Energy Policy* 37 (2009): 4615–4623.

38. U.S. Energy Information Administration, "What Drives Crude Oil Prices? Supply OPEC," http://www.eia.gov/finance/markets/supply-opec.cfm (accessed July 23, 2015).

39. Justin Williams, "Ghawar Oil Field: Saudi Arabia's Oil Future," *Energy and Capital*, Feb 19, 2013, http://www.energyandcapital.com/articles/ghawar-oil -field/3101.

Chapter Four

The Oil Security Approach
of the United States

INTRODUCTION

In the early 20th century, before China was reconstituted into a coherent state, unhindered by civil war and foreign incursions, the United States had gradually ascended to great heights of industrial and economic power, translating that wealth into a burgeoning middle class, heralding the era of the combustion engine and the automobile, ever thirsty for oil. Given ample domestic supply and growing demand, expertise was rapidly developed in oil extraction and refining, resulting in the United States engendering a privileged position that endured through much of the century, witnessing political, military, and economic dominance underpinned by ample domestic sources of petroleum, the capability to secure overseas sources when required, and the expertise needed to extract from ever more complicated sources. From the early development of the U.S. petroleum industry in Pennsylvania in the late 19th century to the supply availability in World War Two,[1] and to the naval dominance of the commons, the United States has been one step ahead of any conceivable competitor, dominating in both industry and technological prowess and oil supply. The oil supply aspect of American power during the 20th century is essential, and it "fueled" the state in a fundamental way.

The History of American Oil Security

A coherent energy security policy on the part of the United States is inherently centered on oil. Much of the approach for the United States was formulated during the initial global oil booms not only in response to the burgeoning auto industry, but later as recognition of the importance of oil to broader industry and military applications.

As with many oil discoveries in the 19th century, finding these resources was almost accidental. Oil seepage from the ground in Pennsylvania would eventually be developed and harnessed by myriad small-scale oil developers, and after the long process of whittling down competition among hundreds of drillers, the industry was eventually consolidated, mostly under the auspices of Rockefeller's Standard Oil.[2] In one way at least, this was a favorable outcome, given that the plethora of developers extracting under intense competition on the same oil patches were quickly and prematurely depleting their own resources, adversely impacting overall recovery rates.

By this time, most U.S. concerns for oil were mostly domestic and being a relatively new country to be proactive overseas, the United States was a bit late to stake out claims in the Middle East, lagging behind the British and French. After spending much of the opening years of the 20th century at war with the oil industry, spurred on by Ida Tarbell's exposé on Standard Oil, this quickly changed due to a single event: World War One. The war was important because it demonstrated that oil was emerging as an integral component to a country's defense materials, and therefore, this meant countries like the United States would need as much oil as they could possibly find. The postwar world saw the Wilson Administration move to support and assist domestic oil companies in their efforts to go abroad for new sources. This was the beginning of the symbiotic relationship between government and the oil industry, and resulted mainly from pragmatic conclusions arrived at by the administration, which understood not only the importance of oil to the military and industry, but also that the country was facing (perceived) domestic oil supply shortages (before Texas oilfields were developed), combined with drastic rises in demand, both of which resulted in rapid price increases.[3] This was also combined with the realization that other states were similarly developing their own overseas oil resources in order to enhance and maintain their own military power, especially the British, who famously under the auspices of Winston Churchill, then First Lord of the Admiralty, began converting the British fleet from coal power to oil, even before the war. In short, after the war, there was in imminent and recognized need to pursue these resources wherever able on the part of the U.S., in stark contrast to the prewar desire for these same companies to pursue overseas markets.

As the roaring twenties commenced, oil began to find a new demand outlet in the automotive industry, among others.[4] This was not a sure thing, as gasoline engines had to compete with both electric and steam-driven automobiles, but the gasoline-fed internal combustion engine finally won out, providing a new market for petroleum, in addition to the already existing lamp oil market. Further development of the oil industry was now not just a military matter, but a domestic matter as well, giving further impetus to expanding overseas.

Although the British were already established in Persia, U.S. oil companies made a dash for Middle East oil throughout the 1930s led by Standard Oil of California, which first struck oil in Bahrain, in 1932. The finds in Bahrain and Kuwait catalyzed increased interest in the Arabian Peninsula, and Standard Oil of California's (Socal) first discovery in eastern Saudi Arabia in 1938 caused an even more frenzied dash throughout the Arabian Peninsula, drawing out competition between the British and the Americans, vying for concessions from Ibn Saud. Oil was a primary overseas concern, right up to and throughout the Second World War, when the dash for Middle East oil was temporarily halted, where some areas had Allied orders to cement wells for fear of German capture, or where other areas were even bombed.[5]

The Japan situation is perhaps the first time where energy security deeply affected the material security of the United States by the accidental cutoff of oil exports to Japan in 1941,[6] catalyzing the subsequent actions taken by the Japanese Empire to redress its disadvantage in oil supplies. The direct consequence of the oil-based leverage exerted by the United States led directly to an attack on its military facilities in Pearl Harbor, consolidation in Manchuria, and the effective loss of an entire oil-producing region, the Netherlands East Indies.

At this point, it's important to recognize the limits of using oil for coercion, as demonstrated by the strategic interaction between the United States and Japan during the lead-up to the Second World War. There exists what can be termed a *coercive threshold* whereby once the compellent state finally proceeds to carry out its oil-related threats, this in turn pushes the "compelled" state towards a rapid kinetic response before current fuel supplies run dry. Out of fuel, and out of options, a state constrained in this manner will act like an injured animal backed into a corner; it will lash out because it simply has nothing to lose, and no other recourse.

As the Second World War wore on, another critical aspect of the war effort involved the United States ferrying supplies to the British. Despite their best efforts in Persia, and the greater Middle East, to source enough secure supplies of petroleum and transport those supplies back to the British Isles, they were simply unable to source enough of the needed supplies. Along with an assortment of desperately needed war materials and supplies, the United States ended up sending large quantities of oil to the British. And, as Daniel Yergin points out, it wasn't necessarily the crude oil that was important, but critically it was the refined petroleum products, ready for immediate use, and high quality. In particular, a new high-octane blend was introduced that allowed British fighter planes to handily outperform their underpowered German attackers in the air, playing a decisive role in the Battle of Britain.[7] Oil supplies were vital to the defense of the island.

During this time, the long-range pipelines were also developed as a countermeasure to the sustained losses suffered by oil tankers due to German U-boat attacks. The first extended-range pipeline was constructed by 1943, stretching from Texas oilfields to the East Coast, bypassing the costly routes hugging U.S. coastlines.[8] U-boats were active off the East Coast, sinking vessels within sight of major U.S. cities, including New York, and up the coast into Canadian waters.

Eventually, as the United States shifted into open warfare against the Axis powers, abundant U.S.-based oil proved even more vital to all Allied countries. The oil, and refined products, flowed through all theaters of combat, supplying the war effort against the German and Japanese forces. In direct contrast, the Axis powers simply did not have the necessary fuel to properly prosecute the war. Recognizing this weakness, Allied forces would eventually engage in a deliberate bombing campaign of German and Japanese oil infrastructure, targeting refineries and oil storage depots, severely restricting the supply of fuel to combat units. The qualitative and quantitative oil and fuel advantage enjoyed by the Allied powers in the Second World War was a deciding factor in the outcome of the conflict. This was a hard truth learned: oil had been lifted to a preeminent position and was utterly vital not only to a country's economy, but also to its military capacity. Embracing this point of view most forcefully was Secretary of the Interior Harold Ickes, in a letter to President Franklin D. Roosevelt in 1943, affirming:

> I said to you once that, next to winning the war, the most important matter before us as a Nation was the world oil situation. I feel this more strongly than I did when I made this statement . . . Despite everything, our supplies are falling below demand. Therefore, it behooves us to find supplies of crude oil elsewhere . . . this war has already demonstrated that, we cannot snuggle up to ourselves on the American Continent. We have assumed obligations in the world upon which we must make good. This means that we should have available oil in different parts of the world.[9]

After the war, both the Americans and the British, more than ever, understood the importance of oil, and began to take further measures in the Persian Gulf to provide overseas supplies for domestic consumption, with the strategic, dual purpose of rebuilding Continental Europe. The United States quickly formed a relationship with the Saudis, solidified by President Roosevelt's secret trip after the Yalta Conference to meet Ibn Saud himself on a U.S. naval vessel near the Suez Canal. This high-level meeting was a stark recognition of the importance of oil in the future of the United States and the world, and so one of the world's more interesting relationships began.[10]

Middle East oil factored heavily into Cold War strategic concerns, not only to keep NATO countries supplied, but also to deny surplus supplies to Warsaw Pact countries.[11] The United States ended up developing great sensitivity to any Soviet encroachments on the Gulf oil supply, beginning with their expulsion from Iran immediately after the war. Additionally, Marshall Plan assistance called for abundant oil supplies to be shipped to Europe, generating new markets for Gulf producers (along with the oil companies) and creating energy sources for a continent embroiled in ideological struggle. There was even further encouragement on the part of the U.S. government, when the emergence of fifty-fifty profit sharing emerged as regional Middle East governments improved their bargaining positions. This was set to raise production costs for American oil companies, but instead the Treasury Department stepped in to absorb these increasing costs through large tax breaks.[12]

Despite the arrangement between the U.S. and Saudi Arabia,[13] there were emerging frictions in the relationship between the United States and Middle Eastern producers: the partition of Palestine with the concurrent creation of the state of Israel and sovereignty issues. These aspects of the political and business relationships with states in the region, including misadventures in places like Iran, would sour relations with the region, fomenting a difficult and contentious relationship that still exists today. It was also crucial for some of these states to maintain governments friendly to the United States, resulting in further complications and involvement in domestic affairs.[14] In addition to these political issues, business was complicated, not just in the Middle East, but in countries around around the world, as they would begin to reassert their sovereignty over their own resources from multinational oil companies that were extracting and exporting supplies at favorable prices.[15] Broad assertion of state sovereignty and renegotiations of contracts, in conjunction with political tensions, would lead to another seminal moment in U.S. energy security: the 1973 oil shock, and the short-lived shift of power from consumers to producers.

If anything, Middle East states grew in importance to the United States, especially as it became clear the region was necessary to maintain stability in global oil markets. For instance, Saudi Arabia was so important that the Saudi government, with encouragement from the United States, heavily promoted Wahhabism, an extreme version of Islam, throughout the entire country and abroad, in order to shore up domestic support and draw a contrast between The Kingdom and Iran, and to provide ideological fodder opposite communism, which was slowly creeping towards the peninsula, especially with the Soviet War underway in Afghanistan.[16]

The shocks of the 1970s, especially the quadrupling of prices in 1973, demonstrated a need to revamp energy security and implement new policies designed to reduce external dependence in the future. The oil shocks were a learning process for Saudi Arabia as well. By engaging in these overtly political actions, they hindered their own long-term export security by alienating customers in developed, Western economies, and were severely impacted by the price drops in the 1980s. The U.S., however, engaged in a multinational effort through the Organization for Economic Cooperation and Development (OECD), composed of largely advanced industrialized, Western energy consumers, to create the International Energy Agency (IEA), based in Paris. The IEA would serve primarily as a coordinating mechanism for oil reserves from participating consumer states, so they would optimally prepare for, and react to, threats to energy supplies. This system is still in place today, and has been relatively effective, especially in its reserve requirements for all member states and coordinated SPR releases. However, the significance of these achievements pales in comparison to the market fallout from politically orchestrated price increases. Through higher prices and government encouragement, multiple new non-OPEC producing regions began exporting supplies to OECD countries, most notably from the North Sea and Alaska. For instance, within a month of the imposition of the embargo and price increases, President Nixon, on November 16, 1973, signed into law the Trans-Alaska Pipeline Authorization Act, removing any hurdles to the establishment of a pipeline from Alaska to the continental United States,[17] and a few days later, proclaimed the goal of energy "self-sufficiency" in an address to the nation.[18] While self-sufficiency remains elusive, the pipeline was completed by 1977. In addition, demand had dropped as a result of the crises by causing new levels of conservation[19] and the development of new energy technologies[20] to reduce consumption, most notably in automobiles. Both supply and demand were working against the OPEC producers, and even as they normalized relations and exports to the West, there wasn't anything to be done, other than brace for the depressed prices of the 1980s.

The Carter Administration also had a prominent role to play in crafting an energy security response. Most notable was the explicit declaration that the Persian Gulf is a vital interest to U.S. national security, and any armed incursions would be met with a military response. This led to the creation of the Rapid Deployment Joint Task Force (RDJTF), which would eventually become Central Command (CENTCOM). In President Carter's own words:

> The region, which is now threatened by Soviet troops in Afghanistan, is of great strategic importance: It contains more than two-thirds of the world's exportable oil. The Soviet effort to dominate Afghanistan has brought Soviet military forces to within 300 miles of the Indian Ocean and close to the Straits of Hormuz, a waterway through which most of the world's oil must flow. The Soviet Union is now attempting to consolidate a strategic position, therefore, that poses

a grave threat to the free movement of Middle East oil. . . . It demands the participation of all who rely on oil from the Middle East and who are concerned with global peace and stability.[21]

He proceeds to state explicitly: "Let our position be absolutely clear: An attempt by any outside force to gain control of the Persian Gulf region will be regarded as an assault on the vital interests of the United States of America, and such an assault will be repelled by any means necessary, including military force."[22] After a decade of deteriorating U.S. ability to shape events in the Middle East, and Soviet encroachments in the region, the explicit nature of Carter's proclamation was quite important, and represented the culmination of several years of effort.[23] These shifting strategic and energy dynamics in the 1980s, along with the explicit declaration of Persian Gulf oil as a vital interest to the United States, lay much of the groundwork and operational capability for the United States in the Middle East in the 1990s and 2000s.[24] While the RDJTF was fashioned as a contingency based, non-NATO, joint operation global task force,[25] it was mainly developed for carrier-based deployment to the Persian Gulf as a deterrent force to the Soviet Union. Later, the designation would be modified, ultimately becoming U.S. Central Command (CENTCOM), and would act on its explicitly stated purpose to protect the Gulf by taking military action in 1991, halting Saddam Hussein's southern advance, and ejecting his military forces from Kuwait.

This force structure, strategy, organization, and business environment carried over into the modern area, and was merely solidified and refined, making adaptations and adjustments where needed. Although there were blunders along the way, this strategy and the system it produced has been remarkably successful and continues to endure.

The Grand Strategy of the United States

The available evidence concerning American grand strategy is well developed and coherent, with many similar themes, and recent history clearly demonstrates key facets of the strategy. One can surmise the explicit and implicit objectives of the United States from multiple sources, but one objective is clear in most of these examinations: Secure access to Persian Gulf oil and maintenance of global oil markets is paramount in America's grand strategic calculations. This grew primarily out of the need to "fuel" Europe's postwar development through the Marshall Plan, and since then it has taken on a broader role for the markets as a whole, becoming guarantor of the free flow of oil for allies and market participants. In addition, opposite China, the United States retains a high degree of strategic flexibility,[26] as the only true state that is not forced to derive and implement its grand strategy under significant security constraints in the post–Cold War period. This may be the defining feature of U.S. grand strategy in the contemporary era as peer competitors, or even compelling threats to the country's interests and its citizenry, do not exist in a serious way, creating issues of their own, especially with the shift from threat-based strategic and military planning to capabilities-based planning,[27] which is lacking in strategic thought entirely, along with the propensity to manufacture threat.[28]

Despite deficiencies, there is still great continuity in U.S. grand strategy, with key aspects that stretch back nearly a century. A good place to start may be with an important overview of U.S. grand strategy from Robert Art, who has clearly delineated everything from the use of force,[29] to a current and past look at America's grand strategy,[30] to his proposed approach for a more effective grand strategy for the United States.[31] Over time, he has developed a rank-ordered list of grand strategic objectives that the United States has pursued for several decades.[32] First on his list is to prevent an attack on the American heartland. Threats to the heartland are meant to have the fiercest of military responses available. His second interest is the maintenance of an open economic order and to combat protectionism. Ranked third is the preservation of access to reasonably priced and secure supplies of oil from the Persian Gulf. In previous iterations of these rank-ordered lists,[33] Art specifically mentions oil from the Persian Gulf as a priority of vital importance to U.S. grand strategy even as a couple other components have shifted and changed. For instance, extremely important to U.S. grand strategy, and previously occupying the number two spot on Art's list, is the prevention of great power Eurasian wars and the security competitions that make such conflicts increasingly likely. This stems from the Realist notion to maintain a balance of power, and to prevent the ascension of a regional hegemon, especially on a highly industrialized landmass. This he ranked as highly important, and would merit a military response, as was done in the two previous world wars and throughout the Cold War. His recent list places this at number four and shifts the language to "the prevention of certain wars." In this category he places Europe, Asia, as well as attacks on Israel and South Korea. He rounds off his list with the promotion of democratic institutions where feasible and the support of humanitarian values. Art's list is important to this study for its consistence in ranking oil supplies from the Persian Gulf as vital to grand strategy and for his clear attempts at reconciliation between not only interests but also the threats and capabilities of the United States to meet those threats, concepts that sorely need incorporation in the energy security literature.

With Art's rankings, one can clearly disseminate a hedging strategy through the various post–World War Two theoretical strands in pursuit of security and prosperity taken by the United States. The combination of Realist and Liberal approaches was determined to be the best way forward. The utilization of hard power with deterrence and military force where needed, in combination with the pursuit of a liberal interdependent global economy, and peace based on adoption of democratic governmental systems is the direct application of these theoretical principles developed over decades.

Other scholars like Christopher Layne promote a relatively simpler approach to U.S. grand strategy as being based primarily on expansion and hegemony,[34] but also highly inclusive of oil. Much of this expansion occurred during the Second World War, but the next phase occurred as the United States recognized its new interests in oil, especially that of the Middle East. Layne believes that since the conclusion of World War Two, the United States has assiduously embarked on a campaign of expansion, and this expansion has naturally led the U.S. to bid for hegemony in the important regions of Western Europe, East Asia, and the Persian Gulf.[35] Layne makes the point several times that this was an endogenously derived policy, developed by planners during World War Two, and before the Soviet Union presented a major threat to U.S. security.[36] This he terms, "extraregional hegemony," and then clarifies the meaning of hegemony as being primarily about hard power and economic supremacy.[37] A hegemon has great military capability in a region and no other power can seriously damage that hard power. Economic hegemony consists of a "preponderance of material resources" securely available to the state.[38] As the war ended, the framework was in place before the emergence of the Cold War, and the U.S. acted quickly to establish a "postwar network of overseas air bases [. . .] intended to ensure that the United States would not be stopped by water from projecting its power into Europe, East Asia, and the Middle East to prevent any potential rival [. . .] from attaining hegemony in Europe or Asia, or threatening America's Open Door interests by cutting off access to Eurasian markets and raw materials."[39] The prevention of hegemony and extreme economic turmoil were advanced as key interests to U.S. security due to the accepted reasoning that such turmoil eventually has the capacity to contribute to conflict and war. But, Middle East policy was oil-driven and the emerging requirement to secure U.S. access to oil from the Middle East, including the sea lines of communication (SLOCs), generated new security commitments and concerns.[40] The Gulf sources, in particular, even drove Washington to include Greece, Turkey, and Iran as a component of their security policy in the region, providing a line of buffer states that would assist in shielding Gulf oil from the Soviet Union. Layne explicitly states "America's regional strategic objectives—gaining control over Middle Eastern and Persian Gulf oil, and establishing the United States (at Britain's expense) as the region's dominant power—were fixed during World War Two, well before U.S. policymakers became concerned about the

Soviet threat."[41] The United States recognized the importance of retaining control of these regions for their own supply security, but also to deny that security to others, in order to increase dependence on the United States. As Layne points out, the United States worked to prevent Britain's re-emergence as a hegemon by forcing currency convertibility, opening British markets, and gaining control of Britain's raw materials resources, such as oil concessions in Iran, making the U.S. the dominant power in the Middle East.[42] As the Cold War progressed, the United States worked to prevent both Eurasian industrial production and additional natural resources, especially oil, from being harnessed by the Soviet Union and distributed to Warsaw Pact countries. Had Soviet expansion on this scale occurred it might have been able to overcome its industrial and resource deficiencies, enabling power projection outside its periphery.[43]

Colin Dueck catalogues the expanse of U.S. grand strategy since the beginning of the 20th century, bringing a degree of continuity based on the marriage between realism and constructivism as determinants of strategic culture. The manifestations of this are built on classical liberalism[44] and the idea of limited liability (the avoidance of costs and commitments),[45] generating grand strategic "sub-cultures" that shift over time, whether internationalist, nationalist, progressive, or Realist.[46] The most recent iteration of this approach coalesces into a mostly unchanged strategy carried over from the Cold War. This, Dueck argues, is due to the "success" of the grand strategy (i.e., ending the Cold War) and the absence of any compelling reason for change, which meant a lot of the existing framework could persist, alongside a resurgence of the limited liability approach, leading to many half-hearted overseas ventures.[47] However, this still meant the United States would be incredibly active overseas, laboring to secure overseas assets and policy preferences.

More sources seem to corroborate many established grand strategy tenets of the U.S. For instance, leaked defense documents in 1992 demonstrate the desire to prevent peer competitors from rising to challenge U.S. dominance.[48] Due to the backlash from these leaks, the next guidance on defense strategy had to be modified so as to be more palatable to the spread of liberalism, and culminated in the release of new guidance from then Secretary of Defense Dick Cheney watering down the more aggressive components,[49] but still stating the U.S. desire to "preclude any hostile power from dominating a region critical to our interests"[50] and in reference to the Middle East and the Persian Gulf, to safeguard "access [. . .] to the region's important sources of oil."[51] This is again demonstrated in the 2002 version, where it is again made clear the United States will not tolerate security threats, and will utilize preemptive measures to prevent such threats, among others.[52]

Bill Clinton's term as president was marked by a tug-of-war of differing grand strategies given the end of the Cold War and the primacy of the United States in its "unipolar moment."[53] Without a major threat to confront, policy vacillated with a certain degree of indecision, but nevertheless formed a more or less coherent policy of "selective primacy."[54] As Posen and Ross demonstrate, cooperative security, selective engagement, and primacy all had roles to play in U.S. grand strategy over the given period, and much of this is demonstrated in Clinton's National Security Strategy, A National Security Strategy of Engagement and Enlargement, where the language curiously shifts between these various aspects of grand strategy.[55] Impressively, when it comes to energy security, the security document is not shy about stating the importance of oil[56] and its place as a "vital interest" to the security of the United States and its allies.[57]

George W. Bush's first National Security Strategy (NSS) also mentions vital interests and briefly mentions the enhancement of energy security,[58] and then in the 2006 National Security Strategy, there is mention of the typical security interests, but it also explicitly mentions the dependence of the United States and its allies on foreign oil from unstable parts of the world as a key security challenge,[59] and proceeds to dedicate an entire section to "Opening, integrating, and diversifying energy markets to ensure energy independence" by focusing on key energy security imperatives.[60] Interestingly, the 2006 NSS also unambiguously states concerns over the China-energy nexus. The administration cites non-transparent military expansion, China's attempts to "'lock-up' energy supplies around world," and the unqualified support of autocratic, resource-rich countries.[61]

Barack Obama's NSS is perhaps the least reflective of past grand strategic and Realist tenets. The loose reference to overseas security exists and there were references to energy security, although mainly regarding the diversification of the domestic energy mix for a new energy economy and to combat climate change.[62] Domestic diversification, including the use of more renewables, and increases in efficiency are important to oil security, since this will reduce overall demand, and will lessen the need for higher import levels. This type of transition has the same impact as the domestic demand response following the 1970s oil shocks.

The overall picture of U.S. grand strategy is one of select rank orders, defensible, vital interests, made secure by an internationalist, or expansionary foreign policy. At the core of these assessments of U.S. grand strategy is oil and the Persian Gulf. The overseas security apparatus of the United States has moved assiduously over time in order to secure key energy centers for the domestic economy and the broader oil markets. This is a particularly secure position today, whereby the U.S. controls three of the key zones in the world that retain the greatest amount of oil and gas reserves: The Persian Gulf, Venezuela, due to U.S. dominance in the Western Hemisphere and close proximity to the U.S.,[63] and North America, including the United States, with its own sizable reserve base.

An Assessment of U.S. Energy Security

The United States has methodically worked to secure overseas sources of oil supplies as seen with its strong consideration given in grand strategic thought, and more specifically, military and political action in the Persian Gulf beginning with the stronger relationship forged by President Roosevelt and ibn Saud at the end of the Second World War. Eventually, the United States would become engaged in many areas to secure its oil supply both overtly and covertly. This has been a continuous security staple, and the United States has had the ability to dedicate the necessary resources to such a task. But, in the immediate past, the U.S. has clearly enjoyed a reign of preponderant military, economic, and political power. Using key aspects elucidated in the previous chapter, the strength of U.S. oil security begins to take shape. However, going forward, one of the biggest issues on the horizon is how the United States will respond to its oil and gas challenges in an increasingly multipolar world, with China a notable challenge.[64]

Availability

Domestic Production

A primary measure of availability is the amount of production occurring within a state's boundaries. Here, the United States, while blessed with reserves and production in the past, went into a state of steady, secular decline beginning in 1985. As a matter of fact, 1986 would be the last year U.S. production would surpass 10 million barrels per day until 2013. Over the course of these 27 years, some which are logged in table 3.1 below, the United States reached a production low of 6.83 million barrels per day in 2006, and then began to slowly increase, until a massive surge in production beginning in 2011–2012 resulting from tight oil extraction. Globally, production was increasing through the course of this study (except from 2005–07); however, so was demand, and global proved reserves were increasingly slow to be discovered, or were in decline, and of the fields that were discovered, they were less economically viable, and less suitable for standard production.[65] It was this supposed convergence between increasing production (the increased velocity at which oil is being removed from the

Table 4.1. Annual Domestic Oil Production (Mbbls/d)

Year	Production	Year	Production
1992	8,868	2003	7,362
1993	8,583	2004	7,244
1994	8,389	2005	6,903
1995	8,322	2006	6,828
1996	8,295	2007	6,862
1997	8,269	2008	6,783
1998	8,011	2009	7,263
1999	7,731	2010	7,552
2000	7,734	2011	7,868
2001	7,670	2012	8,892
2002	7,626	2013	10,003

Source: BP Statistical Review of Energy 2014, Statistical Workbook, Oil Production, http://www.bp.com/en/global/corporate/energy -economics/statistical-review-of-world-energy.html.

ground) and declining reserves (the actual oil left in the ground) that fueled worries over "peak oil" by many analysts.[66]

In table 4.1, we can clearly see a 23 percent decline in production from the 1992 peak to the 2006 trough. Average production through the study was 7.87 million bbls per day with a standard deviation of .78 million bbls per day (780,000 bbls per day). The United States continues to lead in the development of new production technologies, and to apply these advancements to enhance domestic and overseas production. The shale boom is only the latest, and perhaps most dramatic, example of this occurring. Production ability and continuous innovation are distinct advantages to companies originating in the United States and other OECD countries.

Concerning refining operations, it is particularly interesting to note both the dominance of U.S. refining operations, paralleled to the massive increases in domestic refining capacity witnessed in China. For instance, global refining capacity had China at 4.1 percent of the total in 1992, while the United States had 20.4 percent of total global refining capacity. Fast-forward to 2013, when the United States had a slight drop to 18.8 percent of global refining capacity, while China's capacity grew to 13.3 percent of the global total, the result of a massive expansion of refining infrastructure. This is a 413 percent increase in refining capacity for China over the study period, while the United States witnessed a 15 percent increase over the study period. And, there is a great deal of continuity through slow growth on the part of the U.S. refining industry, as demonstrated in table 4.2. Domestic refining operations continue to be a major strength for US oil security. The stretches all the way back to World War Two, and because of the dance for finding operations the United States has been a major product exporter for many decades. The simple fact is, crude oil does not

Table 4.2.   Country-level Refining Capacity (Mbbls/d)

Year	Daily Amount	Year	Daily Amount
1992	15,120	2003	16,894
1993	15,030	2004	17,125
1994	15,434	2005	17,339
1995	15,333	2006	17,443
1996	15,452	2007	17,594
1997	15,711	2008	17,672
1998	16,261	2009	17,584
1999	16,512	2010	17,736
2000	16,595	2011	17,322
2001	16,785	2012	17,824
2002	16,757	2013	17,818

Source: BP Statistical Review of Energy 2014, Statistical Workbook, Oil: Refinery Capacities, http://www.bp.com/en/global/corporate/energy-economics/statistical-review-of-world-energy.html.

do a whole lot of good unless it can be refined into usable products. The United States remains a leader in this area and not only on capacity, but on the diverse fuel types that can be processed. For instance, the United States remains one of the few countries in the world capable of processing heavy crudes on a large scale, giving it a distinct diversification advantage.

Energy Infrastructure

Energy infrastructure in an international context consists of those processes and equipment that move crude oil across national boundaries, and then efficiently and effectively distribute those materials domestically. For the purposes of this study, only pipelines and ports will be considered, given their direct relationship to the external environment. Without this restriction, it would be easy to then catalogue such items as highways and traversable roads throughout the country, where a tallied tanker fleet moved crude and refined products to their destinations. Or to count railroad tracks and the ability to move crude via rail. Cataloguing this would be excessive, especially since these components have other primary uses far beyond the transportation of energy products. But, ports and pipelines are eminently important and directly connected to the extra-territorial aspects of energy security, while also maintaining a direct connection to global markets as they are the primary points of ingress for crude.

Additionally, collecting data on pipeline length and capacity, as well as the number of available ports along with their capacity to offload crude, for use in a time-series analysis has proven quite difficult due to data availability. However, it is possible to capture some of this information for various moments through the progression of each state's oil security. It also may be irrelevant, since the number of ports, lengths of pipelines, and their varying capacities are generally going to be unique to the requirements of the specific the country. Another problem with ports is the same problem mentioned above with highways and trains: they're not used just for oil, but for the millions of other products that pour in and out of both countries every year.

For those who believe pipelines are a vulnerable component of the supply chain, this may not necessarily be true. For instance, after decades of dealing with adverse internal conditions, Saudi Arabia has developed the capability to repair damaged pipelines within a remarkable 36 hours, complete with replacement materials placed along pipeline infrastructure and rapid response teams managed by Saudi security forces.[67] Pipelines may be vulnerable during wartime, but there is a cost to targeting these lines since they inherently would require constant strikes to keep them offline, given their ease of repair. They, however, would be invulnerable under normal or antagonistic conditions. The domestic oil and natural gas pipeline network in the United States is highly developed and has been an effective means of oil transportation in and out of the country, and around the country internally for many decades.

Ports have been an integral part of the economic success of the United States and have been developed and renovated at increasing rates since the founding of the country. The cognizance was always in place that in order for the United States to maintain its own security, it would have to look towards the oceans on either end of the continent: security both in terms of physical and economic harms. Particular to oil, many ports were capable of importing overseas crude, but this capacity was enhanced beginning in the 1950s, when the United States began to import more oil and embarked on port-expansion projects. Since that time, the super tanker has come to dominate the seagoing crude trade, which is an important distinction, because only large, deepwater ports are viable suitors for such large vessels to offload such massive amounts of petroleum. The United States has several such ports but relies primarily on the Louisiana Offshore Oil Port (LOOP) when importing crude, especially from the Middle East.

Current Extractable Reserves

Not too long ago, global extractable reserve growth was projected to decline and many large fields had deteriorating production or were already in a secular, long-term decline,[68] which would have ushered in a new era oil scarcity, reducing overall supply, and driving up prices dramatically in the face of increased global economic growth. However, new technology and techniques have been developed that drastically altered the amount of extractable reserves the United States, and indeed the world, could draw upon. In particular, the ability to profitably extract from tight oil deposits, particularly shale, has dramatically increased domestic reserves, reversing the potential scarcity that would have existed otherwise.

Reserves, for the purposes of this research, adhere to the strict definition utilized in the energy industry. Reserves here do not simply include oil-in-place (OIP), within a given territory, or under the control of the specific country or company. The definition here is the actual amount of recoverable oil that can be extracted at economically permissive levels, and is located within the sovereign's territory. Therefore, proved reserves, also referred to as 1P or P90, are utilized for the study, indicating petroleum that is profitable to produce with current technology and at current price levels. This is petroleum that has a 90 percent chance of being produced under current conditions. Probable (2P or P50) and possible (3P or P10) reserves, may be referenced, and it will be noted when either of these are used. Domestic reserves are, of course, given a premium in terms of energy security, given their strategically secure location within a country's borders. However, the reserves available to individual companies are eminently important as well, contributing to overall energy security under normal market conditions.

Especially interesting to note, in table 4.3, is the trajectory of available proved reserves in the United States. There is a slow but steady decline, with the occasional relapse, through the 1990s, and then a general plateau from 1999 to 2009, before rapidly climbing higher due to both higher prices and the U.S.-based shale revolution. The climb in reserves from 2009 to 2010 was 13 percent, 2010 to 2011, 14 percent, and 2011 to 2012 was 11 percent,

Table 4.3.   U.S. Proved Reserves of Crude Oil (Bbbls)

Year	Proved Reserves	Year	Proved Reserves
1992	31.2	2003	29.4
1993	30.2	2004	29.3
1994	29.6	2005	29.9
1995	29.8	2006	29.4
1996	29.8	2007	30.5
1997	30.5	2008	28.4
1998	28.6	2009	30.9
1999	29.7	2010	35
2000	30.4	2011	39.8
2001	30.4	2012	44.2
2002	30.7	2013	44.2

Source: BP Statistical Review of Energy 2014, Statistical Workbook, Oil—Proved Reserves History, http://www.bp.com/en/global/corporate/energy-economics/statistical-review-of-world-energy.html.

meaning over the 2009 to 2012 period, proved reserves surged by 43 percent, giving the United States an important advantage in secure, domestic supply.

In the interest of devising quantitative comparisons, the reserve amount is not as useful as it might seem. To understand this better, the reserve amount needs to be compared to other measures, especially since what may be large reserve levels for one state may be exceedingly low for another. Energy demands owing to levels of development will be a critical factor to understand reserve amounts better. Alone, the amount simply doesn't reveal much about the level of dependency of the country on those reserves. For this, one could potentially use some metric, such as consumption, in conjunction with the reserve measure. For this, a simple reserves-to-production ratio, modified to use consumption instead of production, is used to gauge the amount of time a country could survive cut off from outside sources. The use of consumption instead of production should prove more accurate for energy security measures, since consumption is the true measure of the oil required for a country in a given year, instead of production, which may be modified for any number of reasons, including increases or decreases in different refined fuel blends or product exports. In this sense, a country like Kuwait will have large production levels for export, despite having low consumption rates, meaning it is an inaccurate measure for its own domestic oil security. The study establishes the reserves-to-consumption ratio by measuring the amount of reserves in a given year by consumption levels in the same year, as noted in table 4.4. The output, given in years, may be a contentious figure, given consumption projections, price volatility, supply, and demand, but it is a useful measure nonetheless. The amount of supply available given a set year of consumption can give a rough conception of the potential of an economy to run with a possible supply cutoff from overseas supplies of crude oil.

Proved reserves are increasing in the United States, at the same time that broader consumption of petroleum and petroleum products is decreasing, increasing the years of available petroleum in the ground for eventual consumption by nearly 20 percent from 2011 to 2012. The majority of the period saw the average years of available supply at 4.6 years, and from 1992 to 2010, the period before the shale boom, the average was 4.3 years. This is a relatively stable amount, given the growth in demand and production over the period.

The stability of the reserve levels for the United States underscores perhaps a careful approach to the development and production of energy in the United States. There hasn't been a "rush" in the new century to develop reserves, and exploration and production has been steady. Only certain amounts of exploration and production of domestic sources has been allowed and this has contributed to the maintenance of stable levels over the period of the study.

Table 4.4.   **Reserves-to-Consumption**

Year	Annual Consumption (MMbbls)	Years of Supply	Year	Annual Consumption (MMbbls)	Years of Supply
1992	6,217	5.02	2003	7,312	4.02
1993	6,291	4.8	2004	7,566	3.87
1994	6,467	4.58	2005	7,592	3.94
1995	6,469	4.61	2006	7,550	3.89
1996	6,682	4.46	2007	7,548	4.04
1997	6,796	4.49	2008	7,113	3.99
1998	6,904	4.14	2009	6,851	4.51
1999	7,124	4.17	2010	7,000	5
2000	7,190	4.23	2011	6,891	5.78
2001	7,171	4.24	2012	6,748	6.55
2002	7,212	4.26	2013	6,893	6.41

Source: BP Statistical Review of Energy 2014, Statistical Workbook, Oil: Consumption, http://www.bp.com/
en/global/corporate/energy-economics/statistical-review-of-world-energy.html

Capital Investment and Efficiency

The energy industry is notoriously capital-intensive. Without the necessary capital equipment for extraction, processing, transport, and distribution, on top of the financial capital to fund operations and make costly investments, on a uniquely extended timeline, an oil company cannot operate, and its performance will certainly suffer over the long term.

U.S. energy companies have access to multiple sources of capital, and typically are able to raise funds for investments and purchases when required. The international energy companies in general maintain higher levels of technological proficiency, so they are also in high demand for joint ventures, which can bring on additional funding, and perhaps more importantly, further risk mitigation. However, much of this is dependent on the vagaries of the market, and all forces subject to it. In an environment, such as the 2007–2008 financial crisis, where credit was scarce, this may serve to hamper and restrict operations and capital investment, forcing companies to forgo opportunities and market share, in place of fiscal discipline. Capital markets, while plentiful and highly developed in industrialized economies, have the potential for volatility, owing to market fluctuations, which can be a potential risk to energy financing. Access to capital, but also the effective use of that capital is incredibly important. There is a widely accepted measure, popularized by ExxonMobil, for capital efficiency in the oil and gas sector: return on average capital employed (ROACE). This is a measure to effectively demonstrate profit as a percentage of the capital utilized in company operations. A company with a higher percentage indicates it maintains higher profit levels from direct operations for every dollar spent. The average amount of capital is derived from the mean of the current and previous year's capital employed in operations. The return is essentially net income with financing expenses added back in, taken as a percentage of the capital employed in the given year. It should also be noted each company computes this metric differently, which means the ROACE listed on balance sheets is not fit for direct comparison between companies. The approach used in this research most closely follows the methodology utilized by Royal Dutch Shell but modified for clarity and data availability.[69] The formula used is as follows:

$$\frac{net\ income + interest}{total\ stockholder\ equity + short\text{-}term\ debt + long\text{-}term\ debt + minority\ interests + capital\ leases\ (if\ available)}$$

This is essentially a compromise measure based on an examination of this measure's use in the company reports of multiple oil and gas firms and more textbook-oriented equations, with the results demonstrated below in table 4.5. For instance, some will include special items, one-time expenses, or use earnings before interest and taxes (EBIT) interchangeably with net income.

With these results, there is quite a range between the companies in terms of their capital efficiency. ExxonMobil is, by a significant margin, the most capital efficient of the three, reaching an average almost three times that of ConocoPhillips. All took significant reductions in their returns during the depressed prices in 2009, after the 2008 crash. They tend to be remarkably consistent, while showing less profitability over time. Speculation to these

Table 4.5.   Return on Average Capital Employed (ROACE)

Year	ExxonMobil (XOM)	Chevron (CVX)	ConocoPhillips (COP)
2005	0.3	0.19	0.22
2006	0.33	0.23	0.19
2007	0.32	0.23	0.12
2008	0.36	0.27	−0.16
2009	0.17	0.11	0.07
2010	0.22	0.18	0.14
2011	0.26	0.22	0.15
2012	0.28	0.19	0.1
2013	0.18	0.14	0.12
Average for All Years	0.27	0.19	0.1

Source: Author's calculations based on data from company reports, Bloomberg Terminal company data, Morningstar, www.morningstar.com and NASDAQ, www.nasdaq.com. Company reports available at ExxonMobil, http://corporate.exxonmobil.com/en/; Chevron, https://www.chevron.com; ConocoPhillips, http://www.conocophillips.com/Pages/default.aspx.

circumstances may point, at least partially, towards the greater capital requirements for extraction, compared with earlier. These averages are then bundled together for direct comparisons with Chinese firms, as a single efficiency ratio meant to represent American-based companies.

Affordability

Pricing and Volatility

Supply and demand ultimately determine the price of petroleum; however, advanced financial markets promote the efficient pricing of commodities and at times can have more influence on pricing than overtly evident. In this case, the United States has the most advanced energy financial network in the world, centered on the WTI benchmark.

Export prices and volatility are both important components for the proper functioning of oil markets. Both affect everything in the market, from the final price paid by consumers to the ability to plan ahead into a stable or unstable environment. For instance, stable pricing is needed in order for companies to plan projects several years in advance, or for countries to plan geopolitical responses to adverse events impacting the supply and price of oil. In order to gauge these outcomes, it is import to recognize the required disaggregation of the "oil price" into proper terms. There isn't a single unified price of oil all over the world, albeit it is similar within specific categories of petroleum grades. For example, a heavier grade of petroleum will be priced similar to other heavier grades, and lighter oils will be priced accordingly as well. For this section, it is best to use the ubiquitous West Texas Intermediate (WTI) price for crude in the United States. This is the primary benchmark for oil produced in the United States and is used in some cases for imports from abroad. However, it is no longer used for oil imports from Saudi Arabia and has been supplanted by the Price Reporting Agency (PRA) Argus Media's index, the Argus Sour Crude Index (ASCI), given its more accurate assessment of oil prices from the Middle East to the United States. However, this change only occurred in 2011, and the impact would be negligible to switch from WTI to ASCI for 2012, so WTI will be used as the main pricing mechanism for the price of oil in the United States. Looking at the price of WTI over the course of the study, shown in table 4.6, one can plainly see the variations in the price of oil, and how difficult it is to predict with any certainty where the price will be too far in the future. However, owing to market mechanisms discussed here, the price of WTI has been relatively stable, with intermittent volatility as the market adjusts to face new realities. This is essentially how anyone would expect a market to operate, and oil bears this out.

Table 4.6.   Annual Price of WTI Crude (West Texas Intermediate, 40 API, Midland Texas), USD per Barrel, and Volatility (Annual Standard Deviations)

Year	Price	Volatility	Year	Price	Volatility
1992	20.56	1.24	2003	31.1	2.21
1993	18.46	1.65	2004	41.45	5.62
1994	17.18	1.59	2005	56.44	6.01
1995	18.43	0.77	2006	66.05	5.24
1996	22.13	2.06	2007	72.29	12.64
1997	20.59	1.7	2008	99.59	27.78
1998	14.42	1.39	2009	61.69	13.18
1999	19.17	4.55	2010	79.4	4.56
2000	30.32	2.54	2011	95.05	7.36
2001	25.87	3.42	2012	94.14	7.19
2002	26.12	3.05	2013	97.93	5.02

Notes: Author took the simple average of the end-of-month price for each year to calculate annual price and calculated the standard deviations for each year.

Sources: Quandl, WTI Crude Oil Price (ODA/POILWTI_USD), https://www.quandl.com/data/ODA/ POILW4TI_USD, sourced from Open Data for Africa, African Development Bank Group IMF Primary Commodity Prices August 2015, http://opendataforafrica.org/efkgejg/imf-primary-commodity-prices -august-2015, and International Monetary Fund, IMF Primary Commodity Prices, http://www.imf.org/ external/np/res/commod/index.aspx.

The data demonstrate a relatively stable price for the commodity over the first half of the study, from 1992 to 2002. The pricing remained largely smooth, averaging a price of $21.20 per/bbl with a standard deviation of $4.39 per/bbl, giving a range of approximately 21 percent on a barrel of oil over the ten-year period. The second half of the study is where the numbers become more volatile. The primary reason for this price surge and volatility is emerging market demand growth, in particular, Chinese demand growth. The average price for the second ten-year period is $72.28 per/bbl with a standard deviation of $22.36 per/bbl yielding a range of approximately 31 percent on a barrel of oil. And, when accounting for not just annual averages, but for the monthly price, the standard deviation rises to $24.97 per/bbl, resulting in a 35 percent variation in the price per barrel.

Prices have increased beyond the level of inflation reflecting supply and demand and volatility has increased over the first ten-year period, almost reverting back to levels seen in the 1980s, where the standard deviation was $15.71, or 33 percent on an average of $48.10. While not that important, the price of oil is destined to change drastically over a twenty-year period, as we have seen with this study. When speaking of price stability, it is not necessarily a concern that the price rises or falls, even by significant amounts, so long as companies and economies have the necessary time to adjust to changes in pricing. No one would realistically attempt to predict

twenty, or even ten, years ahead, what the price of oil might be; this would
be a fool's errand at best, and potentially destructive to anyone that would
rely on such numbers. However, companies and economies should be able
to project a few years ahead, with a certain degree of accuracy, what their
energy costs will be, within a certain bounded range. Broken up into smaller
data chunks, we can see the cost of WTI maintains stability and keeps with
slow adjustments, except for 2008.

Short-term oil price is primarily the consideration of not only long-term
supply-and-demand fundamentals, but the amount of excess supply in the
system at a specific moment in time. This is the primary purpose of Saudi
Arabia's vast reserves, used to stabilize and suppress prices if the situation
calls for it.

It should also be pointed out that price volatility can take two forms;
both pertinent for the U.S. and China. Oil price volatility is essentially a
two-level situation where prices occur at the international level and the
domestic level. Similar levels of price volatility will be seen at the international level for both countries; however, the domestic levels will differ due
to domestic controls. Namely, many price swings and gyrations that occur
then filter down to the consumer in the United States, positively, or negatively, impacting household income levels. However, in China, the companies themselves bear much of the brunt of higher commodity prices as they
are still required to sell to domestic consumers, but at a capped price level,
sometimes resulting in serious financial losses. This additionally demonstrates why Chinese companies are attempting to operate abroad as much
as possible, in order to diversify their sources of income away from China,
in order to reduce financial losses in such situations. The result, however,
is that much of the price volatility in China is shielded from the consumers,
owing its stability to price fixing by the state.

Pricing for oil consumed in the United States is also mostly transparent.
The pricing for oil arriving is generally derived from market conditions,
reflecting the spot price of WTI or Brent Crude. The oil market also derives
pricing indirectly from many long-term contracts that have been established,
some of which have published information, many of which do not. Oil market intermediaries, most notably Argus Media Corp, based in the United
Kingdom, and Platts, a division of McGraw Hill, based in the United States,
both have a very involved role in pricing global oil supplies, as many of the
global financial contracts, and most in the United States, are derived from
pricing data generated by these two firms. For instance, Saudi Arabia, when
contracting oil deliveries to the United States utilizes the Argus Sour Crude
Index, relying heavily on the interpretation of the firm in the pricing of oil
supplies. Many of the processes for pricing within both these organizations

are transparent except for pricing derived from individual, forward contracts in some cases.[70] The WTI and Brent markets represent the most sophisticated oil markets in the world including futures, options, and OTC derivatives, and contribute to the effective pricing of products and ample market liquidity.

It is also worth noting the increase in oil price volatility reflecting the increase in demand and tighter conditions in the global market. The standard deviations steadily increase over the study period, ultimately breaching double digits in the 2007–2009 period, before dropping to still historically elevated single-digit levels. This could be cause for some alarm if the trend of increasing volatility continues, as some suggest.[71] While tight market conditions resulting in increased volatility have yet to be realized, primarily into the tight oil and gas revolution we are currently going through, future demand increases and demographics mean this is a real possibility over the long term.

Reliability

Diversified Sources

The United States has been heavily diversified in its overseas sources for many decades, and this diversity had somewhat plateaued during the period of the study. However, some sources where the U.S. increased its dependence, like Canada, are extremely secure and well established.

One of the more important sources of energy security is the diversity of supplies provided to the state. Diversity in an energy context not only means the number of external states exporting energy to the consuming state, but also diversity among the primary energy sources utilized throughout the government, business, and consumer sectors, the ability to switch between different fuels, as with new vehicles and some power stations, and the ability to use a diverse supply of petroleum products throughout the economy as well. However, in the context of this study, the focus will remain on the geographic aspect since we are dealing primarily with crude oil imports to the United States and China, and the diversity of geographic suppliers will remain the most risk-laden component.

There are surprising numbers of ways to look at diversity of supplies from a state's perspective. However, many of these approaches are flawed, and as such the approach developed here will attempt to refine some of these approaches. As a first step, the raw number of states supplying crude oil to the United States is a promising gauge: the more suppliers, the better. If one state is unable to supply the necessary oil, whatever the reason may be, there are plenty of other suppliers ready to step in and fill the gap. Table 4.7 shows the number of oil suppliers to the United States from 1992 to 2013.

Table 4.7.   Total Number of States Exporting to the U.S. by Year

Year	Number of States	Year	Number of States
1992	46	2003	46
1993	45	2004	48
1994	45	2005	46
1995	55	2006	52
1996	50	2007	45
1997	44	2008	48
1998	41	2009	46
1999	52	2010	43
2000	43	2011	50
2001	44	2012	41
2002	46	2013	42

Source: United Nations Comtrade Database, United Nations, Trade Data Extraction Interface, HS Commodity Code 2709, Petroleum Oils, Oils from Bituminous Minerals, Crude, http://comtrade.un.org.

The number of U.S. suppliers is remarkably steady over the course of the study. There are some aberrations, but the United States steadily maintained suppliers from 41 to 55 throughout the course the entire period. This averages to 46.3 suppliers over the research period, with a standard deviation of 3.6, showing a tight band for the number of suppliers. Furthermore, there is no indication of changing patterns in the 1990s or the 2000s. The average number of suppliers from 1992 to 2000 is 46.8, and the average from 2001 to 2013 is 46, indicating a comfortable diversity of supply for the United States to be in the mid 40s. Interestingly, the lowest number of suppliers for the U.S., at 41, has been reached two times: the first, in 1998, potentially reflecting weakening global economic conditions, and the other, in 2012, most likely the result of the increases in domestic shale oil production. In 2013, the U.S. only added one supplier, and one could expect this trend to continue over the next decade, perhaps even witnessing the number of suppliers dipping below 40. The number of suppliers can be a telling figure, especially when compared to other states with the same energy demands, or when compared to other great powers.

However, in order to conduct a more in-depth examination, going beyond the number of suppliers will be required. The United States has been able to approach diversity of supply from a privileged position compared to China, and has even been able to turn down supplies in the past if the political structure of the states was not acceptable to the U.S. and the West in general. For example, Sudan was frequently rebuked as a supplier because of its internal political issues.

Another innovative approach to measure diversity of supply is a technique borrowed from microeconomics and portfolio theory in finance. In this case, the Herfindahl-Hirschman Index (HHI) measures the variety of the supplies, and balances against the entire "portfolio" of suppliers. In finance, this measure is typically applied by asset managers to determine whether a portfolio is over-exposed to certain company sizes (small, medium, large cap), sectors (technology, energy, consumer durables), or geographical location (domestic and foreign, in addition to particular regions), and allows the manager to plan and adjust accordingly. In microeconomics, this approach is typically used to determine market concentration. This approach has been adapted and refined since introduced as a potential measure for energy security, but further refinement is needed. In this section, a basic HHI approach will be used, and further modifications will be made to produce a composite result in chapter 5. Using the standard HHI approach, with the following equation introduced in Chapter I, we can gain a better understanding of supplier concentration:

$$HHI = \Sigma \ ((\text{export share}_c \ / \ \text{total imports}) * 100)^2$$

or

$$HHI = \sum_{c=1}^{n} es_c^2$$

Where es is the export share of that particular country, c is the country in question, all of which is taken as a percentage over total imports multiplied by 100, and squared for the final product. This formula is applied to all suppliers to the country, regardless of supply amount, and calculated for each year from 1992 to 2012, as demonstrated in table 4.8.

Table 4.8.   Annual Herfindahl-Hirschman Index (HHI) Score

Year	HHI Score	Year	HHI Score
1992	1,336	2003	1,057
1993	1,082	2004	1,030
1994	1,069	2005	1,005
1995	1,104	2006	1,027
1996	1,094	2007	1,055
1997	1,135	2008	1,037
1998	1,077	2009	974
1999	1,005	2010	1,008
2000	1,061	2011	1,145
2001	1,088	2012	1,214
2002	1,044	2013	1,467

Source: Author's own calculations using UN Comtrade Data (United Nations Comtrade Database, United Nations, Trade Data Extraction Interface, HS Commodity Code 2709, Petroleum Oils, Oils From Bituminous Minerals, Crude, http://comtrade.un.org) and above HHI equation derived from multiple sources, including the U.S. Department of Justice (https://www.justice .gov/atr/horizontal-merger-guidelines-08192010#5c); for a more detailed look, reference Stephen A. Rhoades, The Herfindahl-Hirschman Index, Federal Reserve Bulletin, Volume 79, Number 3, March 1993, pp 188–189.

Recalling from earlier, the lower the number, the better the score. In 1992, The United States started out with a relatively higher concentration of suppliers with a score of 1,336, and then dropped to 1,082 the following year. Starting in 1993, the United States remained in a tight band of approximately 1,000 to 1,100 for nearly 20 years. The highest level of diversification was achieved only in 2009, and afterward, the U.S. broke out of the band in 2011, and as of 2013, has less diversity of supply than in 1992, owing to the adjustments resulting from the shale boom and increasing domestic supply. For all years, the average score is 1,096, with a standard deviation of 111. From 1993 to 2011, the standard deviation was only 44, as a result of the tight diversification band achieved during those years, a remarkably stable number.

Short- and Long-Term Protection from Political Interruptions

The ability of the United States to unilaterally respond to overseas political interruptions is perhaps unparalleled by any other country and has acted to overtly and covertly guard global oil markets and maintain the security of the Arabian Peninsula in the past. Aside from military action, the ability of the United States and the protected market structure to respond to politically induced oil shocks is high and resilient. As Gholz and Press go at great lengths to describe, the global oil market itself has four adaptive mechanisms that mitigate the risks to political disruption.[72] These mechanisms are: increases in production; private inventories; government-controlled inventories; and re-routing transportation.[73] All four of these mechanisms are nearly automatic based on the self-interest of market participants and have been tested for durability and robustness multiple times over the past 40 years. Due to the diversification of oil production beginning in the 1980s, increasing production in other parts of the world can typically offset, in a relatively short timeframe, any production loss in another country. Multiple global producing assets can fill this role,[74] and Saudi Arabia typically plays the role of swing producer, increasing output in case of interruptions or if prices climb too high or too rapidly. After production from a set of regional assets, oil is then transported with a flexible and resilient system of tankers capable of shifting routes if necessary. In many cases, the marginal cost increase of re-routing tanker traffic is not entirely prohibitive. These vessels are strong as well, many absorbing missile and mine strikes during previous conflicts, and still surviving with only light damage and casualties, ultimately able to deliver their payload.[75] And, there is no reason to believe this is any different today along key oil transport vectors, especially in the Gulf region.[76] Production and transport resiliency is key to bring in additional product, and then the private and government-controlled inventories allow for quick drawdown, providing crisis supplies and giving time for the supply chain to reorient and adjust.[77] This system has been a remarkably effective strategy where even global actors benefiting from higher prices are naturally incentivized to increase output in response to price rises.

As can be seen in table 4.9, both government- and industry-controlled petroleum stocks have enjoyed relative stability over the course of the study. The total crude stocks of the United States comfortably exceed the minimum amount required by the IEA with plenty to draw on in the case of a crisis. And, the data show these levels continue to climb, with total stocks rising by 9.5 percent over the course of the time period shown, with much of that increase derived from increases in government controlled stocks, reflecting a concerted effort by the U.S. government to increase supply security in the face of price increases seen in the mid-2000s.

Oft mentioned in other contexts, U.S. command of the commons provides substantial security for the United States and its allies, at a level that no other

Table 4.9.   Government-Controlled Petroleum Stocks (SPR), Industry-Controlled Petroleum Stocks, and Total Petroleum Stocks (MMbbl/yr)

Year	Government-Controlled	Industry-Controlled	Total Stocks
1992	N/A	N/A	1,591.97
1993	587.08	1,060.14	1,647.22
1994	591.67	1,061.12	1,652.79
1995	591.64	971.21	1,562.85
1996	565.82	941.60	1,507.42
1997	563.43	996.33	1,559.76
1998	571.41	1,075.57	1,646.98
1999	567.24	925.69	1,492.93
2000	540.68	926.87	1,467.55
2001	550.24	1,036.11	1,586.35
2002	599.09	948.82	1,547.91
2003	638.39	929.92	1,568.30
2004	675.60	969.21	1,644.81
2005	684.54	1,013.06	1,697.60
2006	688.61	1,030.90	1,719.51
2007	696.94	968.40	1,665.35
2008	701.82	1,034.92	1,736.74
2009	726.62	1,049.76	1,776.38
2010	726.55	1,067.55	1,794.10
2011	695.95	1,055.54	1,750.09
2012	695.27	1,112.51	1,807.78
2013	695.97	1,065.40	1,761.37

Source: Energy Information Administration, International Energy Statistics, Annual Stocks (https://www .eia.gov/cfapps/ipdbproject/iedindex3.cfm?tid=5&pid=5&aid=5&cid=regions&syid=1992&eyid=2013& unit=MBBL).

power possesses.[78] Supremacy in the commons is of course a boon for oil security. Command of the commons is a crucial aspect of U.S. oil security that provides overwhelming support underpinning the entire global oil security apparatus. This has primarily a military dimension and although the commons have traditionally been thought of as "naval mastery,"[79] more recently the concept has also included both air and space, traditionally captured by the air force in the United States. For the purposes of oil security, preeminent naval power is still of the utmost importance, maintaining command over the SLOCs that all oil tankers traverse. It is important to understand no other great power could remotely challenge this position over the course of the study, and the security of the commons is of the utmost importance to the entire oil market. From U.S. nuclear attack submarines (SSNs), to multiple Nimitz-class nuclear-powered aircraft carriers (with a new more advanced class on the way), to the Marine Corp VSTOL carriers, and the myriad multi-mission cruisers and destroyers for carrier protection and patrol have cemented the primacy of U.S. naval power over any potential adversaries.[80] And, the "command" aspect is based more on tacit supremacy, not complete domination. Command of the commons does not refer to its denial to certain states, or their militaries, but instead that the United States reaps far more military benefits from the commons, and can convincingly deny their use to other states, and that in any contest for the commons, the U.S. would prevail in its denial.[81]

Furthermore, regarding long-term protection from political events, war is something that must be confronted in the case of oil security. This is not considered enough in studies of this nature, much to the detriment of our understanding of energy security. This is inherently a process heavily reliant on military power, as we witnessed during the Second World War and during the security competition during the Cold War. If, for instance, political interruptions are large scale and prolonged, albeit a rare occurrence, the mitigating factors of the oil market would ultimately not be able to cope with the loss of supply. In a hot, kinetic, military conflict, oil tankers cannot easily traverse the commons in order to deliver any sort of crude supply to any country, putting the whole system in jeopardy with such blatant vulnerabilities. This also goes for the potential for war, where obviously military power, and in particular, a strong naval presence, is of core importance for energy security. This places the United States in a uniquely preeminent position with its large, advanced, and highly capable naval force that has been in command of the global commons for over six decades. The ability of the U.S. to field such a force is next to none and is unlikely to be supplanted in the near to medium term. However, this power has its limits, in the sense that the power can typically only be utilized to its fullest after war has already broken out. This will be discussed further in chapter 5. Furthermore, the United States has been especially active militarily in order to protect against perceived threats to energy security, especially regarding the Saudi peninsula. Active engage-ment with the Saudis on the global supply of petroleum has been a mainstay since the 1940s, and the United States has acted as security guarantor for the region and the Gulf.[82] Much of this was tacit, but the eventual creation of the Rapid Deployment Joint Task Force (RDJTF), and later the progression to Central Command (CENTCOM), solidified the position of the U.S. against the former Soviet Union on the issue of Saudi oil, and while politically active in the region to counter the Soviets, never engaged in full military operations to counter communist influence or control over vital energy supplies. The U.S. did eventually move militarily to counter threats by Saddam Hussein, resulting in the First Gulf War. The Iraqi military presented a colossal risk to Saudi stability, security, and their crucial eastern oil fields that fuel much of the world. The importance of this military power, without true peer competi-tion on open water, provides a decisive strategic advantage, and essentially underwrites the security of the global energy apparatus. Gholz and Press identify the short-term ability of global energy markets to absorb a multitude of shocks, but these responses would not be available without the appropriate military force available to subdue threats.

Military power is essential in other areas as well. Perhaps the most notable lapse in the security of the commons came in the latter part of the study where frequent attacks by Somali pirates caused an international stir with the high frequency of their attacks, and the systematic ransoming of crews and cargos. This is notable, as it is near shipping lanes that transport, among other cargos, oil from the Persian Gulf to the U.S. This was essentially tolerated for some time, but after escalation, the U.S. was forced to increase response and work within a multilateral framework with other countries to halt the piracy. While this level of piracy was not enough to pose a significant threat to the oil supply security of the United States, there were a few incidents for concern, especially when in 2011 pirates hijacked a Very Large Crude Car-rier (VLCC), carrying 2 million barrels of petroleum that was headed for the Gulf of Mexico.[83] This is approximately one-fifth of the daily import volume of crude to the U.S., which is not an entirely insignificant amount. If this had occurred more often, it would have attracted the attention of the navy sooner, but the major threat to oil simply did not materialize and was mostly subdued after the multinational force began securing these shipping lanes.

CONCLUDING REMARKS ON
AMERICA'S ENERGY SECURITY APPROACH

After rising to a privileged position early in the 20th century, the United States has maintained that predominance highly effectively, engaging all instruments of grand strategy in order to retain general and oil supply security. On the indicators available, the data show the United States to be in generally secure position regarding its general oil security. This is due to both active domestic and foreign programs to secure and enhance the availability of oil supplies. Overseas engagement per its grand strategy is particularly successful as evidenced by diversity in its supply, price stability, and domestic stocks. But, much of this security is derived from less quantifiable elements like the command of the commons and security underwritten by the U.S. military that makes market-based security possible, viable, and resilient.

NOTES

1. Daniel Yergin, *The Prize: The Epic Quest for Oil, Money, and Power* (New York, NY: Free Press, 2008), 369–389.

2. Roger M. Olien and Diana D. Olien, *Oil and Ideology: The Cultural Creation of the American Petroleum Industry* (Chapel Hill, NC: The University of North Carolina Press, 2000), 21–54.

3. Yergin, *The Prize: The Epic Quest for Oil, Money, and Power*, 199.

4. Brian C. Black, "Oil for Living: Petroleum and American Conspicuous Consumption," *Journal of American History* 99, no. 1 (2012).

5. Yergin, *The Prize: The Epic Quest for Oil, Money, and Power*, 304.

6. Irvine H. Anderson Jr., "The 1941 De Facto Embargo on Oil to Japan: A Bureaucratic Reflex," *Pacific Historical Review* 44, no. 2 (1975): 201–231. It should also be noted, at that time, Japan received approximately 80 percent of its oil imports from the United States, so any cessation of exports would prove to be fatal to Japanese oil supplies.

7. Yergin, *The Prize: The Epic Quest for Oil, Money, and Power*, 385.

8. Ibid., 378.

9. Harold Ickes to President Franklin D. Roosevelt, August 18, 1943, Box 50, Folder "Saudi Arabian Pipeline," Series 3: Diplomatic Correspondence, FDR Library and Marist College, http://www.fdrlibrary.marist.edu/archives/collections/franklin/?p=collections/findingaid&id=502 (accessed April 2, 2017).

10. Michael T. Klare, *Blood and Oil: The Dangers and Consequences of America's Growing Dependency on Imported Petroleum* (New York, NY: Henry Holt and Company, 2004), 37–45.

11. "Painter, "Oil and the American Century," *Journal of American History*, 29.

12. David S. Painter, *Oil and the American Century: The Political Economy of U.S. Foreign Oil Policy, 1941–1954* (Baltimore, MD: Johns Hopkins University Press, 1986), 165–171.

13. Walter Pincus, "Secret Presidential Pledges Over Years Erected U.S. Shield for Saudis," *Washington Post*, February 9, 1992, https://www.washingtonpost.com/archive/politics/1992/02/09/secret-presidential-pledges-over-years-erected-us-shield-for-saudis/8252af1b-f6f6-43c1-985b-5385b59f90c2/ (accessed March, 7, 2016).

14. Toby C. Jones, *Desert Kingdom: How Oil and Water Forged Modern Saudi Arabia* (Cambridge, MA: Harvard University Press, 2010), 54–89.

15. Valérie Marcell, *Oil Titans: National Oil Companies in the Middle East* (Washington, D.C.: Brookings Institution Press, 2006), 37–53.

16. Rachel Bronson, *Thicker Than Oil: America's Uneasy Partnership with Saudi Arabia* (New York, NY: Oxford University Press, 2006), 170–171.

17. United States Code, 43 U.S.C. 1651: Congressional Findings and Declaration, Chapter 34 Trans-Alaska Pipeline, Pub. L. 93–153, title II, §202, Nov. 16, 1973, 87 Stat. 584, http://uscode.house.gov/browse.xhtml (accessed February 23, 2016).

18. Richard Nixon: "Address to the Nation About National Energy Policy," November 25, 1973, eds. Gerhard Peters and John T. Woolley, The American Presidency Project, http://www.presidency.ucsb.edu/ws/?pid=4051 (accessed February 23, 2016).

19. Especially through Corporate Average Fuel Efficiency (CAFE) standards implemented in the 1990s.

20. Howard Geller, Philip Harrington, Arthur H. Rosenfeld, Satoshi Tanishima, and Fridtjof Unander, "Polices for Increasing Energy Efficiency: Thirty Years of Experience in OECD Countries," *Energy Policy* 34, no. 5 (2006).

21. Jimmy Carter: "The State of the Union Address Delivered Before a Joint Session of the Congress," January 23, 1980, eds. Gerhard Peters and John T. Woolley, The American Presidency Project, http://www.presidency.ucsb.edu/ws/?pid=33079 (accessed February 23, 2016).

22. Ibid.

23. U.S. Department of State, Office of the Historian, Foreign Relations of the United States, 1977–1980, Volume XVIII, Middle East Region; Arabian Peninsula, https://history.state.gov/historicaldocuments/frus1977-80v18/ch1; many documents here show an emerging trend of more and more concern for U.S. security in the region, and the establishment of increased military presence in the region based largely on Persian Gulf oil.

24. Klare, *Blood and Oil: The Dangers and Consequences of America's Growing Dependency on Imported Petroleum*, 45–50.

25. Paul K. Davis, *Observations on the Rapid Deployment Joint Task Force: Origins, Direction, and Mission* (Santa Monica, CA: RAND Corporation, 1982).

26. Fettweis, "Free Riding or Restraint? Examining European Grand Strategy," *Comparative Strategy*, 317.

27. Christopher J. Fettweis, "Threatlessness and US Grand Strategy," *Survival* 56, no. 5 (2014): 53–55.

28. Christopher J. Fettweis, "Threat and Anxiety in US Foreign Policy," *Survival* 52, no. 2 (2010): 73–77.

29. Robert J. Art, "To What Ends Military Power?" *International Security* 4, no. 4 (1980).

30. Art, *America's Grand Strategy and World Politics*.

31. Robert J. Art, *A Grand Strategy for America* (Ithaca, NY: Cornell University Press, 2003).

32. Art, *America's Grand Strategy and World Politics*, 190–192.

33. Art, *A Grand Strategy for America*, 45–81.

34. Layne, *The Peace of Illusions: American Grand Strategy from 1940 to the Present*, 3–5.

35. Ibid., 3.

36. This concept draws heavily from neoclassical realism. For an excellent source on the topic, reference: Steven E. Lobell, Norrin M. Ripsman, Jeffrey W. Taliaferro, *Neoclassical Realism, The State, and Foreign Policy* (Cambridge, MA: Cambridge University Press, 2009).

37. Layne, *The Peace of Illusions: American Grand Strategy from 1940 to the Present*, 7–10.

38. Ibid., 4.

39. Ibid., 45.

40. Ibid., 46.

41. Ibid.

42. Ibid., 47.

43. Ibid., 55.

44. Dueck, *Reluctant Crusaders: Power, Culture, and Change in American Grand Strategy*, 21–26.

45. Ibid., 26–30.

46. Ibid., 31–33.

47. Ibid., 115.

48. Patrick E. Tyler, "U.S. Strategy Plan Calls for Insuring No Rivals Develop," *New York Times*, March 8, 1992, http://www.nytimes.com/1992/03/08/world/us -strategy-plan-calls-for-insuring-no-rivals-develop.html?pagewanted=all (accessed May 23, 2016).

49. Secretary of Defense, Department of Defense, *Defense Strategy for the 1990s: The Regional Defense Strategy*, Washington, D.C., 1993.

50. Ibid., 4.

51. Ibid., 21.

52. The White House, *National Security Strategy*, Washington, D.C.: The White House, 2002, 12, 19, 20.

53. Charles Krauthammer, "The Unipolar Moment," *Foreign Affairs* 70, no. 1 (1990), 23–33.

54. Barry R. Posen and Andrew L. Ross, "Competing Visions for U.S. Grand Strategy," *International Security* 21, no. 3 1996): 44.

55. Ibid., 44–46; The White House, National Security Strategy, Washington, D.C.: The White House, 1995.

56. There are 12 mentions of the word "oil" in document, more than any of the other national security documents surveyed. Furthermore, these mentions are in the context of supply security, without any concern for their environmental impact or attempts to shift towards renewables as we see in later documents. These mentions are in the context of deterrent threats designed to mitigate the danger posed by oil shocks and potential military incursions on the Saudi Peninsula.

57. The White House, National Security Strategy, Washington, D.C.: The White House, 1995, 21.

58. Ibid., 19–20.

59. The White House, National Security Strategy, Washington, D.C.: The White House, 2006, 27.

60. Ibid., 28–29.

61. Ibid., 41–42.

62. The White House, National Security Strategy, Washington, D.C.: The White House, 2010, 1–6, 45, 47.

63. It should also be noted, in the case of Venezuela, the reference is not to direct political control over the country, especially given the recent contentious political relationship between the two countries. It is strategic due to close proximity to U.S. shores, and because, commercially, Venezuela has limited options due to physical distance to other markets. Additionally, refining infrastructure elsewhere in the world that is capable of processing Venezuelan crude is non-existent or limited, leaving the U.S. as one of the few countries in the world that can process this crude in large quantities.

64. Tyler Priest, "The Dilemmas of Oil Empire," *Journal of American History* 99, no. 1 (2012): 236–251.

65. James D. Hamilton, Causes and Consequences of the Oil Shock of 2008–08, Brookings Papers on Economic Activity, Spring 2009; James D. Hamilton, Oil Prices, Exhaustible Resources, and Economic Growth, October 2012, Prepared for *Handbook of Energy and Climate Change* by Routledge.

66. Richard G. Miller and Steven R. Sorrell, "The Future of Oil Supply," *Philosophical Transactions of the Royal Society A* 372, no. 2006 (2014); David L. Greene, Janet L. Hopson, and Jia Li, "Have We Run Out of Oil Yet? Oil Peaking Analysis from and Optimist's Perspective," *Energy Policy* 34 no. 5 (2006): 515–531; Colin J. Campbell and Jean H. Laherrère "The End of Cheap Oil," *Scientific American*, 1998.

67. Anthony H. Cordesman and Nawaf E. Obaid, *National Security in Saudi Arabia: Threats, Responses, and Challenges* (Westport, CT: Praeger Security International, 2005), 305–324.

68. Aleklett, Kjell, and Colin J. Campbell, "The Peak and Decline of World Oil and Gas Production," *Minerals & Energy* 18, no. 1 (2003): 5; Fatih Birol, "World Energy Outlook 2008," International Energy Agency (Paris, FR, 2008) 37–49, 221–248; John Vidal, "The End of Oil Is Closer than You Think," *The Guardian*, April 21, 2005, https://www.theguardian.com/science/2005/apr/21/oilandpetrol.news (accessed April 10, 2016); Nick A. Owen, Oliver R. Inderwildi, and David A. King, "The Status of Conventional World Oil Reserves—Hype or Cause for Concern?" *Energy Policy* 38, no. 8 (2010); R.W. Bentley, "Global Oil and Gas Depletion: An Overview," *Energy Policy* 30, no. 3 (2002).

69. Ryan Opsal, "A Key Tool For Energy Investors," Oilprice.com, August 18, 2015, http://oilprice.com/Finance/investing-and-trading-reports/A-Key-Tool-For-Energy-Investors.html (accessed June 19, 2016).

70. For instance, reference Argus Media's Methodology: Argus Sour Crude Index (ASCI), 2015, Methodology and Specifications Guide, http://www.argusmedia.com/methodology-and-reference/; and see Bassam Fattouh, "An Anatomy of the Crude Oil Pricing System," The Oxford Institute for Energy Studies, WPM 40 (2011): 52–60.

71. Robert McNally and Michael Levi, "A Crude Predicament: The Era of Volatile Oil Prices," *Foreign Affairs* 90, no. 4 (2011).

72. Eugene Gholz and Daryl G. Press, "Protecting 'The Prize:' Oil and the U.S. National Interest," *Security Studies* 19, no. 3 (2010).

73. Ibid., 457–463.

74. Even more sources are available with tight oil and gas production at higher levels.

75. Martin S. Navias and E. R. Hooton, *Tanker Wars: The Assault on Merchant Shipping During the Iran-Iraq Conflict, 1980–1988* (New York, NY: I.B. Tauris and Co., 1996), 101–131.

76. Joshua R. Itzkowitz Shifrinson and Miranda Priebe, "A Crude Threat: The Limits of an Iranian Missile Campaign against Saudi Arabian Oil," *International Security* 36, no. 1 (2011): 167–201.

77. International Energy Agency, "Energy Supply Security, Emergency Response of IEA Countries, 2014" (2015): 29–37; Note: The government stocks typically need to be at least 90 days of oil consumption if part of IEA/OECD system.

78. Barry R. Posen, "Command of the Commons: The Military Foundation of U.S. Hegemony," *International Security* 28, no. 1 (2003).

79. Paul Kennedy, *The Rise and Fall of British Naval Mastery* (Amherst, NY: Humanity Books, 1983), 9.

80. Posen, "Command of the Commons: The Military Foundation of U.S. Hegemony," *International Security*, 11–12.

81. Ibid., 8.

82. Gary Sick, "The United States in the Persian Gulf: From Twin Pillars to Dual Containment," in *The Middle East and the United States: History, Politics, and Ideologies, Fifth Edition*, eds. David W. Lesch and Mark L. Haas (Boulder, CO: Westview Press, 2012), 309–325.

83. Jonathan Saul and Renee Maltezou, "Somali Pirates Capture Oil Tanker Bound for US: Higher Oil Prices Ahead?" *Christian Science Monitor*, February 9, 2011, www.csmonitor.com/World/Latest-News-Wires/2011/0209/Somali-pirates-capture -oil-tanker-bound-for-US-Higher-oil-prices-ahead (accessed March 27, 2016).

Chapter Five

The Oil Security Approach of China

INTRODUCTION

Throughout most of Chinese history, energy security was an afterthought. Home to many advancements and initial achievements in global history, from a highly advanced bureaucracy to gunpowder, China was nonetheless a latecomer to the Industrial Revolution. This lag was maintained, as the country continued to rely heavily on human-based energy for domestic economic activity well through the 20th century, while other parts of the world were steadily moving towards more mechanization and technological bases for their societies. This is striking considering the relative global economic dominance of China until the mid-19th century, when a conflation of factors radically altered China's position and power. However, despite the great delay in energy interest and comparative accessibility, China did start to make weak attempts at developing domestic sources of energy by the early 20th century, only to have its oil fortunes undergo a major positive shift by the mid-20th century,[1] catapulting oil to a central component of Chinese economic and political power.[2] This centrality of oil is often overlooked in the case of China, but the extractive sector under Maoism was arguably the most successful component of the entire economy. This process will be examined more closely in the following sections.

The History of Chinese Oil Security

The history of oil in China begins in much the same way as it began in other countries in the late 19th century, with small amounts of crude seepage that makes its way to surface level, saturating topsoil, or creating oil slicks atop river and lake water, which is in turn sighted and collected by locals with rudimentary tools and little knowledge of what they possess.[3] Eventually, foreign geologists, chemists, and entrepreneurs would realize the capability of this material as an energy source, and first marketed it as a fuel source for lamps. As mentioned in the previous chapter, Standard Oil made their initial profits not from oil for vehicles and industry, but from kerosene for lamps and lighting. But, even before the time of Rockefeller, elite perspectives in China skewed towards self-sufficiency and autarky, which would eventually fuel oil independence and the domestic Chinese energy industry. China's formative "Century of Humiliation," beginning with the first Opium War in 1839, settled with European "spheres of influence" in a severely weakened, carved-up China under the auspices of the Qing Dynasty greatly contributed to this core narrative.[4]

It was these forcibly opened Chinese markets that would give Standard Oil a new market centered on Shanghai as an emerging consumer of kerosene in the late 19th century.[5] The business was well positioned at the time in the Asian market, providing a significantly cheaper alternative to whale oil, the standard product in the region. It was far less difficult to produce in the quantities required for proliferation, diffusion, and broad consumption throughout the local population, a market significantly expanded due to newly accessible pricing. The Shanghai market was certainly opportune, as the most international and advanced urban center of the country, capable of purchasing large enough quantities of the combustible import. Exports of kerosene to Shanghai surged,[6] turning it into a significant market for Standard Oil, creating the first petroleum dependency for China in the emerging era of oil.

Eventually, a new role for oil emerged around the turn of the century: as a reliable and durable fuel source for private industry, multitudes of automobiles, and crucially, military equipment, all wielded in one form or another by countries and economies around the world. As this shift was underway, contending European powers and then Japan would recognize its importance and begin searching for new petroleum sources. After World War One, the European powers were severely weakened in China, and heaped yet another insult on the country by handing over German colonial assets to Japan. Japanese influence and control grew, exerting more control over China, especially in Manchuria, the industrial heartland and the area with the most energy reserves available, at the time. Indeed, this region would eventually become the largest petroleum-producing region in the country, but it would not be under Japanese control.

As Western powers became further consumed with their own affairs in Europe, Japan steadily emerged as the dominant colonial power in China and would eventually be forced to contend with organized combatants in the Chinese civil war between the Communist Party on one hand and the Guomindong on the other. During their time in control of key territorial assets, Japan was never very successful in its search for oil in China, uncovering only a few minor fields in the northwest of the country.

Domestically, in the years leading up to the Second World War, China provided a theater for civil war and many attempts at locating new sources of oil by both contending factions and Japanese colonial forces. While Japan required oil for utilization in the military and broader economy, the Communist forces and Guomindong did not necessarily need to use oil as a fuel in their own conflict, but to harness and sell as a valuable commodity.

In the 1930s, the Chinese Red Army was able to produce small quantities of oil at Yumen and Yanchang after the importation of necessary equipment and techniques, although the amounts were quite limited.[7] Afterwards, the Nationalist Guomindong forces were able to capture and use Red Army excavation equipment for themselves, albeit with less luck than the communist forces.[8] In fact, all forces operating in China had little success in the discovery of new fields, where the Nationalist forces even operated a joint venture with the Soviet Union, ending in failure during World War Two, with further attempts made in Taiwan by Western firms to discover new fields, which also did not yield any successes, and of course Japan's attempts at exploration and refining which were largely failures.[9] Despite the best efforts of the Japanese, Guomindong, and Communist forces, none were able to make significant finds on the mainland, especially not enough to satisfy domestic or overseas demands for energy.

This presented great difficulties for Japan as a resource-poor island country in dire need of energy assets, particularly oil, and would drive its strategy in the interwar years, pushing it deeper into China and Southeast Asia. The Dutch East Indies was the key area for the Japanese to control, along with all the oil supplies derived from discoveries made by Royal Dutch Shell. Japanese officials were well prepared for this endeavor, including the assumed response by the company's staff, which was to destroy the oil-producing facilities in the region and evacuate before Japanese forces arrived. Shell's staff did exactly that, but Japanese engineers were proficient and incredibly effective, able to have the facilities operational and producing oil in around two months.[10] This was, however, all for naught as Japanese power was halted, and pushed back in the region as the Second World War raged on, and the country was eventually deprived of the vital resources required to prosecute a 20th-century war.

After the victory of the Communist Party in China in 1949, a period of consolidation ensued, and the emerging partnership between China and the Soviet Union became a central pillar of China's energy security, with Mao requesting from Stalin, in 1949, that the most important specialists be brought over as soon as possible with expertise in "railroads, electrical energy, steel production, mining, the oil industry, and the military."[11] The Soviets conferred capital equipment, knowledge, personnel, advisors, and technology to China in order to develop their oil industry infrastructure, even allowing Chinese students to study petroleum engineering in Moscow and sending experts to China to teach and otherwise transmit knowledge beginning in 1952.[12] Despite this assistance, it was not enough to produce any significant finds in the country. Given these events, China was ultimately forced to depend on Soviet oil supplies for the vast majority of its consumption, with imports totaling around 14 million metric tons (mmt) through the 1950s.[13] And, despite the gradual souring of relations between the two countries, these high imports from the Soviet Union would continue since it was a mutually beneficial economic arrangement, and China simply lacked any alternative sources for energy.

The deterioration in relations between the Soviet Union and China would eventually culminate in Khrushchev's recall of all Soviet advisors in 1960,[14] a number that had ballooned to 18,000 after Eastern European countries expelled their own Soviet advisors in 1956.[15] This was an extremely vulnerable position for China, politically cut off from its patron, but highly dependent on the Soviets for its oil needs. Unable to rely on the small, insignificant oil fields in the country, these Soviet imports, coupled with poor relations, created a perilous situation for China, both politically and with regard to energy supplies.

Just in time for the previously mentioned Soviet recall, after an arduous and determined effort by the government, the PRC's exploration efforts finally paid off as it made its first significant oil find in 1959 with the discovery of the colossal Daqing field in Heilongjiang Province. As a result of this find, China's oil security position would be significantly transformed from that point forward, as it was large enough to catapult China not only to energy independence, but also to the point where it would become a major exporter.[16] This discovery not only had practical economic and security implications, but also substantial positive ideological consequences. With ample petroleum available for domestic use, the industry effortlessly fit with Maoist ideology calling for a more autarkic approach to the national economy.[17] Energy was extremely important for these reasons, and by 1963, China was largely energy independent, and continued to develop petroleum refining expertise, importing any equipment required for those operations to be successful.[18] These efforts were eventually aided by two new fields that would come online later in the decade.[19]

The well-publicized and propagandized domestic energy industry was so successful for the Chinese government, it would go on to become a model industry. It was touted as an idealistic component of the national economy,[20] as an example for workers in other industries to follow, and even produced such famous "people's heroes" as "Iron Man Wang," a tireless, dedicated model worker for the nation.[21] Viewed independently of other global oil fields, the domestic oil industry was quite successful, especially when compared to other Chinese industrial programs. It grew in importance as output rapidly increased through the 1960s, generating around 20 percent growth year over year,[22] and maintained a high degree of supply reliability, circumstances that did not go unnoticed by the party's cadre members.

Interestingly, through the tumult of this period, from the catastrophic Great Leap Forward, which placed added political pressure on Mao and the CCP due to decreased living standards, to the events of the Cultural Revolution that forced Mao to deploy the military to regain control of the country, the oil industry was essentially left untouched, and even prospered. For instance, during the Cultural Revolution, Premier Zhou Enlai, a powerful political figure, diplomat, and ally to Deng Xiaoping, second in the CCP hierarchy only to Mao, took personal responsibility for the safety of the industry,[23] going so far as to station military units throughout the country to guard oil fields, equipment, infrastructure, and personnel.[24] The effort to safeguard this vital industry was quite effective; oil production hardly dropped, and even eventually grew as the revolution wore on.[25] Production data indicate China was producing 292,000 barrels per day (bpd) in 1966 at the beginning of the revolution, only to have that number increase 50 percent by 1969 to a production level of 437,000 bpd, and then increase further to 1,746,000 bpd in 1976, the year of Mao's death.[26] This amounts to a fivefold increase in oil production over the course of the Cultural Revolution, an event which, by most other measures, proved tremendously detrimental to the economy, society, and the general well-being of the population.

Oil was centrally prominent, and this importance only grew with time. So much so the industry wasn't vital only as a resource meant to supply domestic fuel requirements, or even simply to fuel its military power, but for broader economic reasons as well. As the economy lay in tatters, China desperately needed funding and capital equipment for development and growth, especially after being cut off from the Soviet Union. Specifically, large quantities of foreign exchange would be required to purchase the necessary equipment and supplies necessary for capital investments and economic growth. Oil was one of the only products of value to the outside world that China could reliably export for hard currency in order to purchase those indispensable products.

Opportunities to import capital equipment and knowledge expanded after the Sino-American thaw in 1971. China quickly entered into negotiations in order to import more foreign equipment and technology from both Europe and the United States, in a bid to reverse negative economic trends. In particular, China was keen to draw on American expertise in advanced energy technology, while comfortably relying on Japan and Western Europe for more standard energy-related capital equipment.[27] This process was actually wide-ranging enough to ultimately culminate in the unheard-of transfer of military technology from a NATO member to China. In 1975, the United Kingdom transferred F-4 Phantom aircraft engine schematics, the factory equipment required for indigenous production of the engines, and even temporarily assigned associated personnel for knowledge transfer and training of Chinese engineers.[28] The U.S. role in arranging the transfer of F-4 engine technology was covert due to the potential for domestic, anti-communist backlash, but the U.S. was quite active transferring in other areas, including energy. The first energy-related equipment contracts were signed in 1973 consisting mostly of coal mining materials, but more important was the purchase of advanced seismic-survey equipment consisting of a Raytheon 704 computer and the U.S.-based training required to operate the system.[29] Additionally, large sales of chemical plants and eventually, more advanced, American-made, offshore seismic exploration technology was sold by France in 1976.[30] These transfers were made in a relatively short amount of time, and all when Mao was still alive and head of state.

After the death of Zhou Enlai and Mao Zedong, both in 1976, a power struggle ensued between the "Gang of Four," which included Mao's last wife, and Mao's successor as chairman, who had risen to premier after Zhou Enlai's death, Hua Guofeng. While deftly handling the Gang of Four, Hua was unable to successfully counter the rise of Deng Xiaoping, who was quickly regaining power after his latest purge. In what would be a ruinous error for Hua, he and his coalition would base his political power on Mao's legacy and steady funding from the oil industry to underwrite and provide the resources necessary to make economic development possible,[31] and a return to growth.[32] Hua was unable to fulfill his political promises, especially to the three key factions supporting his rise,[33] one of which was the petroleum industry itself represented by Li Xiannian and his "Oil Kingdom Faction," especially since oil income itself was restrained.[34] Hua based his oil-funded optimism on little more than the assumption that China's spectacular production growth would simply continue, and result in another doubling of production output within a few years. Evidence to support this lofty, hopeful assumption simply did not exist, since an actual reservoir analysis had not been completed on the key producing fields. When it came time to draw on these additional resources, promised production simply did not materialize, leaving the state without enough petroleum for export, ultimately damaging China's ability to import supplies needed to boost development, stretching resources,[35] and severely damaging Hua's political reputation.[36] What had been a spectacular oil growth story ended in 1978, ultimately contributing to the downfall of Hua.

Chinese leadership was left desperately seeking pragmatic solutions to jump-start economic growth and development, fearful that if they did not, the CCP might risk the loss of political power and eventual dissolution. Many avenues for growth were explored, including a return to the structure used during the first and second five-year plans, when growth was more stable; however, Deng Xiaoping would advocate a more liberal approach to economic development.[37] This was done more as a political maneuver to position his liberal faction opposite Hua's more conservative faction. This allowed Deng to circumvent the powerful heavy industry elites[38] at their moment of weakness when oil funding fell through (which was meant to pay for modernization efforts),[39] taking the unfunded "Four Modernizations" with it,[40] and had a resulting loss in political capacity.[41] Deng was able to seize on the weakness of these entrenched interests, recruiting additional political leaders to his faction in a bid to place key members in profitable positions under his liberal economic structure.[42] This conflation of factors, in addition to skilled political maneuvering by Deng Xiaoping,[43] resulted in the removal of Hua Guofeng and the ascension of Deng Xiaoping to party chairman.

Through the 1980s, China would continue its drive to expand, modernize, and restructure the oil sector while attempting to assimilate as much new knowledge and technology and as many techniques as possible. This traditional drive for oil sector technology and expertise stretches back to Stalin and continues well into the 21st century. As part of its modernization drive, the CCP began spinning off ministry assets into various corporate entities, based loosely on the image of companies in the U.S. and Europe. This drive towards "light" privatization was meant to increase oil sector efficiency and capability, with an eye towards long-term, global growth. The three key state-owned enterprises (SOEs) that operate in the Chinese oil sector today are China National Petroleum Corporation (CNPC), China National Petrochemical Corporation (Sinopec), and China National Offshore Oil Company (CNOOC), which are all derivatives of their respective government ministries, the Ministry of Petroleum Industry (MPI) and Ministry of Chemical Industry (MCI).[44] These first few steps coincided with the initial phases of China's "Going Out" strategy, allowing newly formed companies to acquire the skills needed by importing knowledge through joint ventures, which allowed these companies the capability to expand overseas during the following decade.[45]

Although Chinese national oil companies (NOCs) would begin their multi-decade expansion in the 1990s, China would also face its next oil crisis as it transitioned from net exporter to net importer of crude oil in

1993. Complicating China's practical oil industry concerns, politically, this was an extremely difficult time as well. Still recovering from the domestic instability that culminated in the Tiananmen Square Crisis in 1989, the CCP was attempting to manage the collapse of the Soviet Union and communism and the emergence of the United States as the sole superpower in the international system. Chinese political elites became especially concerned by U.S. military power during Operation Desert Storm in 1991,[46] recognizing the technological superiority of U.S. forces along with their ability to conduct and coordinate modern, multi-branch warfare. This was of course contrasted to the dismal state of the Chinese military, which was still based overwhelmingly on superior numbers of low-skilled soldiers and continued to lack any expeditionary capability. The government quickly realized how comparatively weak and dated their hardware and organization were compared to the U.S. military (and even worse to some, Japan),[47] and essentially spurred technological and doctrinal developments from that point forward.[48] Soon after these events, politics would drive China to a direct confrontation with the United States, where China's extensive military exercises in response to President Lee's American visa issuance was met with two U.S. carrier battle groups off the coast of Taiwan. The 1995–1996 Taiwan Strait Crisis was simply another reminder to the political elites that the United States had no problem countering China militarily and that they would need to view the predominance of American power as potentially disrupting force that would eventually need to be countered.

THE GRAND STRATEGY OF CHINA

Current Chinese grand strategy has been focused on adjusting to domestic economic and political realities, how those realities are impacted by, and connected to, the external political economic environment, and to the continuing preponderance of American power in the face of an elusive multipolar environment. This latter constraint on Chinese strategic flexibility[49] is a key defining characteristic of the state's grand strategy, since it is constantly forced into a reactionary position vis-à-vis the United States and its respective grand strategy. As Avery Goldstein explains, this is a somewhat transitional strategy; one in which China is preparing for an anticipated international system of multipolarity after the unipolar moment of the United States has passed, meaning certain strategic aspects necessarily have an "expiration date."[50] Despite its transitional nature, a degree of continuity and strong patterns in Chinese grand strategy, when accounting for the core interests, threats, and objectives of the country, do certainly exist.

At its core, China is a vulnerable country, and views itself as such, especially when politically convenient.[51] Perhaps most important, elite and popular perspectives are drawn from the beginning of the first Opium War in 1839, when Western powers carved out their respective "spheres of influence" in China, imposing their own policies with impunity against a largely ineffective and impotent Qing dynasty.[52] This period, known to China as the "century of humiliation," is still fresh in the minds of policymakers, and forms a core belief among Chinese policy elites that unless development progresses and military strength increases, another event such as this has the potential to occur.[53] It is, however, important to understand a core concern uniting all political elites within the CCP: the preservation of the monopoly of political power for the party.[54] It may hardly come as a surprise that those in power would seek to retain it. This is certainly true, regardless of the political system in question. However, it is important in the case of China, because the communist party has had a relatively short, tenuous, and turbulent existence. The political elites are fearful and concerned that the party could feasibly lose power unless it is assiduously preserved and protected. This is the distinguishing feature for the political center in a country like China. Due to this threat, and persistent perception of insecurity (regardless if it's warranted), it is constantly on the minds of elites in the country, and carefully dictates their actions and policymaking. Internal dissent has been a constant in Chinese politics since the inception of the CCP in 1949. Born out of civil war, China has witnessed mass mobilization campaigns, revolutions, riots, famine, purges, party factionalization, and most recently the Tiananmen Square incident and frequent conflict with the Uigar and Tibetan ethnic groups. The party views its power as precarious, and therefore must do all it can to quell dissent and satiate the broader population.

The government places great value on stability and cohesion, using this as a legitimating factor to maintain internal security.[55] Today, this cohesiveness is built on satisfying the general public with continued economic growth and nationalistic tendencies, used to reinforce policy at critical junctures.[56] This current situation emerged at the end of the Cold War when communism and Marxism were no longer viable, global avenues to maintain ideological coherence. With one ideology broken, economic growth quickly assumed a role as the key point of legitimacy for the communist party. So long as growth continues, most of the population will continue to allow the CCP to remain in power. If acceptable growth does not continue, the party's monopoly on political power will come into serious jeopardy. This cannot be done without energy, and oil in particular. Most of China's activity overseas has been directed towards economic ends, and the grand strategy is largely centered on these core objectives. As Zheng Bijian[57] comments on China's related "peaceful rise" strategy:

The implications of various aspects of China's rise, from its expanding influence and military muscle to its growing demand for energy supplies, are being heatedly debated in the international community as well as within China. Correctly understanding China's achievements and its path toward greater development is thus crucial. . . . For the next few decades, the Chinese nation will be preoccupied with securing a more comfortable and decent life for its people. Since . . . 1978, the Chinese leadership has concentrated on economic development. Through its achievements so far, China has blazed a new strategic path that suits its national conditions while conforming to the tides of history.

In order to meet these objectives, China has been compelled to alter its strategy and methods to secure its lands and polity drastically over the last two decades.[58] Several points have also emerged, giving a glimpse as to how China views and forms its grand strategy. As Robert Sutter points out, the "prevailing evidence shows that Chinese leaders focus on domestic stability and economic growth." Seeing these as the key elements in determining its ability to stay in power, the Chinese Communist Party leadership views them as the top priority.[59] A good starting point are three general points expounded by Thomas Christensen: regime security, territorial integrity, and internationally recognized power, prestige, and respect.[60] The first has been covered here, but the second point is very important to consider in the Asian maritime environment. For starters, territorial integrity includes not only the hotly contested East and South China Seas, but also Taiwan. This is a major flashpoint in relations between the United States and China, and will continue to be so until the situation is resolved. There are also potential oil and gas deposits within the overlapping territorial claims in the surrounding maritime environment. Official estimates do not even exist, since the area is so politically contentious, that no company has been willing or able to explore these areas for oil and gas deposits. As such, a major part of this conflict is nationalism and territoriality, but energy does play a role.[61] Additionally, the maritime environment is home to myriad significant trade routes, whereby China receives nearly 80 percent of its overseas crude oil supplies. This is mainly through the Malacca Strait and then the South China Sea. It should also be noted, that if successful in its irredentist claims regarding Taiwan, China would then have stronger claims regarding their territoriality to some of these waters and trade routes. The third point by Christensen is difficult to gauge, and remains a lesser goal to be attained, so will not be discussed heavily.

Goldstein has a well-viewed volume on China's grand strategy and first points to China's desire to secure its vital interests, meaning its "territorial and political integrity," in his view the "negative purpose" of external security policy, but also to promote a "positive purpose" policy, that would provide for the state's ascension in the global hierarchy, allowing it to shape the international system, instead of merely respond to events that occur.[62] As such, he maintains key continuities in Chinese strategy include coping with American primacy under anarchy, the joint maintenance of secured second-strike nuclear capability and a modernized military undergoing its own revolution in military affairs (RMA), and finally its geographical and historical imperatives that serve to constrain and influence policy.[63]

On top of these core concerns, as mentioned earlier, the stark demonstration of American military power during the First Gulf War, and then the later dispatch of that same military power, in the form of two carrier battle groups, to the Taiwan Strait in 1995–1996, deeply unsettled leadership at the CCP. These two events demonstrated the extreme deficiencies in Chinese military hardware, doctrine, organization, and training compared to modern Western military power, and that the United States would not hesitate to direct that power towards China. Just as important, it also enticed the leadership to plan broadly for U.S. attempts to "contain" China, and devise strategies and tactics to counter this threat.[64] This spurred action on the part of the CCP, as the critical demonstration validated reforms that were currently underway on the part of the PLA, shifting from "people's war under modern conditions" to a focus on "local war," which entails such concepts as preparation for local wars over major wars, the implementation of advanced technologies in combat, the exclusion of nuclear warfare, highly trained professional military members, offensive doctrine, quick battles for quick resolutions, and a redefinition of offense and defense under multi-dimensional modern warfare.[65] These two events were extremely formative, and immediately informed their long-term global and regional strategies.

In a more recent volume by Andrew Nathan and Andrew Scobell, the authors are not shy about the security imperatives of a Chinese grand strategy, recognizing on the first page, that "Vulnerability to threats is the main driver of China's foreign policy. The world as seen from Beijing is a terrain of hazards, stretching from the streets to land borders and sea lanes thousands of miles beyond to the mines and oilfields of distant continents."[66] Insecurity, both internal and external, drives Chinese grand strategy. The authors contend China's first objective is to restore and maintain territorial integrity, which includes domestic stability, suppression of outside support for separatist movements in Tibet, Xinjiang, and the Inner Mongolian Autonomous Region, control over Taiwan, and defense of maritime claims. The second objective is to prevent the domination of Asia by any other state while increasing influence throughout the region using military, economic, and diplomatic power. Third, China desires an international environment compatible to its continued economic growth, including access to energy. And fourth, China's growing clout should be translated into a greater ability to shape its global environment.[67]

Nathan and Scobell characterize these threats as part of "four concentric circles," the first being the territory China administers or claims, under threat from both inside and out, the second circle being China's complex relations with twenty immediately adjacent countries plus the United States, the third circle being the six nearby multistate regional systems,[68] and the fourth ring includes the rest of world which consists of Europe, the Middle East, Africa, and North and South America, which China has only really entered into since the 1990s, seeking energy, commodities, and markets.[69]

In terms of the specific regional strategy employed, M.Taylor Fravel expands on the territorial aspects of the Chinese approach. In a recent article, he lists the following as part of a coherent strategy for China: regime security, territorial integrity, national unification, maritime security, and regional stability.[70] There are three points to consider here. First military engagement and defense along Chinese borders is incredibly important for basic strategic reasons but, if a conflict were to arise, this could potentially give Chinese forces operational capability along land-based energy routes. Most notably, this will include pipelines, and in some cases, trains and trucks that would bring in supplies. Second, maritime security is specifically brought up as increasingly important to the state. Fravel mentions a key point when he asserts:

> Chinese sources also reflect an increased sensitivity to military threats from the sea to China's wealthy coastal provinces, the need to exploit maritime resources for economic development and, as a trading nation, the economy's dependence on the sea lines of communication that could be disrupted in a conflict, especially one near China's coast. The NDU's study of military strategy, for example, notes the growing importance of the 'rights and interests' of our continental shelf and maritime exclusive economic zones, especially the threats facing strategic resources development and strategic passageways.[71]

Retention of maritime assets is incredibly important, as it is an important method for China to secure its economy. It's also the most realistic zone where Chinese military power would find success since it currently lacks meaningful power projection capabilities, both on land and in the maritime environment.

As part of the regional strategy, political stability also plays heavily into the economic and energy security of the state. In order to continue development over the last 30 years, China has also sought a stable environment where trade and business could thrive, and economic assets would not be put in jeopardy. It is for this reason, in the post–World War Two period and despite security concerns, China has welcomed a U.S. naval presence in the area, because it has restrained Japanese rearmament, and secured trade routes throughout Asia, all of which have benefited Chinese growth enormously.[72] It seems fitting that Chinese planners would wish this stable environment to persist, as the core objective of economic growth has not changed. Chinese interests continue to be principally defensive[73] and regionally focused.[74]

As for vital interests to the state, Michael Swaine points out that many of China's "core interests" have only been outlined relatively recently,[75] as they have attempted to adjust to their strategic environment and increasingly powerful role in the Asia-Pacific. Only in 2009 could one reference a truly official statement of core interests by State Councilor Dai Binguo, involved in the formulation of foreign policy for the PRC, when he stated at the end of the U.S.-China Strategic and Economic Dialogue that Chinese core interests are: preserving China's basic state system and national security; national sovereignty and territorial integrity; and, the continued stable development of China's economy and society.[76] It should be noted, that in this list, the reference to territorial integrity does include national unification with Taiwan.

There are also those that feel Chinese grand strategy, when operationalized, is simply not meeting its long-term objectives, and that major issues began to arise in the late 2000s. For example, Edward Luttwak believes China's actions will trigger the oft-mentioned coalition to move against it, but preceding overt actions such as these, there be an increased geo-economic response to this growth in Chinese power. This type of response means actions by external powers to slow China's economic growth by restricting trade, investment, and technology transfers, but most importantly by the denial of raw materials. High levels of economic growth coupled with rapid increases in military spending will arouse "adversarial reactions" in accordance to the "logic of strategy," breeding reactions ranging from caution to coalition building. This sequence of events is at least partially playing out with the United States moving to revive alliances with Japan and the Philippines, moves welcomed by both states. For further evidence of realignment, look also to Myanmar's opening to the West and Vietnam's shift closer to the Washington orbit.[77]

Luttwak is also not kind to Chinese strategic texts (i.e., *The Art of War*), which he cautions drives Chinese strategic thinking, but ultimately amount to intra-cultural, inter-state relations during the brief "Warring States" period and contains logic not always readily applicable to modern, intercultural, interstate relations.[78] This reliance on old strategy based on parochial norms has caused counterproductive missteps in the conduct of modern foreign policy, compounding difficulties. For instance, he mentions one of the calculations by the government is their propensity to provoke crises in order to force negotiations and resolve disputes on their terms, as is the case with the current clash over the South China Sea. However, in modern interstate relations this only "raises the perceived value" of the object of the dispute to all states involved, making settlements and concessions far less likely, and stoking public and elite opinion against China.[79]

Furthermore, Luttwak points out his belief that the grand strategy of "Peaceful Rise" was quite successful and did not trigger any reactions or create adversaries by its actions, but that China largely abandoned this approach in 2009, creating new problems for itself, a contrast to the restraint, engagement, and reassurance of the past.[80] Other states besides the United States have taken note of this shifting approach. For instance, India is beginning to shed some of its ambiguity towards the Indian Ocean in response to Chinese actions in the region.[81] Luttwak is also quick to point to escalation control as another potentially counterproductive approach by China to control its security environment, a point expounded by others.[82]

Echoing some other scholars, Bates Gill recognizes the strategic shifts taking place in China's engagement, and sees a Chinese leadership that is determined to maintain a stable regional and international environment so it may focus on internal development, the concerted use of diplomacy to enhance economic growth and regional persuasion, and to "counter, co-opt, or circumvent" U.S. influence in the Asia-Pacific region while not appearing overly confrontational.[83]

Countering U.S. power, especially on its periphery, is a growing concern for the leadership. For instance, in China's Defense White Papers, there are both direct and indirect mentions of the United States, lending credence to the idea of America as its chief adversary. Although not always directly stated as the United States, it is difficult to determine another power the Defense White Paper would be referring to when it states, "some powers have worked out strategies for outer space, cyber space and the polar regions, developed means for prompt global strikes, accelerated development of missile defense systems, enhanced cyber operation capabilities to occupy new strategic commanding heights."[84] In fact, the White Papers seem to go to some length to vaguely suggest the United States as the primary adversary without actually saying so. This is almost always accomplished by suggesting a needed response to capabilities that are only available to the United States military, like missile defense, or weapons platforms that are utilized by the United States more than other states, such as aircraft carriers. However, as Andrew Scobell warns in the final paragraph of his 2003 text on the subject, even though Chinese strategic aims may be defensive in nature, and certainly perceived to be defensive by party planners, they have been led to the rationalization that any action on their part is defensive, even in cases that are blatantly threatening to external actors.[85]

In testimony on China's grand strategy, Bonnie Glaser cites three core security objectives[86] for China in Asia as exerting control over its near seas,[87] defending and advancing Chinese sovereignty claims to include the East and South China seas and Taiwan, and regional economic integration.[88] Although she doesn't mention this in her testimony directly, it is clear this encompasses the full elements of grand strategy, including not just security, but the economic and political aspects as well. Rather problematic from a perspective of grand strategy, Bonnie Glaser finds China's long-term security objectives elusive, while the past and near term are relatively straightforward.

Another scholar, Jian Yang brings to the fore the Chinese concept of "comprehensive national power" (CNP) as the foundation for Chinese grand strategy. Within this context, it is understood once again that internal security is problematic for Beijing, and economic development is widely understood to be broadly beneficial for all aspects of national power and grand strategy. Planners seem to have taken from the Soviet experience, the main fault, which was the stagnated economy that could not maintain military power, or internal security sufficiently.[89] CNP is broad, and consists of various inputs depending on the writer, but can be roughly understood as: basic power (population, resources, national unity); economic power (industrial power, agricultural power, scientific and technological power, financial power, and commercial power); national defense power (strategic resources, technology, military strength, nuclear power); and diplomatic power (foreign policy, attitude toward international affairs, foreign aid, etc.).[90] At an expansive level, this leads to a grand strategy with three main components: national security strategy, national development strategy, and national reunification strategy.[91] The author deems Taiwanese unification to be not quite at the same level as the other two, but important enough to be in a category of its own. Reflecting the importance of the economic aspect, the author gives more weight to these aspects, and broader development to include technological, social, and cultural development strategies, along with both internal and external economic development and diplomatic and national defense strategies.[92]

Although not an explicit piece on China's grand strategy, David Shambaugh's recent work on China's global presence notes some key aspects of the grand strategic approach. In his section on security requirements, there is a direct mention of China's "rising dependence on imported oil and other natural resources" which is "fundamentally reshaping China's energy security, away from autarky and relative independence toward rapidly accelerating dependence."[93] This ultimately informs security strategy, territorial claims, and naval developments. Another point that warrants mention is the Chinese conception of security, which is something internal as much as external, with the complete recognition that internal security allows greater coherence against external threats. Several other scholars have mentioned the importance of internal security and the maintenance of the CCP as the sole political organ in China, and Shambaugh concurs with this understanding. China conceives of security very broadly, with a great level of focus and concern on internal security threats, given the Chinese government spent more on internal security in 2012 than on external security, at $111 billion to $107 billion, respectively.[94]

Others take a more direct view of China's intentions with malign intent. Masako Ikegami is explicit about the negative aspects of China's rapid growth and extremely critical of "peaceful rise," claiming China is preparing for a new Cold War, referring to "U.S.-China co-management," intent on replacing the Soviet Union in a global role. Ikegami does believe the current approach to be a blatant shield, disguising more malign intentions, since the facts simply do not back China's claims for several reasons.[95] In Ikegami's conception,the "counter-facts" to these claims fall in four key areas: China's rapid military build-up, China's emerging global power projection over natural resources, the aid-for-oil and oil-for-arms deals in Africa, and China's expanding soft power.[96] This view is notable for its explicit focus on energy resources, and its direct inclusion to overall grand strategy. This approach also reconciles resource needs through involvement in Africa, Latin America, and Central Asia, all areas where an expanding Chinese presence is meant to secure resources for the state.

And, finally, much of this amounts to what is, broadly speaking, a defensive grand strategy constrained by American unipolarity as China attempts to close the wide gap in comprehensive national power.[97] This is a result of U.S. power and in line with past Chinese practice adopting accommodationist grand strategies during periods of weakness and more offensive grand strategies during times of relative strength.[98] Further, China is counterbalancing U.S. power by "self-strengthening" through economic growth and military modernization, and through proactive diplomacy in its external environment to maintain stability.[99]

Overall, China's grand strategy is dual purpose: the provision of diplomatic space and stability to allow for economic growth in support of its expanding security obligations. Much of this is drawn from the experience of the Soviets, and their own mishandling of the economy that ultimately could not support the level of military spending required to maintain competitiveness with Western states. China has prosecuted the peaceful rise strategy, then supplanted by the peaceful development strategy for much of the study period, and despite missteps, has seen much success without triggering too many adversarial reactions.[100]

An Assessment of Chinese Energy Security

China is inherently insecure when it comes to its energy supplies, and just as with economic statecraft within a grand strategic context,[101] energy figures heavily as a key component of grand strategy. Energy security is of the utmost importance to the CCP. Without energy, there is no economic growth. Without economic growth, the party's existence is imperiled and likely to falter. It is not mere energy security to China, but political and party security for the political elites. Energy must be secure, and available to the population at acceptable cost or growth will grind to a halt, taking the party with it. Without energy, there is no gas to put in the tanks of the cars of the emerging middle class, or energy to power heating and cooling systems, or fuels for cooking, or running industrial machinery. Energy is vital to the country, and therefore represents a core interest of the CCP in managing its grand strategy.[102]

Despite all that has been done on the part of the CCP, one simple flaw still exists in their multi-decade attempt to secure overseas sources of energy: their naval power is undeniably weak compared to that of the United States, leaving trade routes highly susceptible to naval interdiction. However, despite this weakness, China has made great strides to reduce vulnerabilities in its energy supply chain and has in many ways taken on approaches typically used by Western powers, including the United States. This integration has greatly enhanced Chinese security and efficiency, but there are also limits. China cannot fully rely on a system built by its chief potential adversaries. In this vein, China relies on the market where possible,[103] but only as much as it must, and attempts to find other ways to mitigate weaknesses in the supply chain. For instance, the reliance on equity oil[104] for some of its supplies is viewed as problematic by some analysts and arouses suspicions of China "locking up resources" so others are unable to access them.[105] Others contend this simply isn't the reality of these supplies and that most end up going to the open market anyway. So, do these supplies uniquely contribute to oil security? Some have contended these actions don't even matter since China has maintained a relatively accommodative posture towards its Asian neighbors and the United States,[106] and the market itself stands to benefit. These topics will be confronted in a later section, but it is important to understand the various approaches and perspectives on these approaches to securing a state's supply of energy.

Availability

Domestic Production

For the last 30 years, China has been attempting to mitigate the negative effects of production declines, as the state has had to shift from producer to consumer. Despite these steep declines, with the adoption of modern extractive technologies and advanced production techniques, China has been able to steadily increase production over the course of the study. Regarding table

Table 5.1.   **Annual Domestic Oil Production (Mbbls/d)**

Year	Production	Year	Production
1992	2,845	2003	3,406
1993	2,892	2004	3,486
1994	2,934	2005	3,642
1995	2,993	2006	3,711
1996	3,175	2007	3,742
1997	3,216	2008	3,814
1998	3,217	2009	3,805
1999	3,218	2010	4,077
2000	3,257	2011	4,074
2001	3,310	2012	4,155
2002	3,351	2013	4,180

Source: BP Statistical Review of Energy 2014, Statistical Workbook, Oil Production, http://www.bp.com/en/global/corporate/energy-economics/statistical-review-of-world-energy.html.

5.1, as Chinese firms have acquired skills and equipment, production has increased reversing the declines that began in the 1970s. Production since 1992 has increased almost every year and will most likely begin to accelerate as Chinese firms unlock tight oil deposits domestically. The data also demonstrate a 47 percent increase in production from 1992 to 2013, suggesting gradual, and consistent, growth absent large aberrations, reflecting a methodical approach to increases in production capacity.

Refining capacity has seen high growth as well. A large state such as China cannot properly secure its sources of energy without the ability to domestically process and refine large amounts of crude for use throughout the military and broader economy. The data in table 5.2 reflects China's

Table 5.2.   **Country-level Refining Capacity (Mbbls/d)**

Year	Daily Amount	Year	Daily Amount
1992	3,044	2003	6,295
1993	3,334	2004	6,603
1994	3,567	2005	7,165
1995	4,014	2006	7,865
1996	4,226	2007	8,399
1997	4,559	2008	8,722
1998	4,592	2009	9,479
1999	5,401	2010	10,302
2000	5,407	2011	10,834
2001	5,643	2012	11,933
2002	5,933	2013	12,598

Source: BP Statistical Review of Energy 2014, Statistical Workbook, Oil: Refinery Capacities, http://www.bp.com/en/global/corporate/energy-economics/statistical-review-of-world-energy.html.

concerns with refining capacity, which has grown over fourfold from the period 1992 to 2013. This has been consistent growth in capacity as well, with a steady doubling over both halves of the study period. Beyond raw numbers, the types of crude to be processed have expanded, and the efficiency gains and economies of scale have accelerated as China has moved to consolidate the sector especially with regards to shutting down the litany of independent, "teapot" refiners localized in Shandong Province.[107] Many of the new refineries are even designed to accept varying types of crude oil, allowing China to absorb and process ever greater varieties of petroleum.[108] This refining flexibility allows for the import of a greater number of blends and crude types going forward.

Energy Infrastructure

Information on China's domestic pipeline network is incomplete, but it seems to be growing at a steady pace. As of 2012, China has around 20,000 kilometers of crude oil pipelines crisscrossing its territory, and the majority of domestically produced crude is transported through this network.[109] Much of this has been designed as a way to effectively distribute oil throughout the country, from China's own fields in the northeast and northwest, to more economically active regions, especially those on the coast.

More directly related to import security is the number and capacity of China's transnational pipelines responsible for importing crude from nearby states. The two main pipelines for oil imports come from Russia and Kazakhstan. As Russia has expanded its exports east, through the East Siberian Oil Pipeline (ESPO), a Russia-China spur was built south, off the main line, which goes south 597 miles into China. The spur was operational in 2011, and carries approximately 300,000 b/d. The Kazakhstan-China oil pipeline traverses about 1,384 miles of difficult terrain and was opened in 2006, carrying 240,000 b/d, with an expansion to 400,000 b/d currently underway.[110] Central Asia strongly figures into China's energy diversification strategy, with CNPC sourcing one-quarter of its overseas production in Kazakhstan. It's also notable to mention, CNPC is the only foreign company operating in the energy sector in Turkmenistan, where China receives around 44 percent of its natural gas imports.[111] This line is notable for its technical difficulties: the length and extreme cold can present multiple problems.[112] Length is a problem due to gravity, since these pipelines need force in order to push the oil through the line and eventually out the other end, and several thousands of miles complicates these efforts and increases the number of pumping stations and maintenance required to keep the lines functioning.[113] Inclement weather presents its own problems. Incredibly low temperatures through the areas that the line traverses can cause the oil to simply sludge, and stop. This means additional costs are incurred to overcome this technical obstacle. However, increased costs simply do not trump the importance of diversification from Central Asia.

Perhaps most interesting, however, is the opening of the clearly strategic Myanmar-China oil pipeline. Myanmar doesn't have oil, but it has deepwater ports capable of offloading oil from the Middle East and any other sources requiring seaborne trade through the Malacca Strait. This 479-mile pipeline is purely meant as an alternate route, which bypasses the straits, and feeds petroleum directly to facilities in Yunnan Province. The massive investment required for this project reflects the increasing strategic importance of not only the route itself, but also the expansion of seaborne oil imports from the Middle East. This pipeline is capable of transporting approximately 440,000 b/d from Myanmar's coastal areas to China.[114]

Current Extractable Reserves

This is a weak point for China and was one of the main contributing factors resulting in their "going out" strategy. Chinese oil reserves are significant, and rank at number thirteen in the world,[115] but they simply do not have enough to power the development and economic growth of 1.3 billion people. Furthermore, domestic reserve growth is weak, and the industry has essentially stagnated over the past two decades. This reinforces the desire for the Chinese NOCs to develop their own shale oil and gas technology imported from abroad, as this will be the main avenue for them to get out of this trend.

As a result of China's "going out" strategy, and its push for overseas reserves, Chinese NOCs have attempted to boost recoverable reserves, under their de facto control, since inception of the strategy. In the 1990s, this was an incredibly important component of China's energy security strategy and represents one of the major shifts of the strategy away from economic realism to a more liberal approach, much like the Western states. Loans-for-oil, infrastructure-for-oil, and equity oil agreements have all been used to boost China's reserves of oil under its tangential control. However, in pursuing this approach, it has completely disregarded political risk factors, especially as China has pursued these agreements in places like Sudan and South Sudan, where oil exports are now essentially halted due to domestic politics. China, having invested a great deal in Sudan, is now unable to receive their oil payments on those investments because of the politically contentious climate. But this approach has also remade entire economies and has had only some success in retrospect,[116] where certain countries and regions are more pliable to Chinese interests. For instance, a falling-out over contract details in 2006

Table 5.3.   China Proved Reserves of Crude Oil (Bbbls)

Year	Proved Reserves	Year	Proved Reserves
1992	15.2	2003	15.5
1993	16.4	2004	15.5
1994	16.3	2005	15.6
1995	16.4	2006	15.6
1996	16.4	2007	15.5
1997	17	2008	15.6
1998	17.4	2009	15.9
1999	15.1	2010	17.3
2000	15.2	2011	17.8
2001	15.4	2012	18.1
2002	15.5	2013	18.1

BP Includes gas condensate and natural gas liquids (NGLs).

Source: BP Statistical Review of Energy 2014, Statistical Workbook, Oil: Proved Reserves History, http://www.bp.com/en/global/corpo rate/energy-economics/statistical-review-of-world-energy.html.

had Angola re-auctioning offshore blocs to other energy companies, hindering development and supply out of that country.[117]

As displayed in table 5.3, Chinese reserves, while not nearly sufficient, have been steadily growing as China's NOCs are able to adapt and bring on new skills and technology from abroad. It remains to be seen whether China will be able to unlock shale deposits throughout the country, which will remain challenging not only because of technical reasons, but those of geography. It would require enormous effort to get materials and equipment out to these mostly remote areas, and then build out the infrastructure required to transport these products to market.

Table 5.4 shows China's issues concerning its reserves in stark detail, where despite year-over-year growth in reserves, the actual years available at current consumption levels has gone from over 5 years, to less than 2. This is a significant drop and only underscores China's overseas energy requirements, due to both consumption and the lack of domestically controlled reserves. With current availability, China has very little supply chain flexibility from domestic sources and will instead have to seek that flexibility elsewhere. Additionally, in a state that prides itself on self-sufficiency, this is a particularly weak point within their energy security apparatus.

Capital Investment and Capital Efficiency

The energy industry runs on high levels of capital investment. Oil exploration, extraction, services, transportation, and distribution are all highly capital-intensive processes with a long time horizon for returns on those investments.

Table 5.4.   **Reserves-to-Consumption**

Year	Annual Consumption (MMbbls)	Years of Supply	Year	Annual Consumption (MMbbls)	Years of Supply
1992	2,902	5.24	2003	6,040	2.57
1993	3,221	5.09	2004	7,053	2.2
1994	3,301	4.94	2005	7,230	2.16
1995	3,593	4.56	2006	7,805	2
1996	3,916	4.19	2007	8,184	1.9
1997	4,313	3.94	2008	8,287	1.89
1998	4,401	3.95	2009	8,640	1.84
1999	4,646	3.25	2010	7,000	2.47
2000	4,967	3.06	2011	9,678	1.84
2001	5,102	3.02	2012	10,230	1.77
2002	5,529	2.8	2013	10,713	1.69

Notes: Author converted daily consumption figures to annual, and then calculated years of supply by dividing reserves by the annualized consumption figures, for each year.
BP sourced consumption data combined with Hong Kong SAR, added then rounded.

Source: BP Statistical Review of Energy 2014, Statistical Workbook, Oil: Consumption, http://www.bp.com/en/global/corporate/energy-economics/statistical-review-of-world-energy.html.

Chinese NOCs have never been too concerned about capital since they branched off from their respective ministries, as they have consistently had some type of government support in the form of subsidies or loans. Additionally, off-book assistance to the companies exists, as many loans are made on the companies' behalf by the China Development Bank (CDB) and the Export-Import Bank (Exim) with their notorious oil-for-loan and oil-for-infrastructure loans. This has been a boon for business, granting access to many deposits that would have otherwise been out of reach. However, contrary to popular belief, these companies do not completely run off government support for all projects. They are stable profit-seeking enterprises that are becoming more adroit at seeking out business opportunities and navigating the market. While it would be hard to believe Beijing would allow any of these companies to go bankrupt and dissolve, and there exists at least implicit guarantees by the state, the government does not have a direct hand in day-to-day business operations,[118] nor frequent direct involvement in the international operations of the firms.[119]

Chinese companies, and by extension, Beijing, have the tendency to pay up and over the proper valuation of an asset if they believe their long-term security interests can be served. This was especially the case in the 1990s and early 2000s. For instance, the costly purchase of PetroKazakhstan[120] is one of the deals industry professionals point to when making their case that Chinese firms simply pay exorbitant amounts in order to hoard assets; however, the true benefit to Beijing was not simply the company and oil access, but its ability to open a whole new land corridor for oil supplies, greatly enhancing its energy security. Individual IOCs, such as Exxon or Chevron, do not have to worry about energy security for the United States. Their sole purpose is business and profit. The Chinese NOCs, however, are concerned with both profit and energy security. A deal like the PetroKazakhstan deal is less about overpaying to gain material assets, or missteps in capital efficiency, and more about gaining material assets and an entire new avenue for oil supplies well into the future. This is clearly beneficial to Chinese energy security by increasing the diversity of supply through the addition of an overland route that is less susceptible to attack.

We also have a much better picture of whether China has been a serial overpayer for oil assets beginning in the mid-2000s, when Chinese purchases increased, and more analysts started to take notice. A recent study demonstrates that from the period 2005–2013, Chinese companies did not typically overpay in their M&A transactions overall, although companies would overpay when entering new sectors and sub-sectors, and were generally more capital efficient than NOCs from other countries, but still less capital efficient than IOCs.[121]

Finding enough detailed information on specific oil-related deals over the 1993–2012 period has been difficult to come by, however, there are ways to glean certain information regarding the Chinese mindset for strategic commodities. First, the Chinese government is very price conscious. The companies may have overpaid in the past, but there are many cases in the past decade where China has simply bided its time and made major acquisitions when the market was advantageous. For instance, during the financial crisis in 2008–2009, Chinese companies took the opportunity to go on an asset-buying binge around the world. They were, of course, able to buy at bargain prices, snapping up lucrative assets on the cheap. During major price drops in oil, and other commodities for that matter, Chinese firms always heavily increase their buying. In 2008, China drastically stepped up acquisitions for its first-phase strategic petroleum reserve, simply because prices had crashed after the major run-up.

Another example is the recent deal that China made with Russia to be supplied with natural gas, which took over 10 years to negotiate.[122] China was responsible for the delays in bargaining, simply pushing for a better deal, and waiting. Only when Russia was in major financial trouble in the wake of Ukraine's annexation, steeped in sanctions and a fiscal mess, did China finally accept a deal from a severely economically weakened and constrained Russia. In need of cash, this reduced bargaining power meant Russia was not in a position to push for higher prices especially with the limited export markets available for Siberian gas.

Table 5.5.   Return on Average Capital Employed (ROACE)

Year	China National Petroleum Corp (PTR)	China Petrochemical Corp (SNP)	China National Offshore Oil Corp (CEO)
2005	0.25	0.13	0.32
2006	0.23	0.15	0.3
2007	0.2	0.14	0.24
2008	0.14	0.09	0.28
2009	0.11	0.14	0.16
2010	0.14	0.15	0.25
2011	0.13	0.14	0.26
2012	0.11	0.11	0.2
2013	0.11	0.11	0.14
Average for All Years	0.16	0.13	0.24

Note: Some financial data related to Chinese companies may be inaccurate.

Source: Author's calculations based on data from company reports, Bloomberg Terminal company data, Morningstar, www.morningstar.com and NASDAQ, www.nasdaq.com. Company reports available at ExxonMobil, http://corporate.exxonmobil.com/en/; Chevron, https://www.chevron.com; ConocoPhillips, http://www.conocophillips.com/Pages/default.aspx.

Table 5.5 demonstrates some relatively respectable returns on average capital employed for the three main NOCs in China. The most transparent, and international of the three, CNOOC, with the symbol "CEO" on international exchanges, has the highest return at 24 percent return on capital, on par with levels seen in Western IOCs. It should also be noted, while efficiency might not be as high as IOCs, Chinese companies can still have higher ROACE levels due to other factors, such as below-market petroleum purchases negotiated by the government as with Venezuela.

Affordability

Pricing and Volatility

China employs price controls in the domestic economy in order to cushion its population against any major rises and volatility in the price of petroleum. This is another reason for the desire of the NOCs to go outward and sell their oil in new and different markets: they can't always make money at home in the controlled, domestic market. While it is a captive market for the companies, they are not free to price their final products based on market supply and demand and are unable to adjust their prices higher at the point of consumption if the prevailing market prices are high. If prices are too high internationally, and these firms then refine and sell their products to the domestic market, they will typically incur heavy financial losses. However, after petroleum is procured internationally, they are always able to sell that at market rates overseas, making a profitable transaction on international markets, whereas that same transaction would have been unprofitable domestically. The government cushions the population and businesses from severe price swings, forcing the brunt of these adjustments on the energy industry itself.

However, information on opaque Chinese transactions can be extremely difficult to come by. China operates mainly in international markets, but also engages heavily in bilateral deals with many foreign governments, where much of the transaction history is clouded. These sorts of clouded transaction many times include the oil-for-loans deals, and similar transactions, mentioned earlier. However, at this point, it does not seem to put the NOCs at significant disadvantage, as they are able to price some of their petroleum from distressed countries at lower rates than prevailing market prices.

The data in table 5.6 demonstrate relatively higher levels of volatility in Dubai crude, but still somewhat stable over the course of the study. The average price over the first half, 1992 to 2002, was approximately $18.30 with a standard deviation of $4.04. This results in a 22 percent price variation off the average. In the second half there are higher prices and greater volatility, with the average price at $72.12 and a standard deviation of $27.69. However, using monthly prices for the index, the standard deviation rises to 25 percent and 41 percent respectively. The average price for all years is $45.20 with a standard deviation of 34.23 using monthly figures, resulting in a 76 percent variation. Here, as with the WTI price, 2008 is an aberration, when the culmination of new demand pressures acting on the price of oil reached

Table 5.6.　Annual Price of Dubai Crude (Medium, Fatah, 32 API, USD), USD per Barrel, and Volatility (Annual Standard Deviations)

Year	Price	Volatility	Year	Price	Volatility
1992	17.14	1.23	2003	26.73	1.79
1993	14.91	1.28	2004	33.46	3.06
1994	14.83	1.34	2005	49.2	5.9
1995	16.13	0.83	2006	61.43	4.46
1996	18.54	1.98	2007	68.37	10.41
1997	18.1	1.21	2008	93.78	27.29
1998	12.09	0.84	2009	61.76	12.29
1999	17.08	4.54	2010	78.06	4.81
2000	26.09	2.78	2011	106.03	5.54
2001	22.71	2.74	2012	108.92	7.26
2002	23.73	2.55	2013	105.43	3.25

Source: Quandl, Dubai Crude Oil Price (ODA/POILDUB_USD), https://www.quandl.com/data/ODA/POIL WTI_USD, sourced from Open Data for Africa, African Development Bank Group IMF Primary Commodity Prices August 2015, http://opendataforafrica.org/efkgejg/imf-primary-commodity-prices-august-2015, and International Monetary Fund, IMF Primary Commodity Prices, http://www.imf.org/external/np/res/commod/index.aspx, author took the simple average of the end-of-month price for each year to calculate annual price. Author also calculated the standard deviations for each year.

their breaking point, resulting in the spectacular run up, and subsequent crash, in prices. Similar to WTI, 2008 also reported the highest level of volatility for Dubai crude during the study period.

Reliability

Diversified Sources

This is one of the most critical, and pragmatic, areas for a large state to enhance its oil security, and over the course of the study, the level of import diversification for Chinese oil supplies has gone from dismal to the same level as the United States, while maintaining similar import requirements. An interesting point demonstrated by the data is that China almost seems to be following the energy diversification pattern of the United States. Not only has diversification increased, but China even has the same level of overreliance on Middle East oil, particularly Saudi Arabia, that the United States had for much of the latter half of the 20th century, and especially in the mid-2000s.

As can be seen in table 5.7 below, China has moved to rapidly expand the number of suppliers of oil. From a low of 21 in 1992, all the way to a maximum of 51 in 2010, China now sources from all over the world. With import sources more than doubled by 2013, China has needed to source additional oil from all over the world, not simply to meet domestic demand, but also to increase diversification for security purposes.

The HHI scores displayed in table 5.8 also express an interesting point relating to the timing of Chinese supplier expansion. It is possible that China may have opportunistically taken advantage of the oil price drops resulting from the Asian financial crisis in 1998, in order to initiate purchases from a

Table 5.7. Total Number of States Exporting to China by Year

Year	Number of States	Year	Number of States
1992	21	2003	44
1993	24	2004	44
1994	25	2005	39
1995	29	2006	44
1996	20	2007	46
1997	32	2008	42
1998	30	2009	43
1999	31	2010	51
2000	32	2011	46
2001	32	2012	48
2002	31	2013	45

Source: United Nations Comtrade Database, United Nations, Trade Data Extraction Interface, HS Commodity Code 2709, Petroleum Oils, Oils from Bituminous Minerals, Crude, http://comtrade.un.org.

Table 5.8.   Annual Herfindahl-Hirschman Index (HHI) Score

Year	HHI Score	Year	HHI Score
1992	2,588	2003	891
1993	1,601	2004	847
1994	2,401	2005	915
1995	1,739	2006	951
1996	1,866	2007	904
1997	1,358	2008	1,043
1998	1,117	2009	996
1999	785	2010	915
2000	979	2011	912
2001	940	2012	944
2002	910	2013	943

Source: Author's own calculations using UN Comtrade Data (United Nations Comtrade Database, United Nations, Trade Data Extraction Interface, HS Commodity Code 2709, Petroleum Oils, Oils From Bituminous Minerals, Crude, http://comtrade.un.org) and above HHI equation derived from multiple sources, including the U.S. Department of Justice (https://www.justice.gov/atr/horizontal-merger-guidelines-08192010#5c), but for a more detailed look, reference Stephen A. Rhoades, The Herfindahl-Hirschman Index, Federal Reserve Bulletin, Volume 79, Number 3, March 1993, pp 188–189.

more diversified array of suppliers, all of which would have been in dire need of new export outlets in the midst of a global economic downturn, one which was especially acute in Asia. This entirely fits with the Chinese pattern of taking advantage of economic malaise elsewhere in the world to advance their interests, especially in strategic sectors. This is similar to actions taken during the more recent economic downturn in 2008, when China went on a buying binge in the energy sector (among others), buying all sorts of assets on the cheap, striking profitable bargains with desperate sellers. It would appear that China might have taken the same action during the regional crisis in order to expand suppliers, probably garnering a cost advantage of some sort on equity and loan-for-oil deals. The timing is stark on the HHI index above, where from 1997 to 1999, the reduction in the HHI score craters at 785 from 1358, a 42 percent drop over the two-year period. This, compared to the raw data on the number of suppliers, indicates that China took the opportunity to significantly expand new supplier relationships to gain cost advantages. This was a surprising piece of data, but falls completely in line with Chinese actions in the sector.

The other interesting, and surprising, point demonstrated by the HHI index is how quickly China went from importing from only a few suppliers in the early 1990s to a highly diversified import base by the mid-2000s. As mentioned earlier, the specific point where this happened was over the 1998–1999 period, when China achieved a score of 785 for 1999. After 1999, China's score breached the 1,000 level only once in 2008. This level of diversity is quite remarkable for its rapidity and maintenance at a level in the 900s for about three-quarters of the study period. It is reasonable to assume that the Chinese government recognized this as a critical area for its long-term energy security goals and made concerted efforts to quickly expand its supplier base, coordinated at the highest levels of government.

Short- and Long-Term Protection from Political Interruptions

China spent much of the study period learning to manage political interruptions along its supply chain, typically through the increasing skill levels and knowledge acquired by management teams at the various state-owned companies. This increase in competition and experience enhanced the capacity of companies to understand and mitigate diverse types of political risk.[123] This type of risk mitigation covers many political disruptions, but not all, and certainly not the potential circumstances that come with "containment" or open warfare. These other risks must also be accounted for.

China relies on the global oil market for economic expediency and efficiency, but constantly makes bilateral energy deals directly with governments and generates a great deal of oil through equity deals in several politically risky countries. In particular, the government-to-government deals conducted by China are far more frequent than the United States and members of the OECD. Politics and U.S. dominance, particularly military dominance, of global oil markets will always force China to look for other alternatives to the current market, even if it means less efficiency, prioritizing a more secure supply chain over lower prices. Further, it is the position of this research, that in particular, China's government-led oil-for-loan and oil-for-infrastructure deals and equity contracts are all examples of paths for China to sidestep the current oil market in favor of a greater degree of supply chain control and security. This control and stability may be illusory,[124] particularly in times of stress and political upheaval, but it does provide another avenue of supplies to Beijing, with more control than the global oil market itself.

Many analysts, and Chinese security hawks in Beijing, believe this does supply additional security, but many others feel that this step does nothing of the sort. The truth is somewhere in between. Bilateral transactions may or may not be cheaper depending on the specific agreement, they don't reduce oil price volatility, and they may not necessarily provide ready access to supplies in the case of a crisis, dependent on severity.[125] Most Chinese equity oil is exported to global markets, but one cannot discount the fact that these approaches result in increased control over supply lines. Referencing the proposed model from chapter 2, it makes more sense to think about this from Beijing's perspective in a gradual standoff with the Western powers. Under normal conditions, the market usually works best, but all states must prepare for the worst. Going from this point to open warfare is a stretch as well. If Western powers continue to follow their current path, pressure may be ratcheted up first in the form of sanctions and other forms of economic warfare. China feels the need to prepare for this, and a higher level of supply chain control will result in supplies that are potentially *sanctions resistant*. To understand this approach, think about what would happen to crude supplies sourced from Venezuela or Sudan. These are two host countries on less-than-friendly terms with Western states, both without compelling reasons to cooperate in Chinese containment. These oil sources use Chinese-owned equipment and workers, and may be brought back to the mainland by Chinese companies, using Chinese flagged vessels. This process limits China's susceptibility to oil sanctions by maximizing control over the entire process from field to port, mitigating legal and political complications along the way. At many times, this approach has even paid off, striking deals with desperate governments ready to supply oil at bargain prices for a bailout, whatever it may be. This has happened time and again, not only with troubled African governments, but with Russia and Venezuela as well.[126]

As with the United States, China's strategic petroleum reserve has risen in importance, although it is difficult to quantify since Beijing does not release reputable figures and considers such information a state secret, although promises have been made recently[127] to begin releasing figures on oil stocks. The available information is shown below in table 5.9, and initial estimates were for the reserves to total 500 million bbls by 2020, but that figure has now potentially risen to 600 million bbls,[128] and is roughly the same 90-day consumption average for OECD/IEA countries.[129] The government has pursued this task in a series of three phases that began in mid-2000, with each phase bringing multiple storage facilities online. Table 5.9 demonstrates capacity estimates for the SPR, which is an important distinction from actual stored crude oil, further complicating China's SPR estimates. While capacity has been growing significantly, we also know that official estimates are lower than the capacity available, putting SPR total stocks at around 190 million barrels.[130] In 2013, total SPR capacity was at around 253 million bbls after the completion of phase 1 facilities and partial completion of phase 2 facilities.

Even hazier is information regarding industry stocks, which are even more sparse than numbers for the official SPR. To make matters worse, since the NOCs run SPR facilities for the government, much of the information available on petroleum stocks might have duplicate data. This means there is no clear distinction between government- and industry-controlled

Table 5.9.   Government-Controlled Petroleum Stocks (SPR), Industry-Controlled Petroleum Stocks, and Total Petroleum Stocks (MMbbls/yr)

Year	Government-Controlled	Industry-Controlled	Total Stocks
2003	0	N/A	N/A
2004	0	N/A	N/A
2005	0	N/A	N/A
2006	30	N/A	N/A
2007	30	N/A	N/A
2008	30	N/A	N/A
2009	91	N/A	N/A
2010	91	N/A	N/A
2011	129	220	349
2012	209	N/A	N/A
2013	253	257	510

Note: Government-Controlled stocks refer to storage capacity.

Sources: Various, company reports, news reports,
Michal Meidan, Amrita Sen, and Robert Cambell, China: the 'new normal,' Oxford Energy Comment, Oxford Institute for Energy Studies, University of Oxford, February 2015, pp 9–10
Song Yen Ling, China's end-October commercial crude, oil product stocks fall on month, Platts Oil Service, November, 25, 2014, http://www.platts.com/latest-news/oil/singapore/chinas-end-october-commercial-crude-oil-product-27868887
Christopher J Neely, China's Strategic Petroleum Reserve: A Drop in the Bucket, Economic Synopses, Federal Reserve Bank of St. Louis, 2007, no. 2
Mandip Singh, China's Strategic Petroleum Reserves: A Reality Check, IDSA Issue Brief, Institute for Defense Studies and Analysis, May 21, 2012, http://www.idsa.in/system/files/IB_ChinasStrategicPetroleumReserves_MandipSingh_210512.pdf.

stocks, complicating data quality issues.[131] However, there are estimates that industry-controlled stocks are around 257 million bbls, but this is, again, an estimate.[132]

As with the SPR, there is the need to distinguish between storage capacity and actual petroleum stocks. Commercial storage capacity in China has actually been high for quite some time, but it simply has not been filled. Many new private players rushed into the sector in the 1990s, contributing to the large growth in facilities capable of storing crude.[133] The shortage in actual stocks is most likely due to a lack of incentives as Chinese NOCs have attempted to become more competitive over time, and simply did not deem it necessary to keep large stocks of petroleum since this is typically unprofitable. By some estimates, commercial storage is around 1.6 billion barrels.[134] But, it is still difficult to know realistically how much of that capacity is filled.

As stated previously in the section on the United States, the ultimate guarantor of long-term oil security is sufficient military power to secure sea and land routes back to the homeland. This is difficult to achieve without expeditionary capabilities and impossible to achieve with a weak navy, the latter of which China has been making great strides to correct. Albeit far off, China's naval developments are clearly on a path to develop a full blue-water naval force capable of meeting threats along supply routes, and in China's near-abroad as a complement to forces on the mainland. A less talked-about attempt by the Chinese to secure energy routes is the so called "string of pearls," which refers to the contracting of port usage along Beijing's Indian Ocean supply routes, extending to near the Persian Gulf and Africa's east coast. This can be thought of as not only a strategic placement of bases along critical supply routes, but also as a way to mitigate current and future naval weakness, until the PLAN has the opportunity and ability to "catch-up" with more modern naval powers. While these military plans have not come to fruition yet, China appears to have started laying the groundwork for future military deployments along its supply routes with the establishment of a base in Djibouti and negations for port development and access with Pakistan.

As mentioned, Chinese flagged tankers are a component of the supply response as well. The Chinese tanker fleet has grown rapidly and can carry significant amounts of petroleum. According to Platts, in 2014, Chinese vessels transported approximately 50–60 percent of China's oil imports, and this number is set to increase with the rapid buildup of the fleet.[135] It is interesting to note, many large energy importers do rely on large tanker fleets flagged in their own territory. Japan, one of the clear vanguards of modern energy security, receives approximately 90 percent of its crude oil via Japanese flagged tankers. This measure is also nearly impossible for U.S. tankers given that companies based there do not typically flag their vessels in the home country, a common practice in the shipping industry.[136] The ability to control the transport requirements of crude imports is compelling.

It should be noted that during wartime conditions, the targeting of tankers has been problematic, but this may be less so today. The intelligence capabilities of the United Sates are within reason to be able to properly identify, and isolate or destroy tankers bound for China. But, not even all tankers bound for China would need to be destroyed, since the mere threat of these attacks will have a deterrent effect on any crews slated to sail for the APAC region. Interdiction, and if needed, destruction, is possible, and if it only occurs with limited success, would still provide the desired outcome.

Supply interdiction is also a challenge since this approach has the potential to make oil costlier to everyone in the world.[137] However, this risk is most likely unfounded due to a black-market-pricing mentality within individual economies. Just because some products cost more on the black market within a country does not mean they cost more outside. It's not a matter of supply and demand, but one simply of access. It would raise the cost of imports to China but would not raise the cost to other parts of the world—in fact, it would most likely lower them given large quantities of Chinese oil would be undelivered and in need of buyers.

This is hugely problematic for Chinese supply and the integral nature of sea power has not gone unnoticed in China with respect to grand strategy.[138] The waterways and maritime routes responsible for large volumes of the oil trade are so important they have received considerable attention by top political elites. This area is a key vulnerability for China, referred to by many as the "Malacca Dilemma"[139] after Hu Jintao's first public mention of the strategic issues concerning the Strait in 2003.[140] China has worked assiduously to mitigate and correct vulnerabilities attributed to the dilemma, including worries of supply interdiction, the strengthening of U.S. alliances in the region, and the apparent encirclement by potentially hostile powers at the behest of the United States, first through non-military measures,[141] followed principally by enhancing naval power in the region,[142] and a reorientation of focus to Asia's SLOCs.[143] One of the greater leaps forward for China has been the purchase of a Soviet-era aircraft carrier from Ukraine. Ambitions for carrier deployments have been with China since the 1920s, and feasibility, technical capacity, or funding never culminated to launch a program, until the recent economic boom, when China's resources matched ambitions and the late Admiral Liu Huaqing, who has been called China's Alfred Thayer Mahan and father of China's modern navy, spearheaded efforts to acquire a carrier and begin indigenous production of a carrier fleet.[144]

In a very practical sense, China's PLAN has embarked on a concerted effort to stall and strangle American sea power in the region through the development of anti-access and area denial (A2/AD) capabilities. These developments began halfway through the study period and China continues to deploy these methods as a means to counter a technologically superior military force through degradation, first strikes, and periphery control, operationalized by use of submarines, ballistic and cruise missiles, mines, land-based air strikes, air defense, electronic warfare, cyber warfare, counter-space, and joint operations.[145] China also looks abroad for this security as well. Access to deepwater ports along the Indian Ocean maritime routes will strengthen Chinese naval power in the future, especially in the context of the "String of Pearls" projections across the Indian Ocean, which is also not just about hardened military sites, but perhaps more about maintaining its benign status while making use of dual-use civilian-military facilities highly dependent on bilateral relationships.[146] All of this will need to be balanced by the difficulties in the South China Sea, which present their own security hurdles, if only by the provocation of conflict with neighboring states.[147]

A fascinating aspect of China's maritime approach is that it simply may not be new, or original. The previous adversary of the United States, the Soviet Union, may very well have provided a naval template for a technologically superior adversary with overwhelming naval power brought to bear close to the maritime periphery.[148] Like the Soviets, China faces an intractable opportunity cost with respect to its naval power. The distribution of military funding will have to continue to be siphoned away from the PLA's ground forces, which are also responsible for funding internal security.[149] However, as China grows, and requires more resources to be dedicated to naval advancement and expansion, it will come at a time when internal security will still be challenging and China may well be encountering more external resistance. This will place great strain on the military budget, and represents an intractable, enduring choice that China has wrestled with for centuries, and all continental-based powers must confront.[150] This inherent tension exists through the study period as China has focused on its submarine and missile-based area-denial strategy in its maritime environment, increasing costs and frustrating efforts by any future hostile powers in the region.[151]

CONCLUDING REMARKS ON CHINA'S ENERGY SECURITY APPROACH

As mentioned in the previous section, the most salient concern of China's political elites is the interdiction of seaborne crude under containment or hostile conditions. The NOCs and China have the same security concerns whether the companies ship supplies directly back to China from where they are sourced, or simply buy supplies on the market at the lowest price. Therefore, it makes sense for China to operate in the market as much as possible and reap the benefits of the lowest possible prices for its oil supplies. However, if needed, China can re-direct overseas sources of petroleum back to the homeland without any concern over economics.

They have the facilities overseas, the oil assets, and a growing tanker fleet available to move supplies directly back to the country in extreme scenarios. This level of control over the entire supply chain provides an extra layer of energy security to China, especially with assets retrieved from abroad. A conflict with the United States or other countries may compromise the security from this approach; however, more importantly, in the potential lead-up to a conflict, when embargoes may be put in place, China will have the ability to continue to receive overseas supply of oil due to this control over the entire supply chain. Other energy companies and tankers may be subject to, and willing to comply with, embargoes or restrictions put in place during the lead-up to any conflict, but Chinese companies with Chinese flagged vessels would almost certainly disregard any orders to halt operations and would continue shipments. This essentially makes certain suppliers risky, yet more resistant to sanctions pressures in the event they may be applied in any future conflict by the United States and other Western states.

This would also force the hand of those implementing the embargo, recognizing that any seizure or destruction of Chinese assets or vessels would be an unacceptable escalation, potentially leading to a full kinetic conflict.[152] Therefore, these overseas sources are not necessarily meant to provide security in the sense that supplies will be able to circumvent the U.S. Navy across the world's trade routes, but to instead provide breathing room during any highly hostile points in the relationship between China and its competitors that may ensue. This breathing room, or "buffer," can be very valuable, and lessens the leverage the United States would have over China in any conflict outside of open warfare. This essentially shifts the burden of a hot war onto China's competitors, putting them in a very unenviable position.

This point of view has strong historical precedent, involving the fateful events that brought Japan into open warfare with the United States in 1941. Cutting off energy supplies to a state has very real consequences, and will force that state into open conflict if they have no other means of resupply. President Roosevelt knew this point well. Time and again, Roosevelt told his staff that oil shipments needed to continue to Japan. He knew any cutoff of oil to Japan would back them into a corner, leaving only open conflict. The eventual cutoff of oil supplies was implemented as a Japanese asset freeze in the U.S., where U.S. dollar denominated assets required by the Japanese to purchase oil supplies were made unavailable. This put the Japanese government in a tight spot. They did not own any significant oil-producing assets, as their attempts in Manchuria did not turn up much. They received around 80 percent of their oil consumed from the United States, regarding the halt in shipments as vital. Ultimately, they were forced to seize oil-producing assets owned by Royal Dutch Shell, in the Dutch East Indies. There, they had Japanese forces in control of oil producing assets, and Japanese flagged tankers and vessels, transporting the oil back to the homeland, regardless of economic efficiency. But, the situation would not have been possible unless Japan were able to conduct these operations themselves. This is highly analogous to a Chinese "lesson learned" whereby control over the entire supply chain is vital to oil security.

Chinese energy security approaches have been storied and unique for a great power, absorbing swings back and forth along the producer-consumer scale, forcing drastic re-thinks of energy security throughout the 20th century. But its core strategic goals have remained the same, especially since the inception of the CCP in 1949 as the monopolizing governing body of China. The flow of energy supplies, oil in particular, must continue unhindered for military and economic purposes, and this imperative will not change anytime soon.

NOTES

1. Tang Xu, Zhang Baosheng, Feng Lianyong, Marwan Masri, Afshin Honarvar, "Economic Impacts and Chalenges of China's Petroleum Industry: An Input-Output Analysis," *Energy* 36, no. 5 (2011), 2905–2911.

2. Mikael Höök, Tang Xu, Pang Xiongqi, and Kjell Aleklett, "Development Journey and Outlook of Chinese Giant Oilfields," *Petroleum Exploration and Development* 37, no. 2 (2010), 237–239.

3. Components of this section were used to inform the following chapter: Ryan C. Opsal and Remi B. Piet, "China and the Significance of Energy Security," in *Energy Security and Environmental Sustainability in the Western Hemisphere*, eds., Remi B. Piet, Bruce M. Bagley, Marcelo R. S. Zorovich (Lanham, MD: Lexington Books, 2017).

4. John K. Fairbank and Merle Goldman, *China: A New History* (Cambridge, MA: Belknap Press of Harvard University Press, 2006), 187–254.

5. Irvine H. Anderson Jr., *The Standard-Vacuum Oil Company and United States East Asian Policy, 1933–1941* (Princeton, NJ: Princeton University Press, 1975), 15–38.

6. Ibid.

7. Tatsu Kambara and Christopher Howe, *China and the Global Energy Crisis: Development and Prospects for China's Oil and Natural Gas* (Cheltenham: Edward Elgar Publishing Limited), 8.

8. Ibid.

9. Ibid., 9–10.

10. Yergin, *The Prize: The Epic Quest for Oil, Money, and Power*, 358–359.

11. Dieter Heinzig, *The Soviet Union and Communist China, 1945–1950: The Arduous Road to the Alliance* (Armonk, NY: M. E. Sharpe Inc., 2004), 227–228.

12. Xuetao Hu, Shuyong Hu, Fayang Jin, and Su Huang, *Physics of Petroleum Reservoirs* (Berlin, DE: Springer-Verlag Berlin Heidelberg, 2017), 3–4.

13. Tatsu Kambara and Christopher Howe, *China and the Global Energy Crisis: Development and Prospects for China's Oil and Natural Gas* (Cheltenham: Edward Elgar Publishing Limited), 12.

14. John K. Fairbank and Merle Goldman, *China: A New History* (Cambridge: Belknap Press of Harvard University Press, 2006), 378–379.

15. Hong Zhou, Jun Zhang, and Min Zhang, *Foreign Aid in China* (Berlin, DE: Springer-Verlag Berlin Heidelberg, 2015), 92–98.

16. Xu Tang, Baosheng Zhang, Mikael Höök, and Lianyong Feng, "Forecast of Oil Reserves and Production in Daqing Oilfield of China," *Energy* 35, no. 7 (2010), 3097–3102.

17. Nai-Ruenn Chen and Walter Galenson, *The Chinese Economy Under Maoism* (New Jersey: Aldine Transaction, A Division of Transaction Publishers, 2011) 143.

18. Kenneth Lieberthal and Michel Oksenberg, *Policymaking in China: Leaders, Structures, and Processes* (Princeton, NJ: Princeton University Press, 1988), 182–183.

19. James Dorian, *Minerals, Energy, and Economic Development in China* (Oxford: Oxford University Press, 1994), 25.

20. Lieberthal and Oksenberg, *Policymaking in China: Leaders, Structures, and Processes*, 178–179.

21. "China's 'Iron Man' an Undying Legend," *People's Daily Online*, September 17, 2009, http://english.people.com.cn/90001/90776/90882/6760061.html (accessed November 22, 2014).

22. Author calculation based on data from: China Economic and Industry Database, CEIC Data, https://www.ceicdata.com/en (accessed November 7, 2014).

23. Lim Tai Wei, *Oil in China: From Self-Reliance to Internationalization* (Singapore: World Scientific Publishing, 2010), 145.

24. Yergin, *The Quest: Energy, Security, and the Remaking of the Modern World*, 224.

25. James Dorian, *Minerals, Energy, and Economic Development in China* (Oxford: Oxford University Press, 1994), 25.

26. Data derived from BP Statistical Review Workbook 2014.

27. Kim Woodard, *The International Energy Relations of China* (Stanford, CA: Stanford University Press, 1980), 90.

28. James Mann, *About Face: A History of America's Curious Relationship with China, from Nixon to Clinton* (New York: Alfred A. Knopf, Inc., 1998), 74.

29. Woodard, *The International Energy Relations of China*, 90.

30. Ibid., 91.

31. Lieberthal and Oksenberg, *Policymaking in China: Leaders, Structures, and Processes*, 60–62.

32. Susan T. Shirk, "Internationalization and China's Domestic Reforms," in *Internationalization and Domestic Politics*, eds. Robert O. Keohane and Helen V. Milner (Cambridge, MA: Cambridge University Press, 1996) 193–195; Luke Patey, *The New Kings of Crude: China, India, and the Global Struggle for Oil in Sudan and South Sudan* (New York, NY: Oxford University Press, 2014), 85–87.

33. Robert Weatherley, *Mao's Forgotten Successor: The Political Career of Hua Guofeng* (New York, NY: Palgrave Macmillan, 2010), 153–154, 164–165.

34. June T. Dreyer, *China's Political System: Modernization and Tradition, Ninth Edition* (New York, NY: Routledge, 2016), 120–122.

35. Joseph Fewsmith, *Dilemmas of Reform in China: Political Conflict and Economic Debate* (Armonk, NY: M.E. Sharpe, 1994), 109.

36. Barry Naughton, *Growing Out of the Plan: Chinese Economic Reform, 1978–1993* (Cambridge, MA: Cambridge University Press), 72–74.

37. Susan L. Shirk, *The Political Logic of Economic Reform in China* (Berkeley: University of California Press, 1993), 21–22.

38. Earlier referred to as the Oil Kingdom Faction, but also known as the Petroleum Faction which sometimes broadly used to include not just party members in the oil sector, but also heavy industry.

39. Barry Naughton, *The Chinese Economy: Transitions and Growth* (Cambridge, MA: The MIT Press, 2007), 78.

40. Maurice Meisner, *Mao's China and After: A History of the People's Republic, Third Edition* (New York, NY: The Free Press, 1999), 428–430.

41. Susan L. Shirk, *The Political Logic of Economic Reform in China* (Berkeley, CA: University of California Press, 1993), 33.

42. Ibid., 33–35.

43. Alexander V. Pantsov and Steven I. Levine, *Deng Xiaoping: A Revolutionary Life* (New York, NY: Oxford University Press, 2015), 345–358.

44. Lianyong Feng, Yan Hu, Charles Hall, and Jianliang Wang, *The Chinese Oil Industry: History and Future* (New York, NY: Springer Publishing, 2013), 8.

45. Nargiza Salidjanova, U.S.-China Economic and Security Review Commission, "Going Out: An Overview of China's Outward Foreign Direct Investment," USCC Staff Research Report, March 30, 2011, 4–5.

46. David Scott, *China Stands Up: The PRC and the International System* (New York, NY: Routledge, 2007), 86–87; Kevin J. Cooney and Yoichiro Sato, eds., *The Rise of China and International Security: America and Asia Respond* (New York, NY: Routledge, 2009), 41–43.

47. Russell Ong, *China's Security Interests in the Post–Cold War Era* (London, U.K.: Curzon Press, 2002), 143–145.

48. Melvin Gurtov and Byong-Moo Hwang, *China's Security: The New Roles of the Military* (Boulder, CO: Lynne Rienner Publishers, 1998), 109–113.

49. Fettweis, "Free Riding or Restraint? Examining European Grand Strategy," *Comparative Strategy*, 317.

50. Avery Goldstein, *Rising to the Challenge: China's Grand Strategy and International Security* (Stanford, CA: Stanford University Press, 2005), 38–40.

51. Christian A. Hess, "Keeping the Past Alive: The Use of History in China's Foreign Relations," in *Handbook of China's International Relations*, ed. Shaun Breslin (New York, NY: Routledge, 2010), 47–54.

52. John K. Fairbank and Merle Goldman, *China: A New History* (Cambridge, MA: Belknap Press of Harvard University Press, 2006), 187–254.

53. Alison A. Kaufman, "The 'Century of Humiliation,' Then and Now: Chinese Perceptions of the International Order," *Pacific Focus* 25, no. 1, April 2010, 1–33

54. M. Taylor Fravel, "China's Search for Military Power," *Washington Quarterly* 31, no. 3 (2008): 127; Thomas J. Christensen, "China," 30–39 in Strategic Asia 2001–02: Power and Purpose (National Bureau of Asian Research, 2001), 30–39; Minxin Pei, China's Trapped Transition: The Limits of Developmental Autocracy (Cambridge, MA: Harvard University Press, 2006), 29–30.

55. Andrew Scobell, *China's Use of Military Force: Beyond the Great Wall and the Long March* (Cambridge, U.K.: Cambridge University Press, 2003), 36–38.

56. André Laliberté and Marc Lanteigne, eds., *The Chinese Party-State in the 21st Century* (New York, NY: Routledge, 2008), 8–13.

57. Zheng Bijian, "China's 'Peaceful Rise' to Great Power Status," *Foreign Affairs* 84, 5 (2005): 18–24.

58. Marc Lanteigne, *Chinese Foreign Policy: An Introduction* (New York, NY: Routledge, 2009), 79–83.

59. Robert G. Sutter, *Chinese Foreign Relations: Power and Policy Since the Cold War* (Lanham, MD: Rowman & Littlefield, 2012), 17.

60. Thomas J. Christensen, "China," in *Strategic Asia 2001–2002: Power and Purpose*, eds. Richard J. Ellings and Aaron L. Friedberg (Seattle, WA: National Bureau of Asian Research, 2001), 27–29.

61. Martin Murphy, "Deepwater Oil Rigs as Strategic Weapons, Commentary," *Naval War College Review* 66, no. 2 (2013).

62. Goldstein, *Rising to the Challenge: China's Grand Strategy and International Security*, 23–24.

63. Ibid., 27–29.

64. Sutter, *Chinese Foreign Relations: Power and Policy since the Cold War, Third Edition*, 29, 52.

65. Nan Li, "The PLA's Evolving Warfighting Doctrine, Strategy, and Tactics, 1985–95: A Chinese Perspective," *China Quarterly* 146 (1996): 444–445, 456–458.

66. Andrew J. Nathan and Andrew Scobell, *China's Search for Security* (New York, NY: Columbia University Press, 2013), 3.

67. Ibid., 32–36.

68. They describe these systems as interconnected and include Northeast Asia, Oceania, continental Southeast Asia, South Asia, and Central Asia, totaling around forty-five different countries. The United States is present in all of these regions.

69. Nathan and Scobell, *China's Search for Security*, 3–6.

70. M. Taylor Fravel, "China's Search for Military Power," *Washington Quarterly* 31, no. 3 (2008): 127–129.

71. Ibid., 129.

72. Thomas J. Christensen, "Chinese Realpolitik: Reading Beijing's Worldview," *Foreign Affairs* 75, no. 5 (1996): 40–45.

73. Andrew Scobell, *China's Use of Military Force Beyond the Great Wall and the Long March* (Cambridge, U.K.: Cambridge University Press, 2003), 15–39. Especially 36–38.

74. Lawrence Freedman, "China as a Global Strategic Actor," in *Does China Matter? A Reassessment: Essays in Memory of Gerald Segal*, ed. Barry Buzan and Rosemary Foot (New York, NY: Routledge, 2004), 21–36.

75. Michael D. Swaine, "China's Assertive Behavior—Part 1: On 'Core Interests,'" *China Leadership Monitor* 34 (2011): 2–4.

76. Ibid., 4.

77. Edward N. Luttwak, *The Rise of China vs. the Logic of Strategy* (Cambridge, MA: The Belknap Press of Harvard University Press, 2012), 237–238.

78. Ibid., 72–88.

79. Ibid., 78–82.

80. Avery Goldstein, "The Diplomatic Face of China's Grand Strategy: A Rising Power's Emerging Choice," *China Quarterly* 168 (2001).

81. Jason J. Blazevic, "Defensive Realism in the Indian Ocean: Oil, Sea Lanes, and the Security Dilemma," *China Security* 5, no. 3 (2009): 64–67.

82. Alison A. Kaufman and Daniel M. Hartnett, "Managing Conflict: Examining Recent PLA Writings on Escalation Control," *Report by CNA China Studies, CNA Analysis and Solutions* (February 2016).

83. Bates Gill, *Rising Star: China's New Security Diplomacy* (Washington, D.C.: Brookings Institution Press, 2007), 10.

84. Information Office of the State Council of the People's Republic of China, *2010 Defense White Paper*, March 31, 2011.

85. Scobell, *China's Use of Military Force Beyond the Great Wall and the Long March*, 198.

86. Bonnie S. Glaser, "China's Grand Strategy in Asia" (Statement before the U.S.-China Economic and Security Review Commission, Washington, D.C., March 13, 2014).

87. Specifically, Dr. Glaser refers to "enhancing the PLA's capacity to conduct regional military operations, including what China refers to as counter intervention operations," which "refers to a chain of capabilities and missions aimed at preventing foreign, especially U.S., military forces from intervening in a conflict in China's near seas, which include the East China Sea, South China Sea, and Yellow Sea."

88. Dr. Glaser notes "fostering greater economic dependence on China and promoting regional economic integration are integral to Beijing's strategy of persuading its neighbors of the benefits of China's rise and dissuading them from challenging Chinese interests," and that this strategy was followed previously to relative success.

89. Jian Yang, *The Pacific Islands in China's Grand Strategy: Small States, Big Games* (New York, NY: Palgrave Macmillan, 2011), 47–49.

90. Ibid., 47–48.

91. Ibid., 48.

92. Ibid., 49.

93. David Shambaugh, *China Goes Global: The Partial Power* (New York, NY: Oxford University Press, 2013), 269.

94. Ibid., 47; Dr. Shambaugh goes on to demonstrate the actual amount spent on internal security is potentially close to $250 billion.

95. Masako Ikegami, "China's Grand Strategy of 'Peaceful Rise' A Prelude to a New Cold War?" in *Rise of China: Beijing's Strategies and Implications for the Asia Pacific*, ed. Hsiao, Hsin-Huang Michael, and Cheng-Yi Lin (New York, NY: Routledge, 2009), 21–54.

96. Ibid.

97. Yuan-kang Wang, *Harmony and War: Confucian Culture and Chinese Power Politics* (New York, NY: Columbia University Press, 2011), 192.

98. Ibid., 192.

99. Ibid., 196.

100. Although China does seem to have become more combative in recent years on the issue of the South China Sea.

101. William J. Norris, Economic Statecraft with Chinese Characteristics: The Use of Commercial Actors in China's Grand Strategy, Doctoral Dissertation Massachusetts Institute of Technology, November 12, 2010.

102. Michal Meidan, Philip Andrews-Speed, and Xin Ma, "Shaping China's Energy Policy: Actors and Processes," in *China's Search for Energy Security: Domestic Sources and International Implications*, Suisheng Zhao, ed. (New York, NY: Routledge, 2013), 48–50.

103. Maximilian Mayer and Jost Wübbeke, "Understanding China's International Energy Strategy," *The Chinese Journal of International Politics* 6 (2013): 273–298.

104. Wojtek M. Wolfe and Brock F. Tessman (2012): China's Global Equity Oil Investments: Economic and Geopolitical Influences, *Journal of Strategic Studies* 35, no. 2 (2012): 175–196.

105. David E. Sanger, "China's Oil Needs Are High on U.S. Agenda," *New York Times*, April 19, 2006, http://www.nytimes.com/2006/04/19/world/asia/19china .html?ex=&_r=0 (accessed May 14, 2016).

106. Hongyi Harry Lai, "China's Global Oil Diplomacy: Is It a Global Security Threat?" *Third World Quarterly* 28, no. 3 (2007): 519–537.

107. U.S. Energy Information Administration, China: International Energy Data and Analysis, May 14, 2015, https://www.eia.gov/beta/international/analysis_includes/ countries_long/China/china.pdf (accessed November 20, 2015), 13.

108. Ibid., 12.

109. International Energy Agency, "China," http://www.iea.org/publications/ freepublications/publication/china_2012.pdf (accessed May 22, 2016): 8.

110. Erica S. Downs, "Looking West: China and Central Asia," Testimony before the U.S.-China Economic and Security Review Commission, March 18, 2015, http:// www.uscc.gov/sites/default/files/Downs%20Testimony_031815.pdf (accessed May 15, 2016).

111. Erica S. Downs, "Mission Mostly Accomplished: China's Energy Trade and Investment Along the Silk Road Economic Belt," *China Brief, The Jamestown Foundation* 15, no. 6 (2015).

112. James Fishelson, "From the Silk Road to Chevron: The Geopolitics of Oil Pipelines in Central Asia," The School of Russian and Asian Studies, 2007, http:// www.sras.org/geopolitics_of_oil_pipelines_in_central_asia (accessed June 23, 2016)

113. Andrew Inkpen and Michael H. Moffett, *The Global Oil and Gas Industry* (Tulsa, OK: PenWell Publishing, 2011), 398–403.

114. Adam Rose and Aung Hla Tun, "Oil Pipeline through Myanmar to China Expected to Open in January," Reuters, January 20, 2015, http://www.reuters.com/ article/petrochina-myanmar-oil-idUSL3N0U22PP20150120 (June 23, 2016).

115. Energy Information Agency, "Crude Oil Proved Reserves 2014," International Energy Statistics, www.eia.gov (accessed June 22, 2016).

116. Ana C. Alves, "Chinese Economic Statecraft: A Comparative Study of China's Oil-backed Loans in Angola and Brazil," *Journal of Current Chinese Affairs* 42, no. 1 (2013): 99–130.

117. Ibid., 110.

118. Erica S. Downs, "Business Interest Groups in Chinese Politics: The Case of the Oil Companies," in *China's Changing Political Landscape: Prospects for Democracy*, ed. Cheng Li (Washington D.C.: Brookings Institution Press, 2008), 121–127.

119. Linda Jakobson and Dean Knox, "New Foreign Policy Actors in China," Stockholm International Peace Research Institute (SIPRI) Policy Paper 26 (2010): 24–28.

120. Christopher Pala, "China Pays Dearly for Kazakhstan Oil," *New York Times*, March 17, 2006, http://www.nytimes.com/2006/03/17/business/worldbusiness/ 17kazakh.html?_r=1& (accessed June 25, 2016).

121. Anatole Pang, "Chinese Overseas Oil and Gas M&A Strategy: Assessing the Financial and Strategic Performance of Foreign Upstream Acquisitions by the Chinese National Oil Companies, 2005–2013" (Master's Thesis, Tsinghua University, Beijing, 2014), 39–54.

122. James Paton and Aibing Guo, "Russia, China Add to $400 Billion Gas Deal With Accord," *Bloomberg*, November 9, 2014, http://www.bloomberg.com/news/articles/2014-11-10/russia-china-add-to-400-billion-gas-deal-with-accord (accessed June 25, 2016).

123. Susana Moreira, "Learning from Failure: China's Overseas Oil Investments," *Journal of Current Chinese Affairs* 42, no. 1 (2013): 131–165.

124. Philip Andrews-Speed and Roland Dannreuther, *China, Oil and Global Politics* (New York, NY: Routledge, 2011), 88.

125. Erica S. Downs, "The Chinese Energy Security Debate," *China Quarterly* 177 (2004): 35–36.

126. Iacob Koch-Weser, *Chinese Energy Engagement with Latin America: A Review of Recent Findings*, Report by Inter-American Dialogue, January 2015, 11.

127. Lucy Hornby, "China Releases First Formal Estimate of Strategic Oil Reserves," *Financial Times*, November 20, 2014, http://www.ft.com/intl/cms/s/0/09c47d8e-7084-11e4-8113-00144feabdc0.html#axzz48HlAYZbA (accessed June 25, 2016).

128. Abheek Bhattacharya, "China's Petroleum Reserve Builds Shaky Floor for Oil," *Wall Street Journal*, http://www.wsj.com/articles/chinas-petroleum-reserve-builds-shaky-floor-for-oil-heard-on-the-street-1409755068 (June 25, 2016).

129. Chen Aizhu and Florence Tan, "China Ramps Up Crude Buying, Reserves Purchases Far Ahead of Schedule," Reuters, November, 26, 2014, http://www.reuters.com/article/us-china-oil-stockpiles-idUSKCN0JA0SN20141127 (June 24, 2016).

130. Adam Rose and Chen Aizhu, "UPDATE 1—China's Strategic Oil Reserves Double to 190 mln bbl—Stats Bureau," Reuters, December 11, 2015, http://www.reuters.com/article/china-oil-reserves-idUSL3N1402YL20151211 (February 20, 2016).

131. Hornby, "China Releases First Formal Estimate of Strategic Oil Reserves," *Financial Times* (accessed May 5, 2016).

132. Platts, "China's End-October Commercial Crude, Oil Product Stocks Fall on Month," November 25, 2014, http://www.platts.com/latest-news/oil/singapore/chinas-end-october-commercial-crude-oil-product-27868887 (accessed May 7, 2016).

133. Mandip Singh, "China's Strategic Petroleum Reserves: A Reality Check," *Institute for Defense Studies and Analysis Issue Brief,* May 21, 2012, http://www.idsa.in/system/files/IB_ChinasStrategicPetroleumReserves_MandipSingh_210512.pdf (accessed May 8, 2016): 5.

134. Ibid., 7.

135. James Bourne, "Petrodollars: China Builds Up its Oil Tanker Fleet," *Platts Oilgram News*, August 18, 2014, blogs.platts.com/2014/08/18/china-oil-tankers/ (accessed May 8, 2016).

136. Institute of Shipping Economics and Logistics, "Shipping Statistics and Market Review," *World Tanker Fleet* 56, no. 3 (2012): 4; John Rogers, ed., *Review of Maritime Transport 2014* (Geneva: UNCTAD, 2014), 27–45.

137. Michael May, "Energy and Security in East Asia," Report on America's Alliances with Japan and Korea in a Changing Northeast Asia, Asia-Pacific Research Center at Stanford University (1998) 25.

138. Zhang Wei, translated by Shazeda Ahmed, "A General Review of the History of China's Sea-Power Theory Development," *Naval War College Review* 68, no. 4 (2015): 87–88.

139. Lanteigne, *Chinese Foreign Policy: An Introduction,* 86; Chen Shaofeng, "China's Self-Extrication from the 'Malacca Dilemma' and Implications," *International Journal of China Studies* 1, no. 1 (2010): 2.

140. Ji, "Dealing with the Malacca Dilemma: China's Effort to Protect its Energy Supply," *Strategic Analysis,* 470–473, 476–484.

141. Chen Shaofeng, "China's Self-Extrication from the 'Malacca Dilemma' and Implications," *International Journal of China Studies* 1, no. 1 (2010): 9–12.

142. Ibid., 13–14.

143. Ji, "Dealing with the Malacca Dilemma: China's Effort to Protect its Energy Supply," *Strategic Analysis,* 476–484.

144. Andrew S. Erickson, Abraham M. Denmark, and Gabriel Collins, "Beijing's 'Starter Carrier' and Future Steps: Alternatives and Implications," *Naval War College Review* 65, no. 1 (2012): 16–24.

145. U.S.-China Economic and Security Review Commission, 2011 Report to Congress, Washington, D.C.: U.S. Government Printing Office, 2011), 182–193.

146. Robert D. Kaplan, *Monsoon: The Indian Ocean and the Future of American Power* (New York, NY: Random House Publishing, 2010), 10–11.

147. Michael G. Gallagher, "China's Illusory Threat to the South China Sea," *International Security* 19, no. 1 (1994).

148. Robert S. Ross, "China's Naval Nationalism: Sources, Prospects, and the U.S. Response," *International Security* 34, no. 2 (2009): 50; John B. Hattendorf, *The Evolution of the U.S. Navy's Maritime Strategy, 1977–1986* (Newport, RI: Naval War College Press), 124–127, 148–149.

149. Ross, "China's Naval Nationalism: Sources, Prospects, and the U.S. Response," *International Security,* 58.

150. Ibid., 53–54.

151. Ibid., 58–59.

152. Alison A. Kaufman and Daniel M. Hartnett, "Managing Conflict: Examining Recent PLA Writings on Escalation Control," Report by CNA China Studies, CNA Analysis and Solutions (February 2016).

Chapter Six

The Clash of Grand Strategy

INTRODUCTION

In this section there will be a direct comparison between the United States and China, using both the Oil Security Ratings (OSR) results, derived from the principal components analysis, along with a comparison of several individual indicators, culminating in a broad qualitative and quantitative comparative analysis between both states. As a key component of the analysis, it is important to note the unique PCA weighting process used in this study, which differentiates it from other weighted scores, and even other PCA-based studies used for risk analysis. A key element of the approach in this study is the temporal component, which utilizes data gathered over a 22-year period, and not just over the course of a single year, allowing a quantification of the long-term approaches to oil security. As argued earlier, this allows greater depth and robustness of the importance of the variables included in the analysis and allows this study to capture this in longitudinal form. This study did not weight the individual variables based on a single year as with the previous studies, but instead applied the weights derived from the entire 22-year dataset for all 30 countries in each year. For instance, in Gupta's study from 2008,[1] a single year was used to calculate the scores for the European Union 27-country bloc, yielding 27 data points for seven variables, yielding only 189 data points. By adding the temporal dimension, new variables, and calculating for 22 years, this research generated 660 data points for each of the ten variables (dimensions of oil security), resulting in 6,600 total data points used to generate the principal component analysis and final scores. The aim was not to understand just the importance of different dimensions of energy security in each individual year, but to understand the relative importance of each variable over the long term, since grand strategy and oil security are fundamentally, and crucially, long-term endeavors that must be confronted by assessing enduring security.

Analysis

The data utilized, and subsequent analyses conducted, for this project yielded considerable insights into understanding relative levels of oil security for China and the United States, among many other countries. This contributes greatly to an understanding of why some countries are more successful, or less successful, at achieving supply security. This represents a great stride in understanding the long-term dynamics influencing oil supply security among many countries, and results in an effective policy-oriented measure capable of identifying weaknesses and deficiencies in security planning. This process gives not only the high-level rankings for the two countries under review, but also a view of the individual weightings, indicating important measures for each state. Tables for the correlation matrix, eigenvalues, and eigenvectors can be found in the appendix. After the final PCA, the derived weightings for the study are drawn from the eignenvectors, using only principal components with a variance above one, leaving the weightings to be derived from the first four principal components, resulting in the percentage distributions listed below in table 6.1.

As demonstrated in table 6.3 above, the Herfindahl-Hirschman Index was determined through the principal component analysis to account for the largest amount of variance in the dataset, assigning it the greatest weight at 15.92 percent. This does not come as a surprise, given crude oil import diversity is routinely touted as one of the most import aspects of oil security, and it would make sense higher levels of diversity would pay off over the long run. As will be discussed in greater detail later in this chapter, this is one of the key weak points China moved rapidly to rectify early in the study, attaining

Table 6.1.   Indicator Derived Weights

Indicators	Weights	Percentage
Herfindahl-Hirschman Index (HHI)	0.1592	15.92
MIT Economic Complexity Index (ECI)	0.1211	12.11
Import Dependence	0.1090	10.90
Imports to Gross Domestic Product	0.1079	10.79
Consumption-to-Reserves	0.0925	9.25
Energy Intensity	0.0921	9.21
Production-to-Reserves	0.0873	8.73
Oil of Total Primary Energy Consumption	0.0857	8.57
National Power	0.0796	7.96
Price Volatility	0.0656	6.56

greater levels of diversity than even the United States, by the year 2000. This also seems to validate the intense focus on this specific approach by many countries. This long-term result has importantly, already corroborated a key component of oil security. Interestingly, MIT's Economic Complexity Index measure accounted for the second greatest amount of variance in the dataset. Again, this was included as a proxy measure for the sophistication of the broader economy. This measure is much more robust than a simple GDP per capita measure because it delves deeper to account for technological advancement and inclusion of technology and knowledge in the national economy. This result signifies a high level of importance attached to a strong knowledge base underlying a country's economy, which can then be translated into gains in the energy sector. A good anecdotal illustration is the current massive increase in tight oil and gas extraction taking place since as a result of technological and knowledge-based advancements. It also does not come as much of a surprise that the variable with the lowest weight at 6.56 percent is Price Volatility, owing to the greater degree of similarity in pricing volatility among the countries involved in the study due to these participants drawing from a "global oil market." Since the market for oil is "global," any price differences will typically be arbitraged away as barrels of oil will typically find their way to the highest bidder and pricing gaps are exploited by trading and investment institutions. This will eliminate greater degrees of volatility between various countries, even though there will still be some differences owing to premiums, blends, and location.

Found below, figure 6.1 is perhaps the most important figure in the study, encapsulating the entirety of the ratings process. Using this quantitative process to create a robust scoring mechanism, it is possible to surmise two key insights from the data. First, the United States is the most oil-secure country in the study, by a wide margin. The United States has also maintained a steady level of oil security throughout the study period due to dominance in many key areas that will be discussed throughout the chapter. As a matter of fact, the United States scores in the "6" range throughout nearly the entire 22-year period analyzed, only witnessing a drop through the 6 level in the final year of the study, 2013. Whether this is an aberration or a trend remains to be seen; however, the decline almost certainly has to do with reductions in import diversity due to large increases in domestic production, and the relative increase of China, which is the other key takeaway from the final scores. This other insight is that China ranks as the second most oil-secure country in the study since 1996 after Japan's precipitous drop and has been rising in supply security dramatically. This increase in security represents the most impressive in the study and backs one of the research hypotheses. As evidenced by the main graph comparing the OSR scores between the United States and

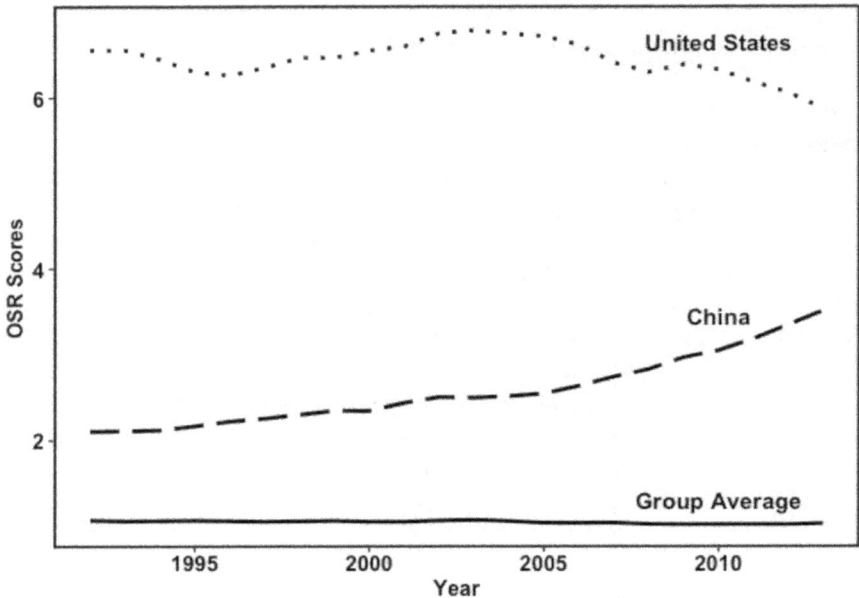

Figure 6.1.   Oil Security Ratings of China and the United States

China, the substantial gap in scores that existed in 1992 has narrowed considerably and it appears this trend will continue. The average score over the 22-year period for the United States is 6.44, while China scores a 2.58, and the score for all thirty countries included in the dataset is 1.05. The average for all countries was curiously steady throughout the study period, vacillating only slightly between 1.07 and 1.02, indicating an overall downward trend for the entire group, with a 4 percent decline. Any number of conclusions can be drawn from this, from a more reticent approach to energy security on the part of non-dominant states in the international system, to the difficulties typical of institutional change in bureaucracy, or to a less important view of energy security as a topic on the whole by policymakers in these countries. This is an area perhaps for further research and study.

Second, a striking feature suggested above is the steep increase in China's oil security mirrored to the decrease witnessed by the United States over the last decade, demonstrating a continuing, trending convergence between the two states. Throughout the entire period, China's oil security has been on a steady upward trajectory, beginning with a score of 2.11 in 1992, and ending with a score of 3.51 in 2013, resulting in a stunning increase of 67 percent. No other country comes close to mirroring these rapid advances in oil security. The average year-over-year gain for China throughout the entire study is

2.48 percent, well ahead of the second highest average belonging to Ireland, with 1.64 percent. The United States, while starting with, and maintaining, a superior level of oil security, ended with year-over-year declines throughout the study period, with a –.51 percent decrease annually.

China's year-over-year advances also accelerated beginning in 2005, when the average jumps to 3.76 percent ending in 2013. The United States, over the same period, witnessed an acceleration in year-over-year declines to 1.52 percent beginning in 2005, and this number rises further to 2.46 percent beginning in 2011. The decreases are clearly accelerating, and these last few years account for the overall decrease in oil security for the United States throughout the entire study period. As a matter of fact, the year-over-year rate for the United States is essentially flat from 1992 through 2006, only dipping into the negatives overall beginning in 2007.

Another fascinating aspect of the OSR results is demonstrated when viewing figure 6.2, which displays the comparison of China's final scores to those of other countries included in the study. One must quickly come to the conclusion that oil security is of incredible importance to the Chinese government, owing to the steady, concerted, long-term increase in oil security compared to these other countries. Policy is purposefully oriented in order to create sustainable gains on this scale, placing China's oil security on a trajectory unparalleled by other consequential actors in the international system.

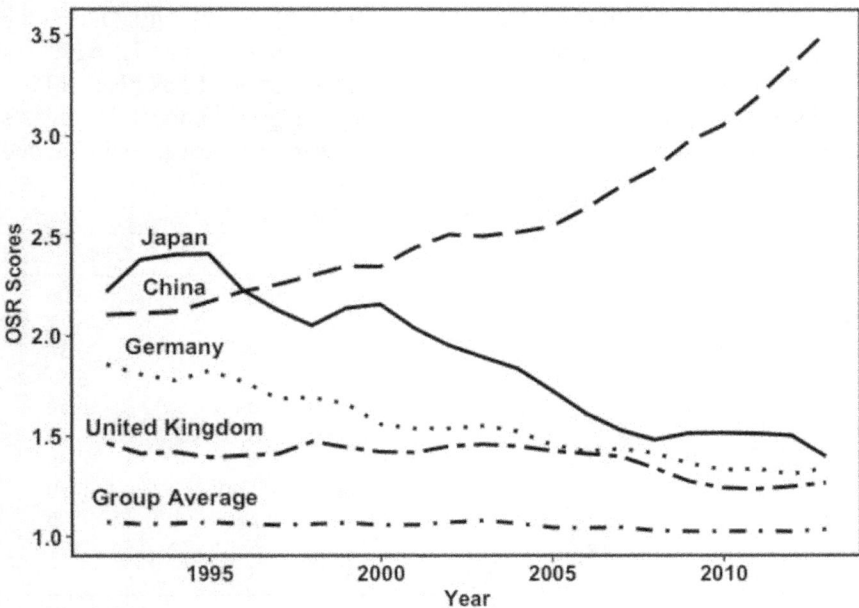

Figure 6.2. Oil Security Ratings (China and select countries)

They are adapting, changing, and introducing best practices developed by the United States over many decades. The following graph demonstrates this, by removing the United States, and allowing for a closer look at other selected countries, this starkly demonstrates China's path as separate from the others.

Gross Domestic Product per Unit of Energy Used

This is a measure of energy intensity in the economy. The higher the dollar amount, the more energy efficient the overall economy is, meaning per unit of energy used, the country will ideally be able to create more wealth from that single unit of energy. As table 6.2 shows, both the United States and China do not score particularly well on this measure compared to other countries. For instance, averaged out through the entire 22-year period, China ranks last out of all countries in the study, coming in at number 30. The United States does not do much better, ranked at 24. However, both did improve efficiency over the study period, and since the data is inflation adjusted at constant 2011 U.S. dollars at purchasing power parity, these were real efficiency gains. Both steadily increased over the study period, with only slight changes in the year-over-year growth rate. Efficiency in the United States rose by a healthy 51 percent, while China more than doubled efficiency for a 116 percent gain over 22 years. Much of this gain in China, however, is the result of the country continuing to shed inefficient, dirty, and small-scale manufacturing and industrial businesses throughout the economy. During the Maoist era and well into the 1980s and 1990s, China's industrial base was wildly inefficient and incredibly energy intensive, so as it has been able to shed some of these legacy industries, efficiency has grown concomitantly. As China continues to transition its economy towards increased value-added

Table 6.2. GDP per Unit of Energy Used (U.S. and China, USD)

Year	China	United States	Year	China	United States
1992	2.45	4.86	2003	4.23	6.06
1993	2.64	4.91	2004	4.05	6.17
1994	2.85	5.01	2005	4.17	6.34
1995	2.94	5.08	2006	4.30	6.57
1996	3.15	5.16	2007	4.66	6.58
1997	3.44	5.34	2008	5.00	6.73
1998	3.69	5.53	2009	5.06	6.88
1999	3.89	5.64	2010	5.11	6.89
2000	4.00	5.71	2011	5.15	7.08
2001	4.24	5.87	2012	5.30	7.41
2002	4.38	5.91	2013	5.30	7.36

Source: World Bank, World Development Indicators, GDP per unit of energy use (constant 2011 PPP per kg of oil equivalent), 2016, http://data.worldbank.org.

businesses and services, it will continue these relatively easy efficiency gains. However, despite these gains, China is wildly inefficient compared to the other countries in the study, with only $4.09 of GDP produced for each unit of energy consumed. The United States produced $6.05 of GDP per unit of energy consumed, while Malta gained the top spot with $12.42, Italy the second spot, with $12.16, and Ireland in the third spot with $12.00. Compared to other advanced industrial economies, both the United States and China have much room for improvement. Curiously, Japan, largely considered highly energy efficient, only ranks at 16 out of the countries in the sample. Japan embarked on an efficiency drive after World War Two after losing the military option to secure its energy sources. While a rank of 16 may not sound impressive, it is when one considers the level of manufacturing in the economy. Despite being an export-oriented, large, industrialized economy, Japan still generates $9.95 per unit of energy consumed, far outpacing efficiency in the United States and China. This is a level similar to Belgium and Germany, and ahead of Australia and the Republic of Korea.

Production to Reserves

The production-to-reserves ratio is an oil security measure used to understand the amount of time a country could produce oil at current levels of production, for each year, given the amount of proved reserves available within the territory of that country. Basically, this adopts the view that the most secure oil supplies a country could possibly draw on are those supplies which are wholly domestic in nature. Shown in table 6.3, on this measure, China comes out ahead of the United States. This is simply due to the lower levels of

Table 6.3. Production to Reserves (U.S. and China)

Year	China	United States	Year	China	United States
1992	0.04327	0.12665	2003	0.06846	0.11839
1993	0.04395	0.12915	2004	0.07005	0.12118
1994	0.04470	0.13066	2005	0.07265	0.11851
1995	0.04547	0.13338	2006	0.07413	0.11611
1996	0.04762	0.13341	2007	0.08588	0.12227
1997	0.04867	0.13476	2008	0.08749	0.12114
1998	0.04864	0.12823	2009	0.08780	0.14476
1999	0.04859	0.13228	2010	0.07421	0.14112
2000	0.04941	0.12777	2011	0.07412	0.13121
2001	0.05019	0.12500	2012	0.07499	0.12683
2002	0.05163	0.12310	2013	0.06566	0.12300

Source: Calculated by author using data derived from Energy Information Administration, International Energy Statistics, Crude Oil Proved Reserves (Bbbls) and Production of Crude Oil, NGPL, and Other Liquids (Mbbl/d), 2016, https://www.eia.gov.

production in China. On the other hand, the United States is a massive importer of crude oil, that also refines a large portion of that crude, and then re-exports the products to other markets. China actually takes the number four ranking at .06, behind Bulgaria at .02, Romania at .04, and India at .05, respectively. The United States ranks at 15, with a score of .13. Several countries received a score of 1, due to a complete absence of reserves or production, or the absence of both reserves and production. This indicates the lowest score possible, and nine countries in the study are at this level. The majority of these nine countries are small, economically advanced countries like Belgium and the Republic of Korea and reflects either a lack of access to domestic sources, or perhaps, the inability to achieve economies of scale on the production side. Another interesting point about this data, is the curious stability witnessed in the scores for the United States, where it vacillates only slightly in the .12 to .14 range for all 22 years. Meanwhile, China has similar levels of stability, but there is an overall trend to the data, showing an increase in the score, despite a hefty reduction in the level of domestic reserves available, beginning in 2003. Even still, China's scores only waver between .04 and .09, where the peak is in 2009 and drops down to .07 in 2013. This level of stability is probably the result of the measured release of property by the respective governing authorities for exploration and production in both territories.

Consumption to Reserves

The consumption to reserves ratio is a measure not unlike the previous production to reserves ratio, where the goal is to understand how long a country could survive off its current stock of domestic crude oil reserves given current levels of consumption for each year. The production versus consumption distinction is crucial, given the importance of both aspects of a state to produce the requisite amounts of crude oil and to then ultimately meet that demand in the form of consumption. As with the previous measure, a lower score is better, indicating less consumption compared the amount of domestic proved reserves available. With this measure, in table 6.4, China exhibits a better score for each of the 22 years considered, but the clear trend for China is negative, with a quadrupling of the score over this period from .04 in 1992 to .16 in 2013. This is due to the combined factors of greatly increased crude oil consumption in China and reduced crude reserves available, a trend that accelerated in 2003. China's massive increases in consumption could not have happened at a worse time for this measure, given the declines in reserves coinciding at the same time, which would most likely be related to these consumption increases. The United States, on the other hand, started in 1992 with a relatively high score of .24, only to rise to

Table 6.4. Consumption to Reserves (U.S. and China)

Year	China	United States	Year	China	United States
1992	0.04048	0.23980	2003	0.11156	0.30438
1993	0.04501	0.25195	2004	0.12875	0.32749
1994	0.04807	0.26780	2005	0.13591	0.33608
1995	0.05115	0.27408	2006	0.14527	0.32803
1996	0.05490	0.28379	2007	0.17064	0.33832
1997	0.05956	0.29139	2008	0.17559	0.31197
1998	0.06244	0.28906	2009	0.18409	0.33334
1999	0.06636	0.31849	2010	0.16032	0.31372
2000	0.07293	0.31038	2011	0.17047	0.27370
2001	0.07479	0.30496	2012	0.18250	0.23312
2002	0.07849	0.30250	2013	0.16129	0.20719

Source: Calculated by author using data derived from Energy Information Administration, International Energy Statistics, Crude Oil Proved Reserves (Bbbls) and Total Petroleum Consumption (Mbbl/d), 2016, https://www.eia.gov.

a peak of .338 in 2007. However, the trend for the United States since then has moved lower, reaching .21 in 2013, below even the beginning score in 1992. This represents a very positive contribution to oil security, and the 2013 score is on trend to reach parity with China in a few years. Among the other countries surveyed, both China and the United States rank relatively well. The worst score goes to Japan, where the lack of meaningful crude reserve levels and extremely high consumption levels catapult it into an extremely unfavorable position regarding this ratio.

Oil as a Component of Total Primary Energy Consumption

For this study, Total Primary Energy Consumption was used instead of the typical Total Primary Energy Production. Preference was given to TPEC because a determination of oil security using a metric like this should reflect final, national level consumption since that is the ultimate end goal of any imports or production. The oil production share of the total amount of primary energy produced doesn't tell much about the structure of the energy demands of a state and is even loosely covered by another measure. Oil as a component of consumption, however, allows one to glean additional information about the ultimate requirements of the state and the general mix among oil, natural gas, coal, renewables, and nuclear energy. Production demonstrates what is produced, but much of that may be exported depending on the country in question. Consumption tells the overall energy requirements and diversification along primary energy components in the economy, which is far more useful. This metric once again takes the lower score as more advantageous, but this is, in a sense, not completely accurate. The true point of

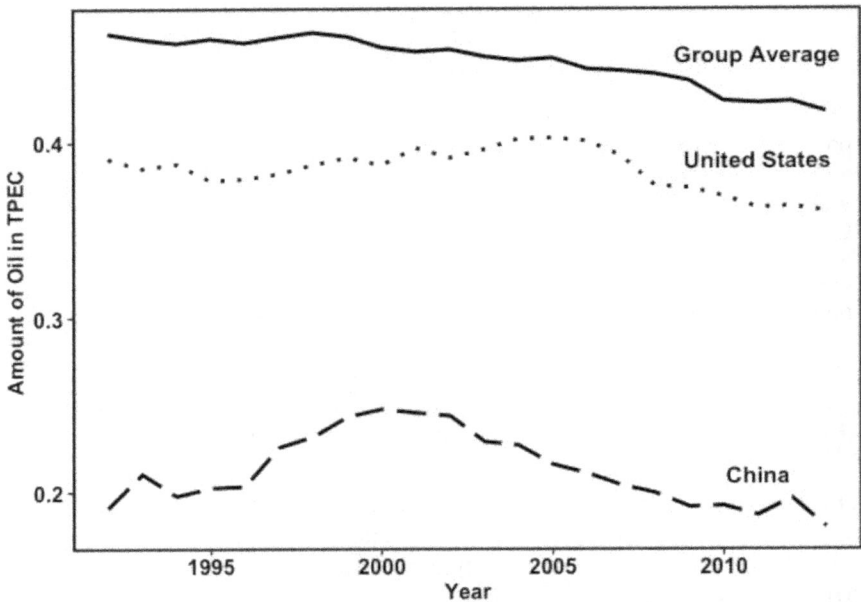

Figure 6.3.   Oil Consumption as a Component of Total Primary Energy Consumption (TPEC)

Source: Calculated by author using data derived from Energy Information Administration, International Energy Statistics, Total Primary Energy Consumption (quadrillion Btu) and Total Petroleum Consumption (quadrillion Btu), 2016, https://www.eia.gov.

gauging primary energy consumption should be to demonstrate some level of diversity, without an overwhelming reliance on any one source of energy. Since the figure represents the percentage of the consumption mix that is at-tributable to crude oil, it is simply assumed that many states, at least in this study, will typically have higher levels of oil consumption compared to other forms of primary energy, and this overreliance can contribute to oil security deficiencies. As shown in figure 6.3, China performs quite well, maintaining lower levels of oil consumption in the domestic economy compared to other energy sources. Even though China has grown rapidly, the greatest amount oil reaches as a share of consumption is 25.8 percent in 2000. After that, it declines to 20 percent in 2007 and finally to 18 percent in 2013. These are very low levels when the 22-year averages are examined for all countries in the study, with China achieving the number two rank behind only Slovakia with an average of 20 percent. It is interesting to note the largely lower levels of oil consumption in the ex–Soviet bloc countries included in the study, plus China, all which mirrored many of the industrialization and development approaches of the Soviet Union. As a legacy of this era, Slovakia, China, Poland, the Czech Republic, Bulgaria, Romania, and Hungary all occupy the ranks one through seven, in that order. Meanwhile, the United States ranks at number 14 with an average level of 38 percent, and witnessed less variability than China over the period, but did report a steady decline beginning in 2008. In 1992 the amount of oil in the mix was 39 percent, with a peak of 40 percent in 2005, and ultimately ended with 36 percent in 2013. The level essentially plateaued from 1992 through 2007, before the earlier mentioned drop.

Massachusetts Institute of Technology Economic Complexity Ratings

The MIT Economic Complexity Rating is one of the most fascinating indicators utilized in the study, and it proved to be a dynamic component to the overall OSR scores. Again, this is meant to be a proxy indicator for economic advancement, the knowledge economy, and to a certain degree, entrepreneurship. Measuring entrepreneurship and creativity in an economy is a relatively new topic, and these more direct measures have only been recorded for the past few years. For instance, the World Economic Forum has a similar measure but doesn't go beyond five years. A measure of this type was sorely needed when one considers something as stunningly impressive as the reserve and production gains resulting from the tight oil revolution occurring in the United States. This materialized only because of domestic technological development in the United States and resulted in a massive impact not only to the supply of oil available for domestic development, but also through the resulting collapse and upending of oil markets.

For this indicator, presented in figure 6.4, the overall average score for the United States turned out quite well, recording a score of 1.69 and coming in at rank 7 for the study. China came down in the rankings at 23 with an average score of .56. There is, however, a trend towards convergence between both countries, where China has greatly increased its complexity over the study period, and the United States had an overall reduction in complexity. As a matter of fact, in 1992, China's score was .18 and the United States' score was 1.93, resulting in a difference of 1.75. By 2013, that gap had narrowed considerably, with China scoring .96 and the United States scoring 1.58, with a difference of .62. China's complexity gains since 1992 have been quick and massive, with gains accelerating in 2001, resulting in an increase of over 400 percent over the course of the study. And, in 2001, China's economic complexity actually doubled year over year, from .26 in 2000 to .55 in 2001. This coincides with the rapid growth in China's economy and its attempts to shed basic manufacturing for higher value-added industries, requiring the dense knowledge-based networks this measure is used to quantify. Over the study period, the score for the United States decreased by 18 percent from 1.93 in 1992 to 1.58 in 2013.

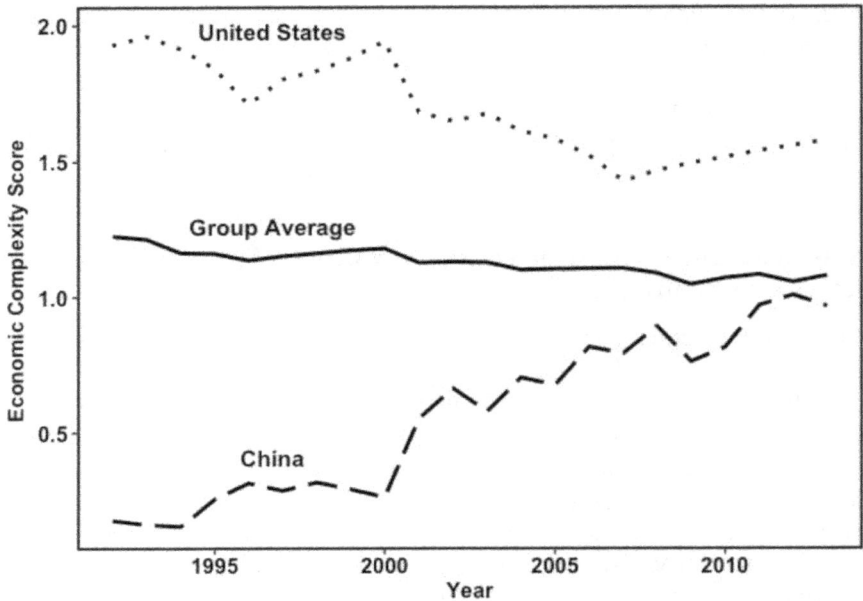

Figure 6.4.   Economic Complexity Scores (U.S. and China)

Source: AJG Simoes, CA Hidalgo, The Economic Complexity Observatory: An Analytical Tool for Under-standing the Dynamics of Economic Development, Workshops at the Twenty-Fifth AAAI Conference on Artificial Intelligence, 2011.

Import Dependence

Import dependence is a simple ratio that has been used heavily by the International Energy Agency as a quick measure for understanding oil import vulnerability. This indicator demonstrates the percentage of crude oil imports to a state as a component of overall petroleum consumption. It measures the ability of the state to supply its own energy needs as opposed to importing to meet those requirements. The higher the level of imports to consumption, the greater the degree of vulnerability a state will witness, along with potential supply issues. Once again, for this indicator, a lower score is better since importing a lower percentage of the economy-wide con-sumption base should lead to less exposure to oil supply security challenges. For much of the study, China had much lower levels of import dependence than the United States, owing to its lower consumption levels in the 1990s and comparatively large resource base. The starting point for this study was determined by capturing China's transition from oil exporter to importer, which means in the 1990s, China still had enough domestic resources to cover most requirements, but rapid economic growth quickly eroded this advantage, and dependence spiked, as can be observed in figure 6.5. As can

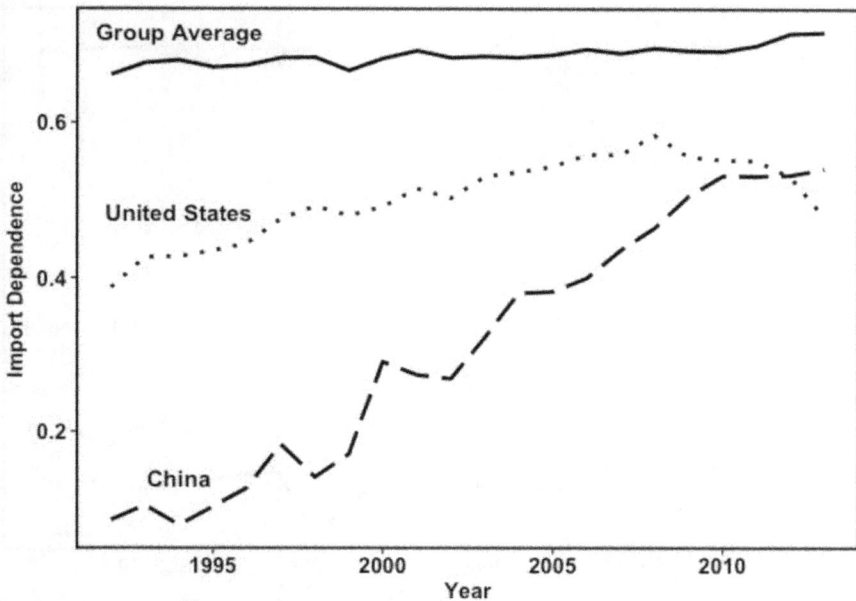

Figure 6.5. Comparison of Oil Import Dependence
Source: Calculated by author using data derived from EIA databases, and included in appendix.

be seen in the graph, there is a huge gap in 1992 between both states, but it is completely gone by 2012, and by 2013 China has a higher level of import dependence, especially as the United States begins to realize production gains from domestic tight oil resources, causing a sharp drop. For much of this period, the United States has a steady increase, which is halted in 2008 before finally decreasing. China on the other hand rapidly increases from .09 in 1992, to .54 in 2013, meaning fully 54 percent of China's crude oil consumption must be met by imports. The United States starts in 1992 at .39, peaks at a high of .58 in 2008, and ends with a .48 in 2013. The averages for all countries adds to our understanding when we see the relative levels of import dependence for both China and the United States, which are quite good, each ranking 5 and 9, respectively. China's average over the period was .31 and the average of the United States was .5.

Herfindahl-Hirschman Index

This is another extremely useful indicator, even outside of more complex models. The ability to diversify import sources increases oil supply security immensely, allowing increases in the capacity of a state to absorb supply losses by importing through established partners elsewhere, mitigating interruptions.

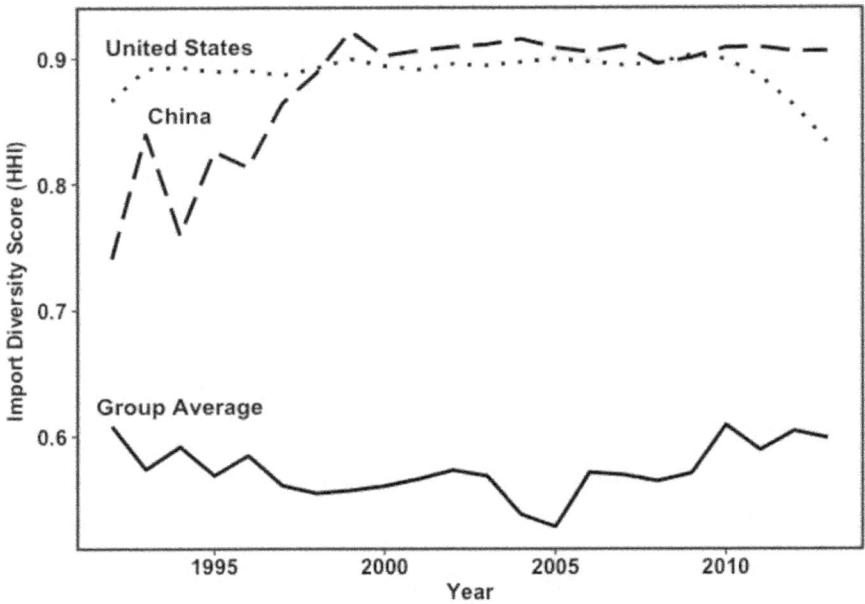

Figure 6.6.   Oil Import Diversity

Source: Calculated by author with data from the UN Comtrade database: United Nations, UN Comtrade
Database, 2016, http://comtrade.un.org/.

Diversity in oil import sources is an extremely valuable tool for oil security. As
indicated in figure 6.6, over the entire 22-year period, the United States ranks as
the second most diverse oil importer, following Spain in the number one spot.
Spain's average rating was a .90, and the United States received a rating of .89.
China ranked at number 4, with a rating of .88.

Digging into the data a little deeper, and referencing the graph, we see an
interesting story between both countries as they strive for diverse oil sources.
First, China moves rapidly to increase the diversity of its oil imports, achieving rough parity with the United States by 1998, and exceeding that level of
diversity in 1999. This represents a rapid increase from .74 in 1992, to .89 in
1998, and .92 in 1999, realizing a 24 percent gain in import diversity from
1992 to 1999. At this point, both states' scores plateau, hovering around the .9
mark, before the United States begins to drop after its peak in 2009 at .90. The
United States ultimately ends up with a .83 in 2013. This drop is most likely
the result of the shifting global oil markets centering on the changes occurring
in the United States as a result of the domestic gains from tight oil production. As this domestic production grows, smaller, ancillary oil exporters to the
United States will necessarily drop exports due to a lack of profitability, and
then move their product elsewhere. Losing supply in this way will negatively
impact import diversity.

Imports to GDP

This is an indicator used to understand the actual dollar amount as a percent of GDP that is spent on crude oil imports economy-wide. This is a clever measure to understand the actual impact of price fluctuations on a national economy, and to measure the depth of oil costs to a state. The more money spent on petroleum as a percentage of GDP, the greater any potential supply disruptions will result in larger shocks to the broader economy. Spending less as a percent of GDP is advantageous in the case of any such unforeseen shocks. On this metric, the trend throughout all countries included is to ultimately spend more on oil over time given price increases in the latter half of the 22-year period in the study. Even if some countries had halted increases in the actual, physical supply of oil imports, the dollar value of those imports would still rise in response to the price increases observed during this time. In figure 6.7, the data reflects this in all participants, and smaller, less oil-reliant states achieve higher levels on this indicator with Luxembourg and Malta taking the top two rankings. However, the United States still ranks at 9 with an average of .0116 (1.2%) and China at a rank of 12 with an average of .0138 (1.4%). The Republic of Korea takes the last spot, with oil accounting for a hefty .0457 (4.6%) of GDP. Looking at

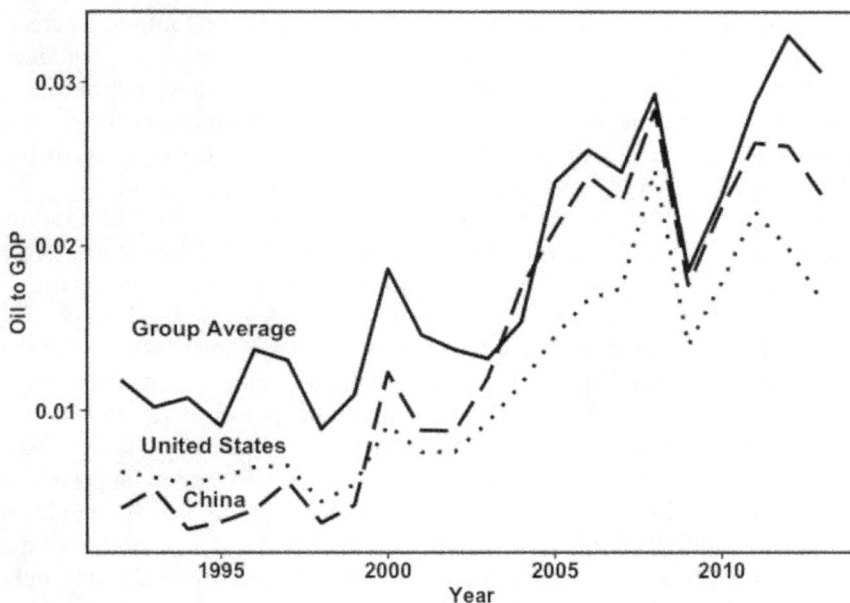

Figure 6.7.   Comparison of Oil Import Value as a Percentage of GDP

Source: Calculations by author with data from multiple sources, including UN Comtrade and the MIT Observatory for Economic Complexity.

the graph we see striking similarities between the United States and China, with both lines plotted quite close to one another. Both seem to be very heavily reflective of the greater oil market, and it is impressive that China has been able to grow its economy sufficiently fast in order to accommodate the massive increases in crude oil imports over the period, which was no small feat. As a matter of fact, the dollar value of Chinese imports swiftly rose from $1.7 billion in 1992 to $220 billion in 2013. However, China's increases in this category were more marked than with the United States. China went from .004 (.4%) of GDP in 1992 all the way to .0232 (2.3%) of GDP in 2013. China surpasses the United States on this measure by the year 2000 and maintains the higher level throughout the study period. The United States starts at .0063 (.6%) of GDP in 1992 and ends with .0167 (1.7%) in 2013, maintaining a healthy separation.

National Power

The power measure comparison is a crucial component to any oil security mix, remains a key method of the United States, and contributes prominently to the higher American OSR score. This measure provides some interesting results, but one should keep in mind, this variable is used to represent preparedness for kinetic conflict, if all other approaches to oil security fail. As such, this is a form of posturing, used to avert a full conflict. There is no shortage of power measures available, as discussed previously, but since this is not a study on power, it was easier to choose a stable, safe measure of national power that could capably provide a quantitative measure for use in the study model. Looking at figure 6.8, it is easy to spot some narrowing of the values between the United States and China; but even in 2013, the United States still scores nearly double what China scores. In addition, the United States' average power score over the study period dwarfs any other states listed, with a 72.47. The second highest went to China, with a score of 24.2, followed by Japan, with a 16.48, and India with a 13.79. It is important to note the rapid advances in national power made by China, paired with the slight decline by the United States in the last few years of the study. Most intriguing, however, is the overall narrowing of the power measures between the United States and China, mirroring that of the final OSR scores from figure 6.1. According to this measure, China actually increases its power by 96 percent over the entire 22-year period, which represents a staggering level of growth, while the United States actually declines by 11 percent over the entire period. Much of the decline comes quite late in the study, and only falls through the 70 level in 2011. However, the narrowing of this measure between both states is glaring.

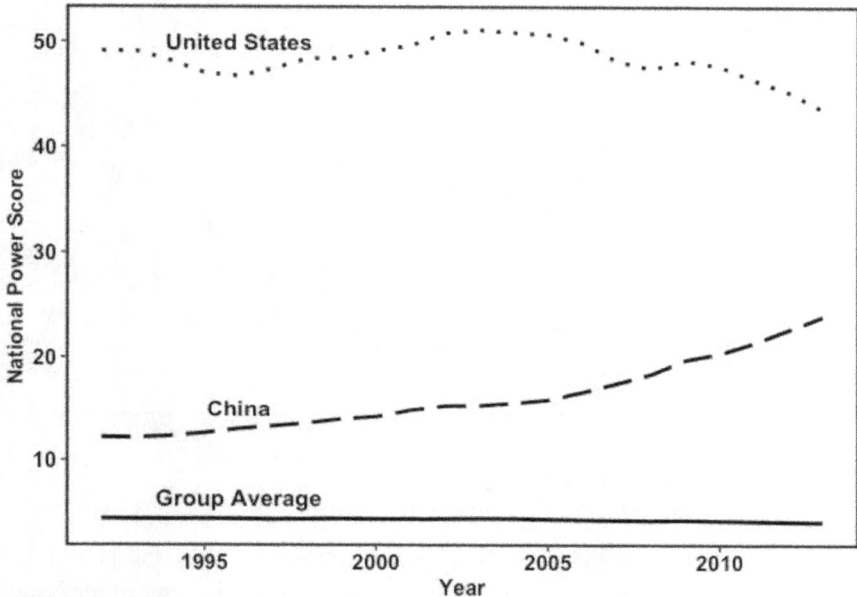

Figure 6.8. National Power (U.S. and China)

Source: Calculations made by author with data from multiple sources including World Bank World Development Indicators and the Stockholm International Peace Research Institute. See appendix for additional information.

Oil Price Volatility

This is ultimately a unique approach to measuring oil price volatility. Instead of looking at the pricing of the dominant crude blends being imported to both countries, which in this case would have been the West Texas Intermediate and Dubai blends, this study utilized trade data that ultimately revealed the average annual price per barrel of crude imported for each individual country in the study. After the average annual price per barrel was calculated, a simple measure averaging the change in the current year with the change in the previous two years is applied, which gives the volatility figure. This is a unique approach in that it allows an examination of pricing at the individual country level, instead of a less precise measure looking at the volatility of specific blends. As for the results, shown in figure 6.9, this is another measure where small states with barely any imports receive the highest scores; however, the United States comes in at the number 4 spot for the average level of volatility over the 22-year period, at a level of 8.34, following Luxembourg, Malta, and Cyprus. China comes in 18th out of the group with a score of 9.94. Looking at the graph, however, volatility

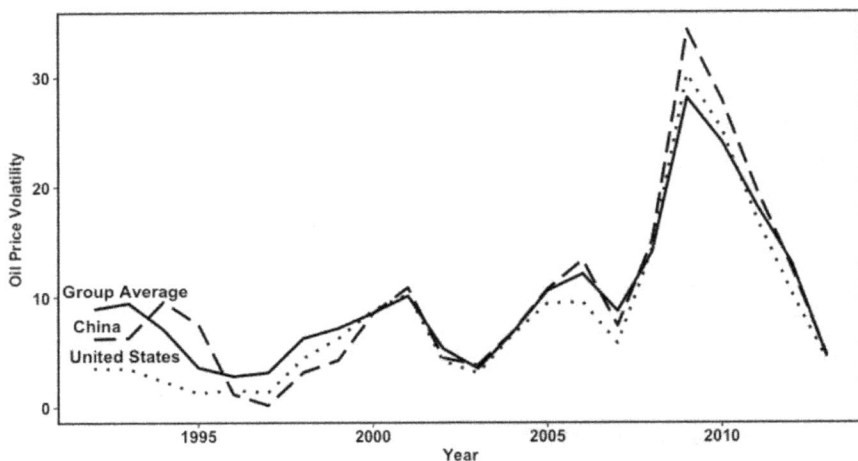

Figure 6.9.　Oil Price Volatility (U.S. and China)
Source: Calculations made by author using data from UN Comtrade.

levels are fairly close between the United States and China. Oil is a global market, so this should be expected to a certain degree, barring other issues involving pricing. For instance, this study showed Bulgaria and Romania to be the subject of extremely high volatility in the early 1990s, quite unlike anything experienced by other countries involved in the study. Figure 6.9 also blatantly illustrates the large spike in volatility, for both states, beginning in 2008, when pricing became much more erratic.

Data Not Included in the OSR Model

Even with other sources of data outside the OSR model above, there is a trend toward convergence. Take data and calculations presented in earlier chapters on capital efficiency from the three largest oil companies in the United States and China. We see both parity and convergence. Figure 6.10 shows the period 2005–2013, with the average, annual Return on Average Capital Employed (ROACE) scores of three major oil companies in each country, roughly estimating capital efficiency for the companies in each state. When viewing figure 6.10, notice the dominance of the American majors included in the study on their capital efficiency measures, except during the 2008 oil price crash and beginnings of the financial crisis. This most likely demonstrates support given to the Chinese NOCs during this period, especially in the form of additional capital to buy assets globally. Being connected to a government benefactor can be beneficial.

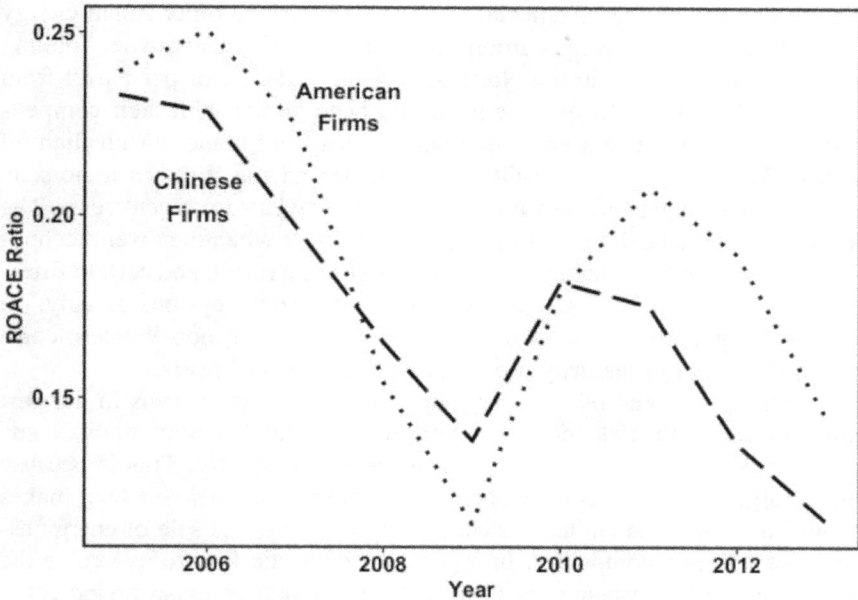

Figure 6.10. Return on Average Capital Employed (ROACE) for Select U.S. and Chinese Energy Companies (Amalgamated)

Note: Some financial data related to Chinese companies may be inaccurate.

Source: Calculations made by author from multiple data sources including Bloomberg Terminal and Morningstar.

Beyond the amalgamated averages, the mean 22-year ROACE score for ExxonMobil was 27 percent, while the second highest out of the group was China National Offshore Oil Company (CNOOC) at 24 percent. Conoco-Phillips performed the worst out of the group at 10 percent. Through much of this period, ROACE movements were relatively similar between the American and Chinese energy companies, indicating the same market forces were at work on both, with a comparable impact. In 2013, ExxonMobil, Chevron, and ConocoPhillips returned 18 percent, 14 percent, and 12 percent, respectively, whereas China National Petroleum Corporation, Sinopec, and CNOOC returned 11 percent, 11 percent, and 14 percent, respectively. While there is a gap, it's not as large as one might think. CNOOC had the same return as Chevron and continued to outperform ConocoPhillips.

Furthermore, despite the constant chorus of Chinese tendencies to "overpay" for assets,[2] recent research on Chinese M&A data would seem to partially disconfirm this hypothesis.[3] Despite the assumption that most Chinese NOCs tend to overpay for their acquisitions,[4] it would seem this is not necessarily the case, especially when compared to other Asian energy companies and other NOCs around the world. For instance, when looking at the average pricing in the North American shale sector per barrel from 2005–2013, Chinese firms have generally been on par with their competitors active in the same area,[5] along with acquisitions made in Canadian oil sands.[6] While the Chinese NOCs are still behind the Western majors on most financial and efficiency metrics, there are caveats for recent years. The large IOCs have been buying into sectors at a time when they were technologically unproven, and garnering lower prices as a result, and certain firms, like CNOOC, have been able to increase capital efficiency considerably.[7] In general, acquisition costs have been in line with other, non-Western competitors, and not necessarily too far behind that of IOC peers.

Additionally, some of the overpaying done by Chinese firms in the past might be part of the risk analysis conducted beforehand, in order to overcome some of the domestic political costs in the target country. This is because many target, domestic constituencies and governments where China makes acquisitions, like the United States, may be hostile to the sale of energy assets to a strategic competitor. In order for a domestic firm to overcome the adverse political consequences, Chinese firms might need to pay an increased premium for the purchase.

Individual costs per barrel are also on par with China's Asian neighbors, reflecting the general "Asia premium" for crude, typically the Dubai blend,[8] and even have similar costs to several European countries, as shown in figure 6.11. While costs per barrel imported to China typically have a significant premium over the cost per barrel in the United States, it is stable and once again, only reflecting region-wide premiums that exist between the major WTI, Brent, and Dubai-Oman blends of crude. Apart from that, per-barrel costs imported to China are typically lower than both the Republic of Korea and Japan, and lower than larger European countries like Germany and France. It is also interesting to note the slowly rising prices per barrel for European economies paired with the increasing costs of Brent crude over time due slowing reserve growth and increased extraction costs.

Direct per-barrel costs between the United States and China provide a unambiguous contrast and clear advantage to the U.S., as shown in table 6.5. Reflecting the Asia premium, China's cost per barrel is considerably higher than that of the United States. In fact, the United States consistently has some of the lowest costs per barrel in the entire 30-country study, and costs in the United Kingdom tend follow close to U.S. costs; although, there is a noticeable change in U.K. and European pricing towards the upside as North Sea crude costs began to rise in the mid-2000s, translating into higher Brent pricing for the continent. U.K. per-barrel costs were cheaper than the United

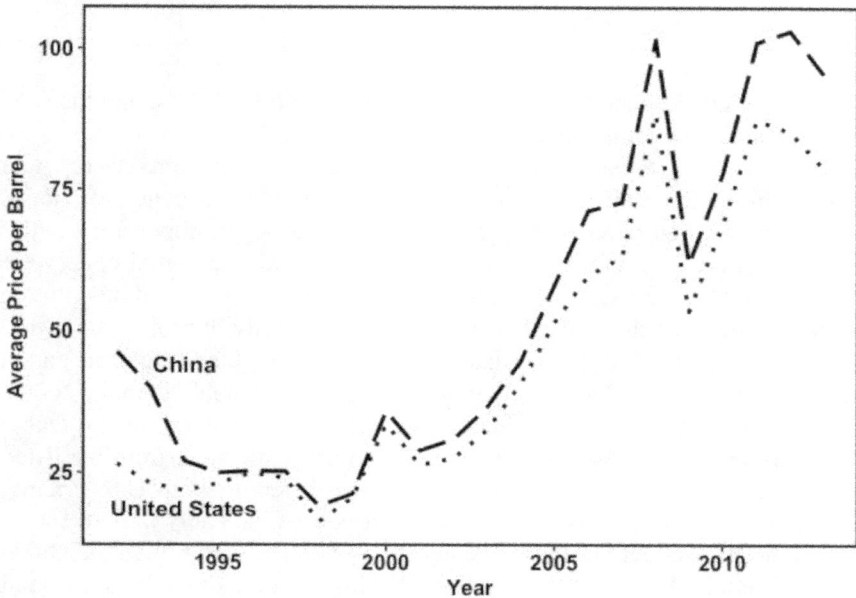

Figure 6.11. Average Price per Barrel (inflation adjusted, 2010 dollars)
Source: Calculations made by author with data from UN Comtrade.

Table 6.5. Comparative Costs for U.S. and Chinese Crude Oil Imports

Year	China ($)	U.S. ($)	China-U.S. (%)	Dubai Crude ($)	Dubai-China (%)
1992	20.54	17.10	−16.74	17.14	19.83
1993	20.35	15.27	−24.97	14.91	36.50
1994	17.11	14.80	−13.49	14.83	15.36
1995	18.48	16.14	−12.66	16.13	14.61
1996	20.30	17.96	−11.53	18.54	9.49
1997	20.82	17.73	−14.87	18.10	15.03
1998	15.48	11.98	−22.63	12.09	28.07
1999	17.07	15.60	−8.62	17.08	−0.01
2000	29.07	26.56	−8.62	26.09	11.45
2001	23.61	21.45	−9.15	22.71	3.95
2002	25.06	22.77	−9.15	23.73	5.58
2003	30.01	27.55	−8.20	26.73	12.27
2004	37.94	35.28	−7.00	33.46	13.40
2005	50.31	46.12	−8.34	49.20	2.25
2006	62.64	55.25	−11.80	61.43	1.97
2007	67.03	59.98	−10.52	68.37	−1.96
2008	99.03	87.39	−11.75	93.78	5.61
2009	59.91	52.66	−12.10	61.76	−2.99
2010	77.98	68.96	−11.56	78.06	−0.10
2011	106.72	90.25	−15.43	106.03	0.65
2012	111.60	89.91	−19.43	108.92	2.46
2013	106.18	84.33	−20.58	105.43	0.72

Notes: All prices are nominal costs countrywide, per barrel.
"China-U.S." and "Dubai-China" categories demonstrate the percent difference anchored in the first listed.

Source: Calculations made by author with data from UN Comtrade Database.

States until 2005, when the two countries switched price levels, and the U.S. retained its lower comparative costs.

The cost differences between the United States and China were quite volatile in the first half of this study, but stabilized in the second half, maintaining a two-digit percentile spread. When China began importing smaller amounts of crude in the beginning of the study period, its initial costs were much higher than the United States, and only sees a drop coinciding with the Asian financial crisis in 1998, when economic activity and oil prices were regionally depressed. But, after that period, China was able to close the gap in costs with the United States, only to see prices rise and stabilize in the 2000s.

It is also notable from the Chinese price differentials that the cost for Dubai blend crude, on a per-barrel basis, is not noticeably different from the listed prices for the region. Here, again, as with the differentials to U.S. pricing, the higher costs are front-loaded in the first half of the study period, showing Chinese costs per barrel on average 14.53 percent higher than the Dubai blend. Then, in the second half, these costs fuse much closer to Dubai blend pricing, averaging only 3 percent higher for that period.

Even on a per-barrel basis, the level of exorbitant pricing thought to exist with Chinese crude purchases doesn't seem to hold up that well. Per-barrel pricing is well above those found in the United States, but relatively close to European costs and generally in line with the Asian premium on crude found with Asia-based buyers.

Finally, although data on individual production and refining levels for both countries have been presented in previous chapters, it is worthwhile to view a direct comparison between the two. In figure 6.12, comparative production and refining levels show China has gained a pronounced level of capacity. Significantly, Chinese refining capacity has quadrupled over the course of the study, allowing China a high degree of crude sourcing flexibility. The United States, already the global leader in refining capacity, had modest increases as well, in addition to fluctuating production levels. These fluctuations are due to lowering overall production in the U.S. before massive increases resulting from the tight oil and gas boom, resulting in a spike, allowing production to surpass levels higher than at any time over the entire 22-year period. Chinese domestic production, on the other hand, merely doubled from an already low level, resulting in modest gains. However, the importance of refining capacity increases is immensely important, and should not go unnoticed.

Section Summary

After a comparative review of the final data generated from the OSR, as well as the individual components unattached to the OSR, it is clear a single word

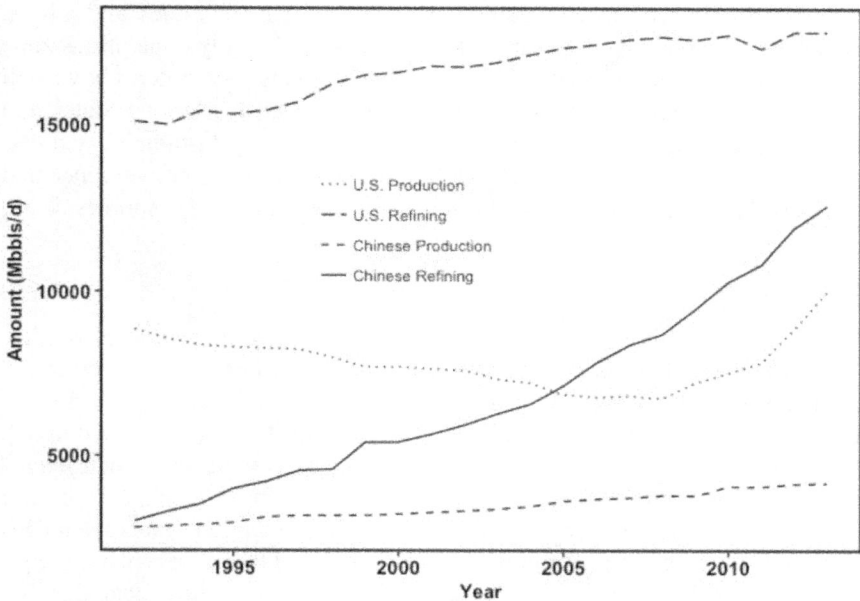

Figure 6.12. National Production and Refining Levels (U.S. and China)

Source: Data sourced from Energy Information Administration, International Energy Statistics, Production (Mbbls/d) and Refining (Mbbls/d), 2016, https://www.eia.gov.

could be used to summarize the relationship between China and the United States: convergence. In nearly every case, it is China that is "catching up" to the United States, adapting its approaches, and in doing so following many of the same paths to oil supply security. Much of this is a concerted effort on the part of the Chinese government; however, it is curious to note that certain components are simply the product of the environment and the size of a consuming state reacting to that environment, meaning massive oil consumers are forced to pursue supply security in a certain way if they want to secure energy supplies at relatively large levels. For example, the power measure certainly represents a deliberate act on the part of the government to increase its economic and military power, while increased levels of import dependence appear to be something that larger, rapidly growing oil consumers simply require in order to accommodate advanced industrialized economies, especially when dealing with limited domestic supplies. However, the trend toward coalescence is clear. Earlier, in chapter 3, the political climate model was introduced with three key "oil security" scenarios, as a state operating in: a politically neutral climate; a politically contentious climate; or an open conflict climate. With respect to this model, it should be noted that these environments, perceived or misperceived, and quite future-oriented, have a direct impact on conflict and cooperation between the United States and China. However, since both states seem destined for the politically contentious zone of the model, it is reasonable to assume the convergence noted above will result in a more confrontational relationship between the United States and China. Since it is the grand strategies of these states, with the elevated element of energy security in their calculations, that has led to convergence and the arrival at similar approaches to secure supplies of overseas sources of oil.

Clashes of Grand Strategy

China has made a concerted effort to minimize its oil security vulnerabilities, but what does this lead to in terms of clashes in grand strategy between the United States and China? China has reduced the oil security gap with the United States; however, it is far from parity. It still has much to accomplish to sustain similar levels of oil security compared to its large petroleum-consuming competitor. The core issues between the two states are best summed up by Daniel Yergin, stating, "Some in the United States see a Chinese grand strategy to preempt the United States and the West when it comes to new oil and gas supplies, and some strategists in Beijing fear that the United States may someday try to interdict China's foreign energy supplies."[9] These core fears then generate several spillover concerns, creating multiple competitive avenues between the two countries.

Most worrisome are the areas of extreme vulnerability for China, which mainly involves areas outside its capacity to secure militarily. For instance, the sea lines of communication running from the Middle East, through the Indian Ocean, into various straits, and finally, through the South China Sea, are particularly vulnerable. This is a path fraught with numerous security challenges and areas where vessels must traverse waters full of current or potential adversaries. If China is to don its veil of security in full, this severe weakness must be mitigated and eventually rectified. And, this weakness, from the Chinese perspective, can only be resolved via political means and military preparedness. Commercial trade can be altered and adjusted, especially in the case of highly fungible goods. But, the oil trade cannot be so easily adjusted, especially since the entire global oil market apparatus is built on institutions and networks created and safeguarded by the United States and its allies. Closing security gaps complements quite well with China's holistic approach to grand strategy in the pursuit of "comprehensive national power." Only with comprehensive power can the great power be sufficiently secure, and energy is, of course, part of that comprehensive power.

One of the core issues to grapple with is whether the existing market-based apparatus, constructed for the efficient and lowest cost distribution of petroleum, is the best way for China to maintain energy security. Outside the market, China has made strides and overtures, strengthening bilateral relationships, establishing equity contracts, and cementing political partnerships. Whether this even provides security beyond the market-based mechanism may be a moot point itself: Chinese policymakers believe it provides additional security. As other authors have pointed out, the efficacy of oil supply redirection based on political relationships may not be at issue, but whether policymakers actually think it is and act on these beliefs. In an important piece of scholarship Levi determines that there is in fact a relationship, regardless of outcome.[10] Foreign policy elites' perceptions of the threat environment, along with proper recourse, have mattered greatly.

Even the perception that China is more energy secure than reality validates may lead to increases in conflict potential with the United States. At various levels of grand strategy, weaker states tend to overestimate their capabilities and underestimate the capabilities of their competitors. In addition, despite the superior material capabilities of the United States it would be difficult to deter Chinese aggression with anything involving territory or nationalism, given these issues tie directly to state security, and by extension, energy security.[11] This course of events is particularly worrisome, given that any threats to Chinese state security, vis-à-vis its energy security, will provoke a particularly strong reaction due to these conjoining threats of overestimation of successful outcome, nationalism, and territoriality. These competing issues have become bound with oil security, and may end up further fused if more energy resources are discovered in the South China Sea.

Increased tensions bring in a host of other issues as well. As mentioned earlier, while sanctions, embargoes, or containment directed toward China do not necessitate outright war, there exists the potential for devastating long-term consequences to the Chinese state in terms of the economy and satisfaction of the general population, which has become accustomed to economic growth and a greater sense of material well-being. Any complications in this intermediate area between war and peace can generate a moral threat to the legitimacy of the CCP, questioning the internal monopoly of power. The monopoly on political power may also be a direct derivative of the Chinese experience before the fall of the Qing Dynasty, when before the forced opening by Western powers, there existed an already weakening state, plagued with internal disorder, rebellion, and revolt, that left the state in a far more vulnerable position to hostile outside powers. Swaine and Tellis touch on this point by their frequent inclusion of the primacy of internal order in their calculations of Chinese grand strategy.[12] Many of the strategists referenced refer to domestic order as a preeminent concern, along the hierarchy of other concerns central to the CCP. The precariousness of the Chinese government has grown progressively, albeit gradually, worse. Although information is now scarce on the level of social unrest within Chinese borders, by the mid-2000s, there were already over 80,000 such protests throughout the country, with more than 100,000 possible later in the decade.[13] However, conceptualized the way Swaine and Tellis do, there is a high level of interdependence between the internal and external threat environment,[14] such that they are completely dependent on one another.[15] Furthermore, in the interaction between the internal and external environment, another key concern is the "level and origin (external or internal) of resources available to the state," bringing strategic energy issues to bear in the internal and external threat environment.[16]

China's Maritime Environment

More so than the Cold War between the United States and Soviet Union, the burgeoning Sino-American competitive arrangement will not primarily take place on land, but instead will take place in the maritime environment. This shift in the primary strategic theater of conflict, for both states, places greater emphasis on naval assets and materials, increasing contention in the maritime environment and greatly increasing its importance. This will also require increasing strategic depth, buffer space, and operating room for Chinese naval assets over the long term, with the potential for added tension at every step.

The recent uptick in territoriality exhibited on the part of the Chinese in the South China Sea is an outgrowth of its attempts to secure its maritime environment, which results in enhanced control over its SLOCs and increases in oil security. China has assiduously employed a strategy to frustrate forward deployed military units and to utilize asymmetric warfare since the 1990s, with the ability to carry out the various components of that strategy more effectively over time as material resources have improved and military doctrine has adapted for modern warfare.[17]

As China grows stronger and feels more secure in multiple areas of state security, including oil security, that sense of confidence will lead to bolder actions. We have already seen this in the escalation of conflict with China since 2011, especially in the South China Sea,[18] and advances to Chinese naval power are notable. It is important to take note that China has surprised analysts, strategists, forecasters, and scholars by advancing military capabilities, economic relationships, and overseas political interests beyond what thought possible for over two decades.[19] And, in some areas, there is actual, or near, technological parity with the United States. As a matter of fact, as Thomas Christensen notes, China may have a certain degree of technological parity with the United States regarding anti-ship ballistic missiles (ASBM),[20] where China has had the CSS-5 Mod 5 (DF-21D) medium-range ballistic missile (MRBM) system deployed for several years. This ASBM weapons system is designed to put vessels at risk, particularly aircraft carriers, within a 1,500-km range.[21] It has yet to be determined how successful this weapons system would be in practice, or how effectively shipboard countermeasures would respond, both causes for great concern. This has the strong potential to frustrate U.S. efforts to control the maritime environment close to Chinese shores and increases the difficulty of countering Chinese maneuvers in the case of a conflict over Taiwan. Additionally, China's naval and air forces that cover China's littoral and near maritime environments extending east and south have grown rapidly, qualitatively and quantitatively.[22]

However, a state cannot provide SLOC defense without a robust naval presence capable of extended, forward deployments, backed by a potent logistics framework. It is also understood that the orientation of China's naval assets, in particular its newest and most advanced hardware, is disproportionately deployed to the South China Sea theater, indicating the prioritization of sovereignty claims in the maritime environment and security of the SLOCs leading to key ports, and not to counter the threat posed by Japan, or even for coercion of Taiwan.[23] A key part of this strategy during China's naval transition phase is the deployment of advanced submarines capable of bridging the gap between a navy attuned to coastal defense and one that is blue-water-capable in addition to closing naval capability gaps with a qualitatively superior adversary.[24]

You Ji expands on this idea of submarines as an effective platform while the PLAN hardware and doctrinal transition is underway, with submarine growth referred to as a "contingency capability" able to fill the "transitional vacuum," and conceiving of submarine use not necessarily as protective, but as a deterrent capable of low-cost threats and attacks on other state's shipping in the region.[25] China has been orienting its fleet toward SLOC operations, especially in the acquisition of nuclear powered attack submarines of which research, development, and deployment has taken precedent.[26]

China is rapidly developing submersible assets and deploying them to the Indian Ocean, along with the relevant support vessels and materials, building a credible deterrent threat, something Chinese military leaders have openly acknowledged as a security gap that needs to be addressed as quickly as possible, broadly an attempt to mitigate this weakness of the "lane" of China's "one point, one lane" strategic disadvantages.[27] For example, the indigenously built Yuan-class attack submarine, unveiled in 2004,[28] represents one of many steps in this direction, amid a larger effort to expand the submarine force both qualitatively and quantitatively, where the underwater force has actually seen the most growth out of advanced naval and air assets indigenously built or acquired abroad.[29]

The PLAN's submarines are gaining familiarity with two key locations as well: the Western Pacific and the Indian Ocean with its multiple-class submarine deployments.[30] China's forward deployed submarine force has begun to familiarize themselves with the Indian Ocean transit corridor first. And, over the past few years, this has expanded to intelligence-gathering missions, exercises involving surface combatants, and the rotations of all four submarine classes available in the Chinese inventory.[31] It is also projected that by 2020, the Chinese navy will field the third largest fleet of nuclear-powered attack submarines in the world, behind the United States and Russia.[32] More recently, by 2015 the number of nuclear-powered attack submarines in the Chinese inventory had grown to five, which is a substantial accomplishment,[33] of which both Han and Yuan class vessels have made recent, lengthy deployments to the Indian Ocean.[34]

It should, however, be pointed out that these naval forces also create a new crisis point if any type of embargo is placed on China and enforced militarily on China's maritime periphery. With the submarine force as the only potential effective means for countering oil embargo operations, the PLAN would face crucial decisions early on regarding optimal deployment of naval assets. For instance, submarine deployment from home bases in the South China Sea is predicated on rather predictable and narrow passageways susceptible to focused monitoring and easier interception by enemy military assets.[35] The submarine force would need to remain in China's immediate maritime environment in order to remain relatively safe; however, if this were the case, the force would lose its coercive power and anti-access and area denial capabilities in the outer island chains, and the Indian Ocean, defeating the purpose of the existence of the force as a security gap while the PLAN force adapts and modernizes. These are crucial decisions to be made early in any crisis.

Embargos, Containment, and Sanctions

Access denial by the United States is a primary concern among Chinese defense planners.[36] Chinese political elites have been concerned over the potential of a blockade of their maritime environment since the early 1990s, around the time China shifted from net exporter to net importer of petroleum.[37] China's oil security is, broadly speaking, centralized on the Middle East and the SLOCs weaving through the Indian Ocean and the South China Sea, and the oil pipelines coming in through Central Asia and Russia, where in all areas, China views itself, even now, as a subject of containment pressures by the United States and its direct or indirect allies.[38]

Once again, due to these pressures, referencing the market as a reliable source of oil security is not plausible. Nor is merely referring to the need for a predominance of naval power in order to militarily secure the sea lines of communication in the case of war. This is important, but it does not deliver the entire story. These both leave out the transitional aspects between peaceful competition and war, which potentially involves increasing political tensions, sanctions, and containment. Why should China not expect and prepare for containment of its power on the part of a Western alliance? This is exactly the sort of long-term, protracted relationship that took place when the last great power attempted to challenge the United States during the 20th century. The Soviet Union could not rely on the "Western" market; nor would China be able to under similar political constraints.

The problem with many market-based analyses for oil security is that they do not account for anything outside these normal market-operating conditions, and also fail to understand that lower prices and higher efficiency is not the end goal in all circumstances. The argument overwhelmingly centers on the fact that petro-nationalism is self-defeating due to the fungibility of oil and the reliability of global oil markets.[39] But, this is simply not an accurate representation of how states would pursue oil security in a politically belligerent climate. Under sanctions, containment, intense competition, or open warfare, pre-existing, politically resilient, and militarily secure energy supply lines do matter. In addition, containment, or in its lesser form, sanctions, typically occur for much longer duration than open warfare. The Cold War, and the concomitant containment and security competition, lasted for the better part of forty years. Warsaw Pact allies did not rely on the global oil market because it was insecure and a Western-designed system, but instead relied on the Soviet Union for such supplies. For instance, many scholars reject the security effects of bilateral, long-term supply contracts and equity oil, since most of this oil is generated from efficient, open-market operations and China sells this same oil to the open market instead of sending equity oil directly back to home ports, thereby eliminating these political approaches as viable energy security strategies.[40] This is patently false if one considers containment or sanctions as an intermediary, and quite feasible step towards open war. If China has established itself as a major political ally, and more importantly, reliable mass importer of oil, a state is more likely to maintain its relationship with Beijing at the cost of political relationships with other countries, like the United States. As power and resources grow in China, more states will find it beneficial to retain a relationship with the Middle Kingdom, and not the United States. This is natural outgrowth of long-term dynamics in the international system.

Even before the Cold War, the idea of oil security was well known and codified, from Churchill's famous quotes on oil insecurity and diversification, to the concept of oil as a core strategic commodity worth fighting over, a "red line" well established in international politics as demonstrated by one of the few actions taken by the defunct League of Nation's against Italy in response to the Abyssinia Crisis in 1935,[41] or Hitler's concern when the Soviets cut off supplies to downstream operations in Germany.[42]

The energy markets themselves were put to the test during World War Two when all involved attempted to fall back on politically and militarily secure energy sources both in the lead-up to war, and during. The great powers didn't put their faith in a "market" but instead supplies they could control for themselves and their allies at any cost. While oil access wasn't as important at that time to the general population, and consequentially economic growth, during both World War One and World War Two oil was primarily a military issue, as this was the only sector that was fully utilizing oil as an energy source, albeit a vital one. The impact of oil deprivation on the general population in many cases would have been negligible, but in some ways was even harsher since any cutoff was more directly an attempt by foreign powers to directly strangle the military of a country.[43] This may not be the case today, but constrained supply can still impact military operations, and certainly affects the broader economy, which is vital to all states, and especially to Chinese Communist Party legitimacy.

Looking back, during the lead-up to World War Two, Germany had access to the global oil market, but decided to begin to synthesize oil domestically, from coal, in order to have its own secure source of supplies. This was a wildly costly and inefficient process, producing sub-standard oil, but Germany knew it would not be able to depend on the market as competition increased between the major European powers. Germany took action to mitigate this market reliance weakness, utilizing any tools or knowledge at its disposal to mitigate this weakness.

In another case, a deciding factor for Japan's attack on Pearl Harbor had to do with secure oil sources: the market-based approach failed as it had become necessarily politicized and militarized and had to expend efforts to secure supplies elsewhere. This shift was underway even before the U.S.' oil embargo on Japan.[44] But, even in this case, an embargo was the first step.

Even other vital commodities would take part in this pattern. Aside from oil, there have been many other strategic resources inducing vulnerability in a state. Take for instance imported foodstuffs to Germany during World War One. The Industrial Revolution dramatically lowered the cost of overseas transport via steam-powered vessels, allowing the country to import cost-competitive food to continental Europe. This created a strategic vulnerability for Germany as Britain embargoed Germany of its desperately needed supplies, contributing significantly to the war effort.[45]

Reasons for Interdiction

Something bold like an embargo or blockade is attractive since it is relatively low risk to the U.S. and allied forces that would be engaged in supportive operations. Vessels can be kept at a relatively harmless range, and vital supplies can still be denied. And, it's not only the actual interdiction of oil transport vessels, or the actual implementation of any embargo, but instead just the mere threat of the world's most powerful naval force moving on any oil transport infrastructure. This could be quite constraining and potentially be crippling, depending on how many other suppliers a state could marshal to their own political alignment in this antagonistic environment.

The United States has a long tradition of interdicting naval vessels, and even more so, has honed these skills in the Persian Gulf since the early 1990s.[46] Furthermore, in 1993, the U.S. Navy even intercepted and boarded the Chinese flagged container ship *Yinhe*, which was potentially carrying restricted chemical weapons materials to Iran.[47] After further inspections in a Saudi port by both American and Saudi personnel, the vessel was deemed to be in absence of any such materials,[48] but for Chinese strategic planners, the contemporary precedent was set: U.S. military vessels will interdict, board, and search Chinese flagged vessels with impunity.

An American embargo against China, including strategic products, is more than a theoretical possibility. With a complete trade embargo in place after the Korean War,[49] including petroleum and petroleum products, and a U.S.-E.U. arms embargo still in place today, the possibilities of the United States utilizing embargoes, sanctions, or interdictions of strategic imports to China is a potent, and realistic threat, more so today given China's massive reliance on imported oil.

The U.S. has even specifically blockaded oil to and from other countries, including Iraq, and considered doing so in the Balkans and North Korea, and has a general proclivity towards denial and coercion when dealing with oil access and adversaries.[50] China has been subjected to Soviet oil cutoffs and has even embargoed oil going to North Korea, if only for a short period.[51]

Another issue is many scholars simply do not think far enough down the supply line for interdictions or cutoffs. For example, there is no reason to restrict naval interdiction to waters even remotely close to the East Asia SLOCs, which tend to be the point of reference when referring to these types of interdictions. Many analysts prefer to focus on the Malacca Strait, with relatively close proximity to Chinese waters. However, interdiction can oc-cur anywhere along the SLOCs from the Persian Gulf to Chinese ports. The farther out interception occurs, the greater advantages and lower costs and risks afforded to the U.S. Navy. However, supply can also be interdicted in foreign ports, export countries, subversion of oil-extracting assets in countries like Sudan or South Sudan, where ramifications of such tampering would be minimal. Even a state like Saudi Arabia could potentially be coerced to restrict supplies given its reliance on the dense, long-standing security arrangements with the United States.

Interdiction Capability

Other scholars have pointed out that if open war is to commence, it is more difficult to track and intercept oil tankers than many would typically believe. Even if this is the case, although it is quite doubtful this would be beyond the capabilities of the U.S. Navy, replete with new technologies and numerous satellites used to identify and eliminate targets, the U.S. would not necessarily need to intercept tankers in transit but could exercise military options in the foreign port or in the oil facilities themselves, halting the flow anywhere along the supply lines.

Could they be interdicted? It would be logistically difficult, and may require enhanced cooperation in sea lanes with allies and non-belligerents, but it is feasible. First, there is still only a limited number of vessels that go through these waters daily, and interdictions need not impact all vessels, only some. Chinese indigenously produced vessels, which China has been assiduously building up, will be more readily identifiable in the future. For instance, about 18 million barrels of oil transit through the Strait of Hormuz every day. Let's say in any given day, Very Large Crude Carriers (VLCCs) are carrying these supplies, resulting in nine VLCCs transiting the Strait daily, well within the capabilities of the U.S. Navy for targeting and interception.

The Malacca Strait is a similar story, with 11 to 15 daily VLCC transits. This is a total amount, indicating two-way traffic in 2014, with total VLCC transits at 4,993.[52] This means anywhere from five to seven loaded tankers are inbound to the Asia-Pacific region, through the Straits, coming from the Indian Ocean. Again, this is not an insurmountable number of vessels for interdiction operations and embargoes. It's also important to mention, in order to be successful, naval forces do not need to intercept and halt all traffic; only some will be sufficient.

As mentioned earlier in this study, the "tanker wars" between Iraq and Iran during the Iran-Iraq War are typically brought up to reassure those worried about military operations targeting oil tankers, which are incredibly well built, sturdy, and essentially armored vessels. However, this is a false comparison. During the tanker war in the 1980s, these tankers were attacked with Cold War–era weapons systems used by two regional actors that included serious deficiencies in targeting and logistics. Even still, about a quarter of tankers in the Persian Gulf were sunk or damaged beyond repair. Many analysts claim this is a low amount, demonstrated as evidence that tankers are relatively impervious to military operations, but strategists should learn the exact opposite lesson. With extremely limited capabilities, the belligerents were able to debilitate a quarter of the tanker fleet. Today, technology has advanced to the point where the limitations realized by both states are not an issue, especially for a force like the U.S. Navy.

SLOCs, Indian Ocean, South China Sea, String of Pearls

China's naval power, and by extension, its energy trade is inexorably linked to its larger grand strategic framework and ambitions, and may very well be central to it, aside from the continuing adaptation to, and coping with, the preponderance of American global military, economic, and political power.[53] Sea lanes continue to matter greatly.

Given the increasing difficulties in conducting U.S. naval operations in China's maritime environment, along with a general aversion to a direct confrontation with a militarily capable, nuclear-armed force, the U.S. may be drawn to impact Chinese oil security farther abroad, well outside the effectiveness of China's most potent military assets and configurations. The only sensible areas for U.S. military intervention to proceed with minimal, to no losses, would be in oil-related areas where China is unable to project its own military forces. More and more it seems the battle for China's oil security will be fought in the Indian Ocean, far from the diligently built-up military support in the East and South China Seas.[54] Chinese strategic planners, of course, know this is an area of extreme vulnerability in times of conflict.

Despite many analysts claiming the demise of the Chinese "string of pearls" approach to the Indian Ocean, developments over the past two years seem to have resurrected this approach with fervor. The pearls extend from one end of the Indian Ocean to the other, potentially connecting East African states and Pakistan, to Sri Lanka and the Seychelles, and the Malacca terminus in the east with Indonesia and Malaysia.[55] In recent years, we have seen more active diplomatic and military engagements along SLOC corridors, whether with political overtures to the Seychelles, or the strengthening of political ties with Malacca Strait associated countries, including Indonesia and Malaysia.

Perhaps the largest leap for China has been the initial construction of its first overseas military facility in Djibouti.[56] This is a burgeoning military facility in a relevant, strategic location along China's key SLOC running from the Middle East to Chinese ports, essentially representing a revival of the pearl necklace approach, where this facility would be the first pearl.[57] In building this base, China also seems to be signaling militarily to Japan, as well as to the United States, that military materials will be established in-kind in the region.[58] Japan, a core strategic competitor and neighbor to China, imports much of its oil from the same sources simply due to geography, and may be even less willing to tolerate a strong and overt Chinese military presence along its own SLOCs through the Indian Ocean and in foreign ports where its own supply security is at stake.

China's forward deployed and force projection naval capabilities are oriented along the route from the mainland through the Indian Ocean to African and Middle Eastern ports. The first long-term force projection exercise on the part of the PLAN was the deployment of a three-vessel task force to the Gulf of Aden in 2009, for the purpose of participating in a multinational naval force to counter the astonishing increase in piracy in the region. However, this task force never left, remained deployed, and continues to patrol these waters, increasing familiarity and developing operational fluency in the region.[59]

Additionally, even though the maritime territorial grabs in the South China Sea are related to territoriality and nationalism, they are also important for securing the SLOCs, the potential for undersea energy resources, and the denial of forward strategic operating areas for China's adversaries, including Taiwan and United States. Chinese control over the South China Sea maritime environment is compounded by competing claims of other potential adversaries, that also recognize the strategic importance of the sea lanes not only for uncontested movement of military assets, but also to control the flow of vital resources, like oil. Senior officials in the Ministry of National Defense have mentioned this in the past,[60] where control over sea lanes, using the Spratly Islands as a base, and submarine warfare, could be used to intercept oil tankers bound for China.

The ability to connect to Middle East and East African oil is vital to Chinese oil security. China's interest especially in the Middle East has always been one of oil security,[61] and the region's importance has been a cornerstone of Chinese energy security policy since the 1990s, has only grown since then, and will continue to intensify in significance as it is the only current global source for oil that can satisfy its growing requirements.[62] This situation presents itself as a realistic long-term flashpoint along China's SLOCs from the Persian Gulf to its domestic deepwater ports.

OVERVIEW

China must treat outside powers as hostile or potentially hostile to further justify the communist party's existence, alongside uninterrupted economic growth, creating a dependency for the economy and security from foreign threats. China's intense military focus on short-term conflicts is further validated by the reality that in wartime, the United States has the clear ability to cut off oil supplies, eroding its ability to conduct a war over long periods of time. This is a major weakness the Chinese government will attempt to rectify over time. In the meantime, China will deploy naval assets to the Indian Ocean and shore up relationships with key partners in the region, establishing military, resupply, and logistics bases. Political relationships can be built on resistance to a specific country, or group of countries. For instance, China's strong political and resource relationship with Iran is built largely on distrust of United States.[63] Even if oil security ultimately is not at stake, certainly the perception exists that it is, and China is responding to this threat politically and militarily.

In a way, China is being socialized into the system by adapting to the best practices of similar states. This is happening with oil security, but in a broader sense, with China's preparation for import restrictions via sanctions or containment, and war. In this sense, as Kenneth Waltz may have articulated, much of China's approach as demonstrated both qualitatively and quantitatively, represent a socialization to the best practices of the system in which the state inhabits, hand in hand with competition which "encourages similarities of attributes and of behavior" and where "socialization and competition are two aspects of a process by which the variety of behaviors and of outcomes is reduced."[64] Competition and security can be socialized in the same way norms and patterns of behavior can be established in the international system. The United States established the precedent for the "right" way to establish and maintain oil security and compete for these critical resources, and it makes sense that China would follow a similar, successful pattern. And, as with the United States and past actions by the Axis powers, China would certainly go to war over a U.S. blockade of Chinese energy supplies.[65]

It should, however, be noted that an oil cutoff offers no real power unless war is imminent or highly probable, since any cutoff would reduce China's ability to prosecute a long war, go against its recently revamped doctrine of fighting "short wars," and would leave it unable to contemplate any political efforts to reduce tension;[66] its only course in such a situation is war. With respect to the question of oil security, China will have the United States in a position where the onus is on them to take the first military action, meanwhile being prepared for containment and sanctions that may arise in the politically contentious phase of the relationship. This has precedents with both Japan and Germany in the lead-up to World War Two as political relationships broke down and the situation worsened in both countries. This subsequently forced both states to take drastic and desperate action in order to directly control and enhance their oil security, including Japan's surprise attack at Pearl

Harbor and its push south into the East Indies' oil fields,[67] and Germany's development of synthetic fuels and its own disastrous push East into the Soviet Union, of which a "prime motive" was oil.[68]

As we see a narrowing of capabilities between the United States and China, we also see a convergence of geographic areas critical to their oil security. The ramifications of this convergence apply directly to both states as it reduces operating states and creates overlapping interests and threats. As Charles Glaser has pointed out in a recent article, this is extremely problematic. The idea of an oil- or energy-based security dilemma is profoundly more difficult to manage than a typical security dilemma, because no two states can be satisfied at the same time with any level of security present along the energy sensitive SLOCs, as these areas are necessarily mutually exclusive to one another.[69] In a typical security dilemma, there is a possibility of passivity in the dilemma according to some theoretical approaches based on the primacy of offensive or defensive military technology, or a clear delineation between offensive and defensive platforms. This is simply not possible in a situation involving sea-lanes since any type of military asset must be deployed to the same location and the distinction between offense and defense is rendered a moot point given the overlap in location. In fact, besides SLOC security, the United States and China have several points of contention regarding oil supply security as codified by Glaser including SLOC security, alliance entrapment, especially regarding Japan, near sea resources, and access vulnerabilities.[70]

This is all quite challenging as the United States will ultimately resort to a less accommodationist approach towards China. For instance, under the Obama presidency, Colin Dueck describes the Obama doctrine as one of retrenchment and accommodation so that American resources could be redirected towards domestic purposes; however, while U.S. grand strategy under the Obama administration was marked by the drawdown of American military forces globally, one region has been the exception: the Asia-Pacific. And, the key foreign policy successes for the administration came when the president employed more traditional, Realist-driven strategies, including responses to Chinese maritime aggression in the East and South China Seas, where deterrence proved the most effective approach.[71]

In some ways, this situation demonstrates an oil-based security dilemma within the confines of preparatory containment. This idea for oil security is independent of what is typically thought of in terms of hard power and military strength. A state normally does not have to prepare separately for containment as opposed to open warfare; military materials are used to counter hard power in containment scenarios and those same materials will be used in the case of open conflict, and that military power will be subjected to the same doctrinal discipline and strategic orientation. The political and economic statecraft conducted under each scenario, however, will matter greatly, and will represent a reversion back to the mercantilism of the 18th and 19th centuries.

Given the relative success of deterrent approaches, it is reasonable to assume this will occur with higher frequency going forward, as this transition is already underway. The United States was largely accommodating to China during the latter's economic liberalization and opening to the West but has been more confrontational as China has stepped up territorial claims in the South China Sea, threatening vital SLOCs and key regional allies. Moving forward, these SLOCs will remain crisis prone as China continues to draw on the market, but ultimately prepares for containment and war.

NOTES

1. Eshita Gupta, "Oil Vulnerability Index of Oil-Importing Countries," *Energy Policy* 36 (2008): 1195–1211.

2. Andrews-Speed and Dannreuther, *China, Oil and Global Politics*, 80–81.

3. Pang, "Chinese Overseas Oil and Gas M&A Strategy: Assessing the Financial and Strategic Performance of Foreign Upstream Acquisitions by the Chinese National Oil Companies, 2005–2013," 39–54.

4. Ibid., 2–4.

5. Ibid., 62.

6. Ibid., 57.

7. Ibid., 51.

8. Bassam Fattouh, "An Anatomy of the Crude Oil Pricing System," *The Oxford Institute for Energy Studies*, WPM 40 (2011): 61.

9. Yergin, "Ensuring Energy Security," *Foreign Affairs*, 77.

10. Clayton and Levi, "The Surprising Sources of Oil's Influence," *Survival*, 107–122.

11. Thomas J. Christensen, *The China Challenge: Shaping the Choices of a Rising Power* (New York, NY: W. W. Norton and Company Inc., 2015), 99–115.

12. Michael D. Swaine and Ashley J. Tellis, *Interpreting China's Grand Strategy: Past, Present, and Future* (Santa Monica, CA: RAND, 2000), 16–19; Robert D. Blackwill and Ashley J. Tellis, "Council Special Report No. 72: Revising U.S. Grand Strategy Toward China," Council on Foreign Relations (April 2015).

13. Kevin O'Brien and Rachel Stern, "Introduction: Studying Contention in Contemporary China," in *Popular Protests in China*, ed. Kevin O'Brien (Cambridge, MA: Harvard University Press, 2008).

14. Reminiscent of nei luan wai huan (internal strife, external threat).

15. Swaine and Tellis, *Interpreting China's Grand Strategy: Past, Present, and Future*, 17.

16. Ibid., 18.

17. Thomas J. Christensen, "Posing Problems Without Catching Up: China's Rise and Challenges for U.S. Security Policy," *International Security* 25, no. 4 (2001).

18. Most recent reports indicate China is further militarizing its presence in the South China Sea by installing military hardware on its network of artificial islands.

19. Amy Chang, "Indigenous Weapons Development in China's Military Modernization," U.S.-China Economic and Security Review Commission Staff Research Report (2012): 38–41.

20. Christensen, *The China Challenge: Shaping the Choices of a Rising Power*, 102–103.

21. Office of the Secretary of Defense, "Annual Report to Congress: Military and Security Developments Involving the People's Republic of China 2016" (2016): 61. Reports indicate a new version of the DF-21D is operational and ready to be deployed, the DF-26, which has a potential range out to 4,000 km, with the ability to target medium-sized vessels.

22. Andrew S. Erickson, "China's Modernization of Its Naval and Air Power Capabilities," in *Strategic Asia 2012–13: China's Military Challenge*, Ashley J. Tellis and Travis Tanner eds. (Seattle, WA: National Bureau of Asian Research, 2012), 61–125.

23. James C. Bussert and Bruce A. Elleman, *People's Liberation Army Navy: Combat Systems Technology 1949–2010* (Annapolis, MD: Naval Institute Press, 2011), 185.

24. Gurpreet S. Khurana, "China's 'String of Pearls' in the Indian Ocean and Its Security Implications," *Strategic Analysis* 32, no. 1 (2008): 2–4.

25. Ji, "Dealing with the Malacca Dilemma: China's Effort to Protect its Energy Supply," *Strategic Analysis*, 481.

26. Ibid., 482.

27. Khurana, "China's 'String of Pearls' in the Indian Ocean and Its Security Implications," *Strategic Analysis* 32, 9. This is an important reference to energy "shunt" routes and mentions a quote from PLA General Qian Guoliang where he states the "threat perception is centered on the danger of one point [and] one lane," where the "one point" is Taiwan and the "one lane" is the route through the Indian Ocean.

28. Chang, "Indigenous Weapons Development in China's Military Modernization," U.S.-China Economic and Security Review Commission Staff Research Report, 8.

29. Ibid., 10.

30. Office of the Secretary of Defense, "Annual Report to Congress: Military and Security Developments Involving the People's Republic of China 2016" (2016): 69.

31. U.S.-China Economic and Security Review Commission, "2016 Report to Congress of the U.S.-China Economic and Security Review Commission, One Hundred Fourteenth Congress Second Session" (Washington, D.C.: U.S. Government Publishing Office, 2016), 263.

32. Ibid., 266.

33. Office of the Secretary of Defense, "Annual Report to Congress: Military and Security Developments Involving the People's Republic of China 2016" (2016): 108.

34. Ibid., 22.

35. Avery Goldstein, "First Things First: The Pressing Danger of Crisis Instability in U.S.-China Relations," *International Security* 37, no. 4 (2013): 56–57, 69–73.

36. Ji, "Dealing with the Malacca Dilemma: China's Effort to Protect its Energy Supply," *Strategic Analysis*, 472–473.

37. Jacqueline Newmyer, "Chinese Energy Security and the Chinese Regime," in *Energy Security and Global Politics: The Militarization of Resource Management*, Daniel Moran and James A. Russell eds. (New York, NY: Routledge, 2009), 203.

38. Pak K. Lee, China's Quest for Oil Security: Oil (Wars) in the Pipeline?" *The Pacific Review* 18, no. 2 (2005): 281–289.

39. James M. Griffin, "Petro-Nationalism: The Futile Search for Oil Security," *The Energy Journal* 36, no. 1 (2015); Gholz and Press, "Protecting 'The Prize': Oil and the U.S. National Interest," *Security Studies*, 457–463.

40. Andrews-Speed and Dannreuther, *China, Oil and Global Politics*, 82.

41. Cristiano A. Ristuccia, "1935 Sanctions in Italy: Would Coal and Crude Oil Have Made a Difference?" Discussion Papers in Economic and Social History, Oxford University, March, 1997, http://www.nuffield.ox.ac.uk/economics/history/paper14/14paper.pdf (accessed August 4, 2016).

42. Yergin, *The Prize: The Epic Quest for Oil, Money, and Power*, 332.

43. Daniel Moran, "The Battlefield and the Marketplace: Two Cautionary Tales," in *Energy Security and Global Politics: The Militarization of Resource Management*, Daniel Moran and James A. Russell eds. (New York, NY: Routledge, 2009), 30–31.

44. The oil import cutoff was actually the result of Japan's inability to access frozen, dollar-denominated assets in the United States, which were needed in order to make petroleum purchases. The actual inability of Japan to import oil from the United States was opposite President Roosevelt's wishes, who stated consistently that he did not wish to cut off Japan's oil supply.

45. Moran and Russell, "The Battlefield," *Energy Security and Global Politics: The Militarization of Resource Management*, 27.

46. Bruce Blair, Chen Yali, and Eric Hagt, "The Oil Weapon: Myth of China's Vulnerability," *China Security* 3 (2006): 40.

47. Kai He, *China's Crisis Behavior: Political Survival and Foreign Policy After the Cold War* (Cambridge, U.K.: Cambridge University Press, 2016), 49–55.

48. Patrick E. Tyler, "No Chemical Arms Aboard China Ship," *The New York Times*, September 6, 1993, http://www.nytimes.com/1993/09/06/world/no-chemical-arms-aboard-china-ship.html (accessed September 8, 2016).

49. Shu G. Zhang, *Economic Cold War: America's Embargo Against China and the Sino-Soviet Alliance, 1949–1963* (Stanford, CA: Stanford University Press, 2001), 17–49, especially 32–33.

50. Blair, Yali, and Hagt, "The Oil Weapon: Myth of China's Vulnerability," *China Security*, 39; The United States even had a plan to destroy Saudi Arabia's oil infrastructure during the Cold War if deterrence failed against the Soviet Union, simply to deny them access and control to such a valuable resource base.

51. Ibid.

52. Marcus Hand, "Malacca Strait Traffic Hits an All Time High in 2014, VLCCs and Dry Bulk Lead Growth," *Seatrade Maritime News*, February 27, 2015, http://www.seatrade-maritime.com/news/asia/malacca-strait-traffic-hits-an-all-time-high-in-2014-vlccs-and-dry-bulk-lead-growth.html (accessed October 28, 2016).

53. Thomas M. Kane, *Chinese Grand Strategy and Maritime Power* (London, U.K.: Frank Cass Publishers, 2002), 62–64, 139–145.

54. Avery Goldstein, "Parsing China's Rise: International Circumstances and National Attributes," in *China's Ascent: Power, Security, and the Future of International Politics*, Robert S. Ross and Zhu Feng, eds. (Ithaca, N.Y.: Cornell University Press, 2008), 82–83.

55. Khurana, "China's 'String of Pearls' in the Indian Ocean and Its Security Implications," *Strategic Analysis*, 6–8.

56. U.S.-China Economic and Security Review Commission, "2016 Report to Congress of the U.S.-China Economic and Security Review Commission, One Hundred Fourteenth Congress Second Session," November 2016, Washington, D.C.: U.S. Government Publishing Office 2016), 218–219.

57. François Dubé, "China's Experiment in Djibouti," October 5, 2016, *The Diplomat*, http://thediplomat.com/2016/10/chinas-experiment-in-djibouti/ (accessed September 5, 2016).

58. Assaf Orion, "The Dragon's Tail at the Horn of Africa: Chinese Military Logistics Facility in Djibouti," The Institute for National Security Studies, Insight No. 791 (2016).

59. Andrew S. Erickson and Austin M. Strange, *Six Years at Sea . . . and Counting: Gulf of Aden Anti-Piracy and China's Maritime Commons Presence* (Washington, D.C.: The Jamestown Foundation, 2015).

60. "MND Admits Strategic Value of Spratly Airstrip," *Taipei Times*, January 6, 2006, http://www.taipeitimes.com/News/taiwan/archives/2006/01/06/2003287638 (accessed September 29, 2016).

61. Jin Liangxiang, "Energy First: China and the Middle East," *Middle East Quarterly* 12, no. 2 (2005).

62. Toshi Yoshihara and Richard Sokolsky, "The United States and China in the Persian Gulf: Challenges and Opportunities," *Fletcher Forum of World Affairs*, 26, no. 1 (2002): 67–69.

63. Toshi Yoshihara and Richard Sokolsky, "The United States and China in the Persian Gulf: Challenges and Opportunities," *Fletcher Forum of World Affairs*, 26, no. 1 (2002): 66.

64. Kenneth N. Waltz, *Theory of International Politics* (Reading, MA: Addison-Wesley Publishing Company, 1979), 76–77.

65. Blair, Yali, and Hagt, "The Oil Weapon: Myth of China's Vulnerability," *China Security*, 41–43.

66. Charles L. Glaser, *Rational Theory of International Politics: The Logic of Competition and Cooperation* (Princeton, NJ: Princeton University Press, 2010), 280–281.

67. Yergin, *The Prize: The Epic Quest for Oil, Money, and Power*, 316–319.

68. Ibid., 334.

69. Charles L. Glaser, "How Oil Influences U.S. National Security," *International Security* 38, no. 2 (2013): 122.

70. Ibid.,131–142.

71. Colin Dueck, *The Obama Doctrine: American Grand Strategy Today* (New York, NY: Oxford University Press, 2015), 101.

Chapter Seven

Conclusion

A BRIEF VIEW OF ENERGY SECURITY

States necessarily prepare either for war, meaning open, kinetic conflict in order to secure energy supply lines, or they prepare for containment and sanctions. Mixing these two, along with the third, current, natural state of the oil market is folly and will conflate any analysis or understanding when attempting to determine how states secure their sources of energy. This is a future-oriented enterprise where states must prepare for political scenarios that are not conducive to the optimal pricing and delivery of petroleum assets, under multiple circumstances, including kinetic conflict.

Energy security is an enduring conflict, fought by all species. It is the fundamental conflict of the natural world. From the smallest species to the largest, all strive for energy security daily, whether through food consumption or photosynthesis, and embark on a struggle to gather, economize, protect, and conserve sufficient amounts of energy at an affordable cost, whether demarcated monetarily or in the level of bodily risk. Looking at the span of human civilization this is certainly true as confidence surrounding food security was the first critical form of energy security. These concerns were eventually scaled up in the form of agriculture to support growing political units, where a sufficiently nourished population was needed to translate human energy to productive energy for use in the broader economy, and in many cases, for military power.

A favored strategy, then as now, has been to cut off this energy source by destroying sources of sustenance: burning crops, destroying granaries and other food stores, sieges, and slaughtering livestock all to starve out an enemy or to deprive of them of their most fundamental source of strength. Later, in addition to human-based energy, horse-based energy became incredibly important for military power, requiring even more food sources to power this military weapon that would dominate the battlefield for nearly six millennia.

In the 18th century, other forms of energy and mechanical power began to take root. With the Industrial Revolution the proliferation of many new technologies proceeded, among them, was the steam engine and the consequent diffusion of this new form of energy production into industry, complementing and enhancing human-based energy itself, and in some cases, beginning to supplant it entirely. By this time, coal had become a vital source of energy, but its reign would not last long. Finally, the 20th century introduces yet another radical shift in energy use, as more facets of society and the military were mechanized, increasing efficiency, output, and lethality to untold heights as states ported over combustion technology to military assets, which would begin to have a meaningful impact in World War One.

This is a shift that would impact not only the military, heralding naval advancements along with the eventual use of air power, but motorized transportation, with roads strung out across countries like veins through a human body, became deeply ingrained and integral to our societies, and our economies. Oil would fuel this shift and would become the lifeblood of economies and militaries, utterly vital to the survival of both, and the key to their success and efficacy. Just as previous societies were forced to secure their granaries and food stores as the core energy stores of the day, so today states must do the same, on a grander scale, with petroleum, while attempting to prepare for a murky future.

The Research

This analysis of this monograph primarily utilized a focused, comparative case study approach, mixed with several data driven aspects, and ultimately a principal components analysis (PCA) that was used to create an "Oil Security Rating" (OSR) system for added clarity and insights. This informed the comparative case study approach, resulting in an intuitive study, illuminating the key questions posed earlier.

Before setting out to answer these questions, however, the concept of grand strategy as a theoretical referent was introduced and thoroughly explored. Although at times difficult to grasp as a coherent concept due to its fluidity, a grand strategy is necessary for any state wishing to survive over the long term and is neglected only at the greatest peril. Any contest for survival can be lost at the outset with a poorly developed grand strategy that does not properly utilize, or account for, all forms of statecraft, including not just military, but also economic and political, and in the context of this work, oil. Focusing only on the military aspects of grand strategy constrains and confuses, robbing the state of the necessary synergies for coherent and cohesive national policies that, when properly coordinated, can be adroitly employed to appropriate effect. When fighting for survival, why focus on only one mean to that end, when there are multiple approaches that can be used?

Despite the inherent difficulties present concerning grand strategic scope, it became understood in this work to entail the "national reconciliation of security related means and ends, consistent with all available resources to the state, under the constraints of an indeterminate future." It is the state's answer to the question of its long-term viability as a secure, independent, sovereign, political entity, engaging all forms of power, influence, leverage, and purpose at its disposal. At its core, it accounts for the temporal and relative threat environment, posing any number of risks to the state.

An understanding of energy security presents its own difficulties. Again, this is a relative concept based on the specific threat environment to a state, the structure of the economy, and even the dominant forms of fuel used throughout the state. In restricting the scope of this research to petroleum, it was more methodologically pragmatic, and allows for an in-depth examination of the global, 20th-century focal point for energy security. The oil market itself is highly developed and interconnected, and depending on crude blend, results in a "global" price for oil. This means, for instance, Iceland, a country notorious for its reliance on renewable sources of energy, will still pay the same global rate for oil imports, regardless of the amount of geothermal energy generated and used by the local population and industry. When it comes to affordability, the market is highly dependent on international politics and the state of the oil industry in general.

Energy security, as Yergin put it, can seem vague, and difficult to pin down. And, it is much more complex than usually defined, as simply being, "affordable access to reliable supplies." Just as with grand strategy, it is no use to limit the way a state pursues something as crucial as the security of its energy supplies, the core lifeblood of any economy. A commodity such as oil is so vital, without it, all modern equipment and technology would cease to operate, from commercial vehicles and military aircraft, to medical equipment and the lights in a household. All is dependent on this strategic resource and should be treated and equipped as such. And the threats have only expanded, now including sophisticated attacks on the technological infrastructure of oil and gas companies. It should also be noted that the frequently trotted out objective of energy independence is illusory and unviable, and even negates important aspects of energy security, specifically diversification. In general, an understanding of energy security is akin to that of grand strategy, where a means-end chain is necessarily attached to feasible energy objectives consistent with the specific threats presented to the state, in order to maintain enduring, broadly resilient (including in multiple political scenarios), and affordable energy supplies. With the United States, the oil security stakes are even wider, considering its political and economic stake in the actual global oil market itself, as a coordination and supply mechanism, replicated as a source of supply for numerous allies around the world. This process is also highly dependent on the current global political scenario in which these states operate. For instance, a state operating in a non-contentious political environment will have more options and is more able to rely on sources for petroleum, like the market, without fear. But, given the temporal dimension of energy security, a state must be prepared for worsening political conditions, and perhaps even war, where these varying scenarios necessarily produce different conditions under which states operate and pursue their objectives.

In terms of oil security, the United States has occupied an enviable position for many decades, especially for a state with such massive demand requirements. It has an explicit strategy to militarily intercede on the Arabian Peninsula and maintains command of the commons with the world's most capable, forward deployable, naval force. The strategy of the U.S. is also global and expansive, with strong stakes in international markets to the benefit of militarily weaker allies without access to domestic oil sources or the capabilities to secure foreign sources. Oil is explicitly and demonstrably a key part of U.S. grand strategy, meaning the two are essentially fused in objectives and approach.

Similarly, China has elevated oil concerns to the top of its own agenda and did so rather quickly after the country became a net importer of oil in 1993, for the first time in over three decades. This was a pivotal, watershed moment for China, with oil company executives and government officials appearing on television in tears, overwrought with shame after failing to domestically provide what was required for the country to sufficiently function and grow. Despite the rhetorical autarky, no country is capable of providing for 1.3 billion people in an advancing, growing economy based on purely domestic sources. This is simply impossible for any large oil consuming state, even the United States including with additional supplies from its recent tight oil and gas flood. Just as oil is a primary concern for the United States, so it is with China, where overseas expansion, especially through the Indian Ocean, appears to be directly related not just to trade routes, but oil routes. The "String of Pearls" appears to be alive and well.

After analyzing the "loose" data not attached to the OSR, and the OSR itself, some of these concepts become much clearer. Perhaps the most intriguing results were the final OSR scores themselves, which demonstrate the overall oil security approach of the United States to be dominant over the entire study period, while China is clearly, rapidly "catching up," and moving towards convergence with the United States. Both countries are quite conscious of their oil security compared to the other 28 countries in the study, even, surprisingly, Japan. Looking again at figure 6.2, China is clearly moving up and away from the other top importers in the study, mirroring Japan's conspicuous drop. For the overall scores, the United States averaged 6.44 throughout the study while China averaged 2.58, with the group average at 1.05. Perhaps fueling further concern is the noticeable increase in the OSR for China in contrast to the decrease for the United States over the past ten years. Although the drop for the U.S. is not entirely outside the 22-year average, adjustments may be required if the trend continues.

Other key metrics, for better or worse, also demonstrate convergence between the two countries. Both production-to-reserve and consumption-to-reserve ratios demonstrate China to be in a better position than the U.S., and despite China's reputation as being notoriously energy inefficient, it is not as energy intensive as once thought, consistently raising GDP output per unit of energy consumed, slowly closing the gap with the United States. As China continues to encourage growth in renewables and clean energy, this should continue to rise. China has also been able to restrict the growth of oil as a component of its primary energy consumption, and unexpectedly scored better than the United States, most likely due to the heavy American reliance on Canada and new domestic sources resulting from the tight oil boom. Per-barrel costs, refining, and return on average capital employed scores also demonstrate similar convergence.

Both states have parallel import dependency after China closed that gap over the past few years, indicating a much higher dependence on overseas oil for China despite U.S. moderation and slight decrease, and nearly identical trajectories indicated concerning oil value as a component of GDP. Oil price volatility is also extremely similar, indicating no major differences in price swings in the per-barrel dollar costs between both countries.

The U.S. however, maintains large leads in other key areas, namely with MIT's economic complexity scores signifying the highly diverse, technologically advanced, and industrially competitive American economy, which continues to significantly outperform what China has on offer, although here the gap is also slowly closing. Most expectedly, the United States scores significantly higher than China, and the other countries in the study, on the power measure, although one can observe notable increases in Chinese ratings here as well. As a reminder, this indicator measures not just direct power, but encompasses the entirety of state power, including latent measures such as the economy and population size. This was noteworthy in a study on oil security, as previous studies had simply not included such measures, or marginalized the importance of power in securing overseas supplies.

Questions Covered in this Monograph

Specifically, early in chapter 1, the following questions were posed: How do the United States and China approach the issue of oil security? Where have their approaches converged or diverged? And, do their respective approaches pose a threat to each other's oil security needs? Ultimately, it was stated this research aims at determining if and how both states' approaches created an atmosphere whereby they affect or even prevent acceptable levels oil security. And, if so, what would this imply for greater management of international life?

It was determined that due to their large size and oil requirements, both the United States and China deploy highly complex and diverse strategies in order to secure their respective oil supplies. These are multifaceted efforts designed to create and protect multiple diverse avenues to achieve optimal supply security. On many of the indicators, referenced earlier, China has made significant gains in security, especially in terms of diversification, which was given the highest weighting by the results of principal components analysis displayed in chapter 6. In recent years, China has even surpassed the U.S. diversification score due to American increases in domestic supply concentration resulting from the North American tight oil boom. Broader economic and technological advancement which catalyze new energy technologies and general state power are two more important measures where China is behind but has gained significant ground. The other indicators, data, and comparisons gleaned many other insights as well.

Chinese convergence with the United States is clearly revealed on multiple independent indicators, other data presented, and the final OSR scores. China has been able to learn much from the United States and through observation of global events pertaining to weaknesses in the oil supply chain. For instance, even though China has yet to experience any significant oil supply shocks, it has embarked on a multi-year effort to construct a potent strategic petroleum reserve, filling available capacity during times of low pricing. This is clearly a learned practice from the experience of the United States (and The Netherlands) in 1973, and the subsequent construction and earmarking of strategic reserves in OECD countries, along with the concomitant formation of the International Energy Agency. There is convergence in many areas including the militarization of supply lines and increasing technological proficiency in the energy sector. There is also convergence in some negative areas including increases in overseas supply dependency and a concentration in overseas supply centering on the Middle East, given the region's proximity and large reserves.

Over the course of the study, the oil security gains made by China were not necessarily encroaching on the security, or directly on the oil security, of the United States. But, judging by the model, outside indicators, and the comparison conducted throughout this work, the United States will eventually enter a critical stage with the maritime supply routes running from the Middle East, where it has overlapping core interests with China. As time goes on, this maritime region will become more critical and militarized, as is already starting to occur, projecting insecurity and strategic vulnerability across the Indian Ocean to the South China Sea.

Final Thoughts

Throughout this analysis, many of the oil security approaches of both states were not mutually exclusive, and in many cases, were complementary. For instance, China's exploration and exploitation of new sources of oil only adds to global supply, in turn facilitating lower prices and increasing market flexibility. But, the harmonizing benefits end when political rivalry grows between the two powers, and the view of oil quickly becomes one not of arteries to keep flowing, but arteries to cut for political, economic, or military gain, in a competition between two serious opponents. To that end, it was necessary that this research had contended, counter to arguments made by Gholz and Press[1] and Andrews-Speed,[2] that market-based, "cost-effective" approaches to energy security are not the key ways to conceive of oil security in the cases of the United States and China. While eminently important, there are still other factors to consider, and these states cannot be taken out of their unique context, especially with Chinese perceptions that relations with the U.S. will deteriorate, presaging conditions where individual relationships, political comradery, and military assets will matter a great deal. Consideration of the future state of politics is imperative.

The expansive nature of American grand strategy, in particular its enduring dominance of the global commons, and the Persian Gulf, is in direct conflict with oil supplies directed through China's sea lines of communication. Growing desire and proficiency as demonstrated in this study to close capability gaps on the part of the Chinese mixed with SLOCs connected to the South China Sea issue, come together in a potentially toxic mix. This presents many difficulties, as discussed in chapter 6, but especially in the non-exclusivity of oil-related SLOCs that necessarily must be occupied by both powers at the same time in order to provide security, creating frictional overlap, especially given China's proclivity to prepare for a point when containment is a political reality. When it comes to the maritime oil routes, there are too many significant points of contention and as China has consistently built up its oil security capabilities, one can only begin to expect a confrontation over vital supplies.

That is perhaps one of the most pertinent issues in light of a holistic view of this study, as within the military dimension, there is a focus on maneuvering over a key element that can be used as a form of strategic coercion, or at least something with the perceived ability to be used successfully for strategic coercion. As China's "comprehensive" power has grown over the last thirty years, so too has its multiple levers of power which gives it multiple symmetric and asymmetric points of leverage to utilize during, or leading up to a conflict. This of course leads to counter-coercion capabilities to be deployed against the United States and its allies in such a conflict. Although the power relationship between the two is considerably wide, it is important to recognize China does have a growing array of political, economic, and military levers to deploy if needed, but critically it does not have a credible threat to counter American naval operations in the Indian Ocean, promoting a key area of vulnerability that is still years off from being rectified, creating a major area of perpetual insecurity.

These problems become more acute as political conditions worsen. When taken as a unified component of grand strategy, oil security is intertwined and securitized by both states at high levels. As contention arises politically into the second zone outlined in chapter 2, many of these issues intersect or have the potential to be used as levers against one another, particularly given the disproportionate power relationship between the U.S. and China. This is fundamentally the most flawed part of previous works on energy security, and oil security in particular. If one does not consider changes in political scenarios in which states operate and are ultimately constrained by, then analyses will be inaccurate. Under normal conditions, now, and during the study period, there is not much in the way of overlap between the United States and China in terms of securing their oil supply; however, this all changes as political conflict escalates, and further convergence occurs between both states in their security methods. If tensions escalate, supply lines will be constrained and targeted. China will no longer be able to rely as heavily on the market and will need to fall back on political allies for "sanctions resistant" oil supplies, and security dilemmas (both traditional and oil-based) are enhanced and brought to the fore. China is no longer part of the global market but a bifurcated market reliant on political allies and those that are well enough integrated and dependent on China for exports, income, and investments.

States necessarily prepare either for war, meaning open, kinetic conflict in order to secure energy supply lines, or they prepare for containment and sanctions. Mixing these two, along with the third, current, natural state of the oil market is folly and will conflate any analysis or understanding when attempting to determine how states secure their sources of energy. This is a future-oriented enterprise where states must prepare for political scenarios that are not conducive for the optimal pricing and delivery of petroleum assets, under multiple circumstances, including kinetic conflict.

For instance, one can consider the indicators production-to-reserves and consumption-to-reserves, when looking at the long-term domestic availability of oil reserves in terms of producing assets located in-state, and the other long-term domestic availability of oil reserves in terms of local consumption. Both indicators tell us something different about the longevity of reserves on hand within the state in question, but have varying importance whether a state has free, unabated access to global markets, or is being "contained" in some manner, offering potential restrictions to that supply. In this case, domestic, fully controllable resources jump in importance as the political scenario worsens, and a state is required to fall back on its most politically reliable sources of oil. Power will, of course, also have a heightened status in these more implacable political scenarios as both hard and soft power have roles to play, along with political power, especially that derived from economic dependence. This delineation of potential future scenarios is important to include in analyses about oil security, otherwise the analyst will be prone to miss crucial aspects of the security apparatus. One must appreciate these are approaches to counter, not necessarily as they exist currently, but to instead prepare for what is to come. Having secure supply lines direct to China allows for future relief of political pressure should it be exerted through sanctions or containment from the United States and its allies. If China was not preparing its energy supply lines, then it would simply model its security exactly like the United States and rely on the market with a strong naval force acting as guarantor to patrol the commons and ensure the flow of oil.

Finally, it should also be noted, at the time of this writing, the world is awash in inexpensive oil. This can certainly ameliorate some of the negative impacts and irritants to the U.S.-Chinese energy relationship and may reduce the possibility for conflict based on oil supplies. However, two items should be noted. First, oil prices mostly likely will not stay low for an extended period. Oil price cycles have had more than a century to play out, with plentiful examples of high and low pricing periods, with multiple peaks and troughs. And, as noted in the introductory chapter, some companies are even beginning to position for a recovery based on drastically reduced capital investment in the sector. Additionally, decline rates of tight oil wells have been particularly high, conveying a degree of uncertainty as to how long, and how much, these wells will ultimately produce,[3] even if producers have developed some techniques to mitigate this problem.[4] Second, and perhaps more important, is the irrelevance of price if the political relationship significantly deteriorates between the two countries, and if China is forced to rely on more direct means to secure its oil supplies. Despite the pessimistic outlook, there remain many avenues for a cooperative relationship between the United States and China when it comes to oil, assuming amicable political relations are maintained. Joint patrols of the SLOCs, an accommodating political settlement between the various parties in the South China Sea dispute, and China's assistance as an intermediary in political disputes, not to mention active exploitation of new resources by Chinese NOCs, adding liquidity to the global supply of oil, are all positive outcomes of such a relationship. All these cooperative measures are possible, especially in a low-price environment where oil-related tensions are necessarily reduced. Furthermore, U.S. and Chinese grand strategy need not clash in the future given the joint desire of both states for economic growth and limited appetite for any type of armed conflict. However, none of these issues discount the variability of possibility over the long term, where worst-case scenarios must be taken seriously.

This book set out to understand the dynamics of two countries that have had enormous demands and impacts on the global supply of oil. The United States, which has been concerned with oil supply security since the beginning of the 20th century, is responsible for countless innovations in exploration, extraction, and refining, as well as developing the necessary approaches to securing this vital resource, including the use of ample military power. This approach has largely been successful. Comparatively, China, a relative newcomer to global oil supply concerns, not overly concerned or reliant on oil until the late 20th century, and with no real background in dealing with massive demand issues or overseas supplies, has seemingly at times, been "crossing the river by feeling the stones," trying new approaches, discarding those that fail, and retaining those that succeed. In both cases, there is new understanding of these oil security approaches and how they may serve to create, or abate, conflict in the future. Grand strategy and oil security are both complex, future oriented enterprises: as with many theoretical approaches in international relations, the shadow of the future looms large.

NOTES

1. Gholz and Press, "Protecting 'The Prize:' Oil and the U.S. National Interest," *Security Studies*, 453–485.

2. Philip Andrews-Speed, "Do Overseas Investments by National Oil Companies Enhance Energy Security at Home? A View from Asia," in *Oil and Gas for Asia: Geopolitical Implications of Asia's Rising Demand*, edited by Philip Andrews-Speed, Mikkal E. Herberg, Tomoko Hosoe, John V. Mitchell, and Zha Daojiong, NBR Special Report no. 41, 2012.

3. Henrik Wachtmeister, Linnea Lund, Kjell Aleklett, and Mikael Höök, "Production Decline Curves of Tight Oil Wells in Eagle Ford Shale," *Natural Resources Research* (2017): 1–15.

4. Ernest Scheyder and Terry Wade, "U.S. Shale Oil's Achilles Heel Shows Signs of Mending," Reuters, July 1, 2016, http://www.reuters.com/article/us-usa-shale-declinerates-idUSKCN0ZH3RQ (accessed April 10, 2017).

Bibliography

Acemoglu, Daron, and James A. Robinson. *Why Nations Fail: The Origins of Power, Prosperity, and Poverty*. New York, NY: Crown Publishing, 2012.

Achen, Christopher H., and Duncan Snidal. "Rational Deterrence Theory and Comparative Case Studies." *World Politics* 41, no. 2 (1989): 143–169.

Aizhu, Chen, and Florence Tan. "China Ramps Up Crude Buying, Reserves Purchases Far Ahead of Schedule," Reuters, November 26, 2014. http://www.reuters.com/article/us-china-oil-stockpiles-idUSKCN0JA0SN20141127.

Aleklett, Kjell, and Colin J. Campbell. "The Peak and Decline of World Oil and Gas Production." *Minerals & Energy* 18, no. 1 (2003): 5–20.

Alves, Ana C. "Chinese Economic Statecraft: A Comparative Study of China's Oil-backed Loans in Angola and Brazil." *Journal of Current Chinese Affairs* 42, no. 1 (2013): 99–130.

Anderson, Irvine H. Jr. "The 1941 De Facto Embargo on Oil to Japan: A Bureaucratic Reflex." *Pacific Historical Review* 44, no. 2 (1975): 201–231.

———. *The Standard-Vacuum Oil Company and United States East Asian Policy, 1933–1941*. Princeton, NJ: Princeton University Press, 1975.

Andrews-Speed, Philip, and Roland Dannreuther. *China, Oil and Global Politics*. New York, NY: Routledge, 2011.

Andrews-Speed, Philip. "Do Overseas Investments by National Oil Companies Enhance Energy Security at Home? A View from Asia." In *Oil and Gas for Asia: Geopolitical Implications of Asia's Rising Demand,* Edited by Philip Andrews-Speed, Mikkal E. Herberg, Tomoko Hosoe, John V. Mitchell, and Zha Daojiong. NBR Special Report no. 41, 2012.

Argus Media. "Argus Sour Crude Index (ASCI), 2015, Methodology and Specifications Guide." http://www.argusmedia.com/methodology-and-reference/.

Art, Robert J. "To What Ends Military Power?" *International Security* 4, no. 4 (1980): 3–35.

———. *A Grand Strategy for America*. Ithaca, NY: Cornell University Press, 2003.

―――. *America's Grand Strategy and World Politics*. New York, NY: Routledge, 2009.

Badea, Anca C. "Energy Security Indicators." European Commission Joint Research Centre, Institute for Energy Security Unit 2010. http://www.jrc.ec.europa.eu/.

Beaufre, André. *Introduction à la Stratégie*. Paris: Armand Colin, 1963. In *Strategy: The Logic of War and Peace*, by Edward Luttwak. Cambridge, MA: Harvard University Press, 2003.

Bentley, R.W. "Global Oil and Gas Depletion: An Overview." *Energy Policy* 30, no. 3 (2002): 189–205.

Bhattacharya, Abheek. "China's Petroleum Reserve Builds Shaky Floor for Oil." *Wall Street Journal*, September 3, 2014. http://www.wsj.com/articles/chinas-petro leum-reserve-builds-shaky-floor-for-oil-heard-on-the-street-1409755068.

Bijian, Zheng. "China's 'Peaceful Rise' to Great Power Status." *Foreign Affairs* 84, 5 (2005): 18–24.

Birol, Fatih. "World Energy Outlook 2008." International Energy Agency. http://www.worldenergyoutlook.org/media/weowebsite/2008-1994/weo2008.pdf.

Black, Brian C. "Oil for Living: Petroleum and American Conspicuous Consumption." *Journal of American History* 99, no. 1 (2012): 40–50.

Blackwill, Robert D., and Ashley J. Tellis. "Council Special Report No. 72: Revising U.S. Grand Strategy Toward China." Council on Foreign Relations, April 2015. http://carnegieendowment.org/files/Tellis_Blackwill.pdf.

Blair, Bruce, Chen Yali, and Eric Hagt. "The Oil Weapon: Myth of China's Vulnerability." *China Security* 3 (2006): 32–63.

Blazevic, Jason J. "Defensive Realism in the Indian Ocean: Oil, Sea Lanes, and the Security Dilemma." *China Security* 5, no. 3 (2009): 59–71.

Bourne, James. "Petrodollars: China Builds Up its Oil Tanker Fleet." *Platts Oilgram News*, August 18, 2014, blogs.platts.com/2014/08/18/china-oil-tankers/.

BP. "Statistical Review 2014: Data Workbook." http://www.bp.com/en/global/corpo rate/energy-economics/statistical-review-of-world-energy/downloads.html.

Brands, Hal. *What Good is Grand Strategy? Power and Purpose in American Statecraft from Harry S. Truman to George W. Bush*. Ithaca, NY: Cornell University Press, 2014.

Bronson, Rachel. *Thicker Than Oil: America's Uneasy Partnership with Saudi Arabia*. New York, NY: Oxford University Press, 2006.

Bussert, James C., and Bruce A. Elleman. *People's Liberation Army Navy: Combat Systems Technology 1949–2010*. Annapolis, MD: Naval Institute Press, 2011.

Buszynski, Leszek. "The South China Sea: Oil, Maritime Claims, and U.S.-China Strategic Rivalry." *Washington Quarterly* 35, no. 2 (2012): 139–156.

Campbell, Colin J., and Jean H. Laherrère. "The End of Cheap Oil." *Scientific American*, 1998. https://www.scientificamerican.com/article/the-end-of-cheap-oil/#.

Center for Energy Economics (The University of Texas at Austin) and PA Government Services Inc. for USAID New Delhi. "USAID Energy Security Quarterly." USAID South Asia Regional Initiative for Energy, USAID SARI/Energy, January 2008. http://www.beg.utexas.edu/energyecon/ESQ1/ESQ1_w/ESQ1updateFeb06.pdf.

Chang, Amy. "Indigenous Weapons Development in China's Military Modernization." U.S.-China Economic and Security Review Commission, 2012, Staff Research Report. https://www.uscc.gov/sites/default/files/Research/China-Indige nous-Military-Developments-Final-Draft-03-April2012.pdf.

Chang, Chin-Lung. "A Measure of National Power." Fo-guang University, Taiwan.

Change, Ssu-li, and Yen-yin Chen. "The Analysis of Oil Supply Security and Diversification Policy in Taiwan—A Shannon-Weiner Index Approach." National Taipei University, Institute of Natural Resource Management.

Chen, Nai-Ruenn, and Walter Galenson. *The Chinese Economy Under Maoism*. New Jersey: Aldine Transaction, A Division of Transaction Publishers, 2011.

Cheng, Joseph Y. S. "A Chinese View of China's Energy Security." *Journal of Contemporary China* 17, no. 55 (2008): 297–317.

China Economic and Industry Database, CEIC Data, https://www.ceicdata.com/en.

China Vitae Reference Library. www.chinavitae.com/library.

China Vitae. "Zhang Gaoli." http://www.chinavitae.com/biography/Zhang_Gaoli.

———. "Zhou Yongkang." http://www.chinavitae.com/biography/Zhou_Yongkang.

Christensen, Thomas J. "China." In *Strategic Asia 2001–2002: Power and Purpose*, edited by Richard J. Ellings and Aaron L. Friedberg, 27–70. Seattle, WA: National Bureau of Asian Research, 2001.

———. "Chinese Realpolitik: Reading Beijing's Worldview." *Foreign Affairs* 75, no. 5 (1996): 37–52.

———. "Posing Problems Without Catching Up: China's Rise and Challenges for U.S. Security Policy." *International Security* 25, no. 4 (2001): 5–40.

———. *The China Challenge: Shaping the Choices of a Rising Power*. New York, NY: W. W. Norton and Company Inc., 2015.

Clausewitz, Carl von, edited and translated by Michael Howard and Peter Paret. *On War*. Princeton, New Jersey: Princeton University Press, 1984.

Clayton, Blake, and Michael Levi. "The Surprising Sources of Oil's Influence." *Survival* 54, no. 6 (2012): 107–122.

Clifford, Catherine. "Oil's Record High, One Year Later." Cable News Network, July 2, 2009. http://money.cnn.com/2009/07/02/markets/year_oil/index.htm.

Clinch, Matt. "Oil CEO Sees 'Significant' Impact on Capacity in the Coming Years." *Consumer News and Business Channel (CNBC)*, January 20, 2017. http://www .cnbc.com/2017/01/20/oil-ceo-sees-significant-impact-on-capacity-in-the-coming -years.html.

Cline, Ray S. *The Power of Nations in the 1990s: A Strategic Assessment*. Lanham, MD: University Press of America, 1994.

Cohen, Gail, Frederick Joutz, and Prakash Loungani. "Measuring Energy Security: Trends in the Diversification of Oil and Gas Supplies." International Monetary Fund, Working Paper 11/39 2011). https://www.imf.org/external/pubs/ft/wp/2011/ wp1139.pdf.

Cooney, Kevin J., and Yoichiro Sato, editors. *The Rise of China and International Security: America and Asia Respond*. New York, NY: Routledge, 2009.

Coq, Chloé Le, and Elena Paltseva. "Measuring the Security of External Energy Supply in the European Union." *Energy Policy* 37 (2009): 4474–4481.

Cordesman, Anthony H., and Nawaf E. Obaid. *National Security in Saudi Arabia: Threats, Responses, and Challenges.* Westport, CT: Praeger Security International, 2005.

Davis, Paul K. *Observations on the Rapid Deployment Joint Task Force: Origins, Direction, and Mission.* Santa Monica, CA: RAND Corporation, 1982.

Deutch, John, and James R. Schlesinger. "National Security Consequences of U.S. Oil Dependency." Council on Foreign Relations, Independent Task Force Report No. 58, 2006.

Deutch, John, James Schlesinger, and David Victor. *National Security Consequences of U.S. Oil Dependency.* Council on Foreign Relations, Independent Task Force Report No. 58, 2006. http://www.cfr.org/oil/national-security-consequences-us -oil-dependency/p11683.

Dorian, James. *Minerals, Energy, and Economic Development in China.* Oxford: Oxford University Press, 1994.

Down, Erica S. "Looking West: China and Central Asia." Testimony before the U.S.-China Economic and Security Review Commission, March 18, 2015. http://www .uscc.gov/sites/default/files/Downs%20Testimony_031815.pdf.

———. "Business Interest Groups in Chinese Politics: The Case of the Oil Companies." In *China's Changing Political Landscape: Prospects for Democracy.* Edited by Cheng Li, 121–141. Washington D.C.: Brookings Institution Press, 2008.

———. "Mission Mostly Accomplished: China's Energy Trade and Investment Along the Silk Road Economic Belt." *China Brief* 15, no. 6 (2015).

———. "The Chinese Energy Security Debate." *China Quarterly* 177 (2004): 21–41.

Downs, Erica S., and Michal Meidan. *Business and Politics in China: The Oil Executive Reshuffle of 2011. China Security* 19 (2011): 3–21.

Dreyer, June T. *China's Political System: Modernization and Tradition,* Ninth Edition. New York, NY: Routledge, 2016.

Dubé, François. "China's Experiment in Djibouti." *The Diplomat,* October 5, 2016. http://thediplomat.com/2016/10/chinas-experiment-in-djibouti/.

Dueck, Colin. *Reluctant Crusaders: Power, Culture, and Change in American Grand Strategy.* Princeton, NJ: Princeton University Press, 2006.

———. *The Obama Doctrine: American Grand Strategy Today.* New York, NY: Oxford University Press, 2015.

Earl, Edward M., editor. *Makers of Modern Strategy.* Princeton: Princeton University Press, 1971.

Elkind, Jonathan. "Energy Security: Call for a Broader Agenda." In *Energy Security: Economics, Politics, Strategies, and Implications.* Edited by Carlos Pascual and Jonathan Elkind, 119–148. Washington D.C.: Brookings Institution Press, 2010.

Elton, Edwin J., Martin J. Gruber, Stephen J. Brown, and William N. Goetzmann. *Modern Portfolio Theory and Investment Analysis,* 8th ed. Wiley Publishing, 2009.

Energy Information Administration. "International Energy Statistics." http://www .eia.gov/cfapps/ipdbproject/IEDIndex3.cfm.

———. What Drives Crude Oil Prices? Supply OPEC. http://www.eia.gov/finance/ markets/supply-opec.cfm.

Energy Information Agency. "Crude Oil Proved Reserves 2014." International Energy Statistics. www.eia.gov.

Erickson, Andrew S., "China's Modernization of Its Naval and Air Power Capabilities." In *Strategic Asia 2012–13: China's Military Challenge*, edited by Ashley J. Tellis and Travis Tanner, 61–125. Seattle, WA: National Bureau of Asian Research, 2012.

Erickson, Andrew S. and Austin M. Strange, *Six Years at Sea . . . and Counting: Gulf of Aden Anti-Piracy and China's Maritime Commons Presence*. Washington, D.C.: The Jamestown Foundation, 2015.

Erickson, Andrew S., Abraham M. Denmark, and Gabriel Collins. "Beijing's 'Starter Carrier' and Future Steps: Alternatives and Implications." *Naval War College Review* 65, no. 1 (2012): 15–55.

Fairbank, John K., and Merle Goldman. *China: A New History*. Cambridge, MA: Harvard University Press, 2006.

Fattouh, Bassam. "An Anatomy of the Crude Oil Pricing System." The Oxford Institute for Energy Studies, WPM 40, 2011.

———. "Oil Market Dynamics Through the Lens of the 2002–2009 Price Cycle." The Oxford Institute for Energy Studies, WPM 39, 2010.

Feng, Lianyong, Yan Hu, Charles Hall, and Jianliang Wang. *The Chinese Oil Industry: History and Future*. New York, NY: Springer Publishing, 2013.

Fettweis, Christopher J. "Free Riding or Restraint? Examining European Grand Strategy." *Comparative Strategy* 30, no. 4 (2011): 316–332.

———. "Threat and Anxiety in US Foreign Policy." *Survival* 52, no. 2 (2010): 59–82.

———. "Threatlessness and US Grand Strategy." *Survival* 56, no. 5 (2014): 43–68.

Fewsmith, Joseph. *Dilemmas of Reform in China: Political Conflict and Economic Debate*. Armonk, NY: M.E. Sharpe, 1994.

Fishelson, James. "From the Silk Road to Chevron: The Geopolitics of Oil Pipelines in Central Asia." The School of Russian and Asian Studies, 2007, http://www.sras.org/geopolitics_of_oil_pipelines_in_central_asia.

Fravel, M. Taylor. "China's Search for Military Power." *Washington Quarterly* 31, no. 3 (2008): 125–141.

Frederick II of Prussia and ed. and trans. Jay Luvaas, *Frederick the Great on the Art of War* (New York: Da Capo Press, 1999), 120.

Freedman, Lawrence. "China as a Global Strategic Actor." In *Does China Matter? A Reassessment: Essays in Memory of Gerald Segal*. Edited by Barry Buzan and Rosemary Foot. New York, NY: Routledge, 2004.

Fucks, Wilhelm. *Mächte von Morgen: Kraftfelder, Tendenzen, Konsequenzen*. Stuttgart: Deutsche Verlags-Anstalt, 1978.

Gaddis, John L. "Containment and the Logic of Strategy." In *The National Interest: A National Interest Reader*. Edited by Benjamin Frankel, 19–36. New York: University Press of America, 1990.

———. "What is Grand Strategy?" Lecture Given at Yale University, New Haven, CT, February 26, 2009.

———. *Strategies of Containment: A Critical Appraisal of American National Security Policy During the Cold War*. New York: Oxford University Press, 2005.

Gallagher, Michael G. "China's Illusory Threat to the South China Sea." *International Security* 19, no. 1 (1994): 169–194.

Geller, Howard, Philip Harrington, Arthur H. Rosenfeld, Satoshi Tanishima, and Fridtjof Unander. "Polices for Increasing Energy Efficiency: Thirty Years of Experience in OECD Countries." *Energy Policy* 34, no. 5 (2006): 556–573.

George, Alexander L. "Case Studies and Theory Development: The Method of Structured, Focused Comparison." In *Diplomacy: New Approaches in History, Theory and Policy*, edited by Paul G. Lauren, 43–68. New York, NY: Free Press, 1979.

George, Alexander L., and Andrew Bennett. *Case Studies and Theory Development in the Social Sciences.* Cambridge, MA: MIT Press, 2005.

George, Alexander L., and Richard Smoke. *Deterrence in American Foreign Policy: Theory and Practice.* New York, NY: Columbia University Press, 1974.

German, F. C. "A Tentative Evaluation of World Power." *Journal of Conflict Resolution* 4, no. 1 (1960): 138–144.

Gholz, Eugene, and Daryl G. Press. "Protecting 'The Prize:' Oil and the U.S. National Interest." *Security Studies* 19, no. 3 (2010): 453–485.

Gill, Bates. *Rising Star: China's New Security Diplomacy.* Washington, D.C.: Brookings Institution Press, 2007.

Glaser, Bonnie S. "China's Grand Strategy in Asia." Statement before the U.S.-China Economic and Security Review Commission, Washington, D.C., March 13, 2014.

Glaser, Charles L. "How Oil Influences U.S. National Security." *International Security* 38, no. 2 (2013): 112–146.

———. *Rational Theory of International Politics: The Logic of Competition and Cooperation.* Princeton, NJ: Princeton University Press, 2010.

Gnansounou, Edgard. "Assessing the Energy Vulnerability: Case of Industrialized Countries." *Energy Policy* 36 (2008): 3734–3744.

Goldstein, Avery. "First Things First: The Pressing Danger of Crisis Instability in U.S.-China Relations." *International Security* 37, no. 4 (2013): 49–89.

———. "Parsing China's Rise: International Circumstances and National Attributes." In *China's Ascent: Power, Security, and the Future of International Politics*, edited by Robert S. Ross and Zhu Feng, 55–86. Ithaca, N.Y.: Cornell University Press, 2008.

———. "The Diplomatic Face of China's Grand Strategy: A Rising Power's Emerging Choice." *China Quarterly* 168 (2001): 835–864.

———. *Rising to the Challenge: China's Grand Strategy and International Security.* Stanford, CA: Stanford University Press, 2005.

Greene, David L., Janet L. Hopson, and Jia Li. "Have We Run Out of Oil Yet? Oil Peaking Analysis from and Optimist's Perspective." *Energy Policy* 34, no. 5 (2006): 515–531.

Griffin, James M. "Petro-Nationalism: The Futile Search for Oil Security," *The Energy Journal* 36, no. 1 (2015): 25–41.

Gupta, Eshita. "Oil Vulnerability Index of Oil-Importing Countries," *Energy Policy* 36 (2008): 1195–1211.

Gurtov, Melvin, and Byong-Moo Hwang. *China's Security: The New Roles of the Military.* Boulder, CO: Lynne Rienner Publishers, 1998.

Hall, Camilla, and Javier Blas. "Qatar Group Falls Victim to Virus Attack," *Financial Times*, August 30, 2012, https://www.ft.com/content/17b9b016-f2bf-11e1-8577-00144feabdc0.

Hamilton, James D. "Causes and Consequences of the Oil Shock of 2008–08." Brookings Papers on Economic Activity, Spring 2009.

———. "Oil Prices, Exhaustible Resources, and Economic Growth." October 2012, Prepared for Handbook of Energy and Climate Change by Routledge.

Hand, Marcus. "Malacca Strait Traffic Hits an All Time High in 2014, VLCCs and Dry Bulk Lead Growth." *Seatrade Maritime News*, February 27, 2015. http://www.seatrade-maritime.com/news/asia/malacca-strait-traffic-hits-an-all-time-high-in-2014-vlccs-and-dry-bulk-lead-growth.html.

Hart, B. H. Liddell. *Strategy: Second Revised Edition*. New York, NY: Praeger Publishers, 1991.

Hattendorf, John B. *The Evolution of the U.S. Navy's Maritime Strategy, 1977–1986*. Newport, RI: Naval War College Press, 2004.

He, Kai. *China's Crisis Behavior: Political Survival and Foreign Policy After the Cold War*. Cambridge, U.K.: Cambridge University Press, 2016.

Heinzig, Dieter. *The Soviet Union and Communist China, 1945–1950: The Arduous Road to the Alliance*. Armonk, NY: M.E. Sharpe Inc., 2004.

Hess, Christian A. "Keeping the Past Alive: The Use of History in China's Foreign Relations." In *Handbook of China's International Relations*, edited by Shaun Breslin, 47–54. New York, NY: Routledge, 2010.

Hilyard, Joseph F. *The Oil and Gas Industry: A Nontechnical Guide*. Tulsa, OK: PennWell Publishing, 2012.

Höhn, Karl H. "Geopolitics and the Measurement of National Power." PhD Dissertation, Universität Hamburg, 2011.

Höhn, Karl. "New Thinking in Measuring National Power." Paper presented at the 2nd Global International Studies Conference by the World International Studies Committee (WISC) at the University of Ljubljana, Ljubljana, Slovenia, July 23–26, 2008.

Höök, Mikael, Tang Xu, Pang Xiongqi, and Kjell Aleklett. "Development Journey and Outlook of Chinese Giant Oilfields." *Petroleum Exploration and Development* 37, no. 2 (2010): 237–249.

Hornby, Lucy. "China Releases First Formal Estimate of Strategic Oil Reserves." *Financial Times*, November 20, 2014. http://www.ft.com/intl/cms/s/0/09c47d8e-7084-11e4-8113-00144feabdc0.html#axzz48HlAYZbA.

Hu, Xuetao, Shuyong Hu, Fayang Jin, and Su Huang. *Physics of Petroleum Reservoirs*. Berlin, DE: Springer-Verlag Berlin Heidelberg, 2017.

Ickes, Harold. Letter to President Franklin D. Roosevelt, August 18, 1943. Box 50, Folder "Saudi Arabian Pipeline." Series 3: Diplomatic Correspondence. FDR Library and Marist College. http://www.fdrlibrary.marist.edu/archives/collections/franklin/?p=collections/findingaid&id=502.

Ikegami, Masako. "China's Grand Strategy of 'Peaceful Rise' A Prelude to a New Cold War?" In *Rise of China: Beijing's Strategies and Implications for the Asia*

Pacific. Edited by Hsin-Huang Michael Hsiao and Cheng-Yi Lin, 21–54. New York, NY: Routledge, 2009.

Information Office of the State Council of the People's Republic of China. "2010 Defense White Paper." March 31, 2011. http://news.xinhuanet.com/english2010/china/2011-03/31/c_13806851.htm.

Inkpen, Andrew, and Michael H. Moffett. *The Global Oil and Gas Industry*. Tulsa, OK: PenWell Publishing, 2011.

Institute of Shipping Economics and Logistics. "Shipping Statistics and Market Review: World Tanker Fleet." 56, no. 3 (2012).

International Energy Agency. "China." http://www.iea.org/publications/freepublications/publication/china_2012.pdf.

———. "Energy Supply Security, Emergency Response of IEA Countries, 2014." https://www.iea.org/publications/freepublications/publication/energy-supply-security-the-emergency-response-of-iea-countries-2014.html.

———. *Statistics*. https://www.iea.org/statistics/.

———. "World Energy Outlook for 2016." http://www.iea.org/newsroom/news/2016/november/world-energy-outlook-2016.html.

International Monetary Fund. *IMF Data*. https://www.imf.org/en/Data.

Itzkowitz Shifrinson, Joshua R., and Miranda Priebe. "A Crude Threat: The Limits of an Iranian Missile Campaign against Saudi Arabian Oil." *International Security* 36, no. 1 (2011): 167–201.

Jakobson, Linda, and Dean Knox. "New Foreign Policy Actors in China." *SIPRI Policy Paper* 26 (2010).

Jewell, Jessica. "The IEA Model of Short-term Energy Security (MOSES) Primary Energy Sources and Secondary Fuels." International Energy Agency 2011.

Ji, You. "Dealing with the Malacca Dilemma: China's Effort to Protect its Energy Supply." *Strategic Analysis* 31, no. 3 (2007): 467–489.

Johnson, Gregory R. "Luttwak Takes a Bath." *Reason Papers* 20 (1995).

Jones, Toby C. *Desert Kingdom: How Oil and Water Forged Modern Saudi Arabia*. Cambridge, MA: Harvard University Press, 2010.

Kalicki, Jan H., and David L. Goldwyn. "Introduction: The Need to Integrate Energy and Foreign Policy." In *Energy and Security: Toward a New Foreign Policy Strategy*. Edited by Jan H. Kalicki and David L. Goldwyn, 1–16. Washington, DC: Woodrow Wilson Center Press, 2005.

Kambara, Tatsu, and Christopher Howe. *China and the Global Energy Crisis: Development and Prospects for China's Oil and Natural Gas*. Northampton, MA: Edward Elgar Publishing, 2007.

Kane, Thomas M. *Chinese Grand Strategy and Maritime Power*. London, U.K.: Frank Cass Publishers, 2002.

Kaplan, Robert D. *Monsoon: The Indian Ocean and the Future of American Power*. New York, NY: Random House Publishing, 2010.

Kaufman, Alison A. "The 'Century of Humiliation,' Then and Now: Chinese Perceptions of the International Order." *Pacific Focus* 25, no. 1 (2010): 1–33.

Kaufman, Alison A., and Daniel M. Hartnett. "Managing Conflict: Examining Recent PLA Writings on Escalation Control." CNA China Studies Report, 2016, CNA

Analysis and Solutions. https://www.cna.org/cna_files/pdf/DRM-2015-U-009963
-Final3.pdf.

Kennedy, Paul. *The Rise and Fall of British Naval Mastery.* Amherst, NY: Humanity Books, 1983.

Khurana, Gurpreet S. "China's 'String of Pearls' in the Indian Ocean and Its Security Implications." *Strategic Analysis* 32, no. 1 (2008): 1–39.

Kim, Kyungnam. "Face Recognition using Principal Components Analysis." Department of Computer Science, University of Maryland College Park. http://www
.umiacs.umd.edu/~knkim/KG_VISA/PCA/FaceRecog_PCA_Kim.pdf; Federal Bureau of Investigation, https://www.fbi.gov/about-us/cjis/fingerprints_biometrics/
biometric-center-of-excellence/files/face-recognition.pdf.

Kirby, Paul. "Russia's Gas Fight with Ukraine." British Broadcasting Corporation, October 31, 2014. http://www.bbc.com/news/world-europe-29521564.

Klare, Michael T. "Energy Security." In *Security Studies: An Introduction*, Edited by Paul D. Williams, 483–496. New York, NY: Routledge, 2008.

———. *Blood and Oil: The Dangers and Consequences of America's Growing Dependency on Imported Petroleum.* New York, NY: Henry Holt and Company, 2004.

Kock-Weser, Iacob. "Chinese Energy Engagement with Latin America: A Review of Recent Findings." Report by Inter-American Dialogue, January 2015. http://www
.thedialogue.org/wp-content/uploads/2015/05/IAD9783ChinaLAweb.pdf.

Krauthammer, Charles. "The Unipolar Moment." *Foreign Affairs* 70, no. 1 (1990), 22–33.

Lai, Hongyi Harry. "China's Global Oil Diplomacy: Is It a Global Security Threat?" *Third World Quarterly* 28, no. 3 (2007): 519–537.

Lake, David A., and Robert Powell. "International Relations: A Strategic Choice Approach." In *Strategic Choice and International Relations*, edited by David A. Lake and Robert Powell, 3–38. Princeton, NJ: Princeton University Press, 1999.

Laliberté, André, and Marc Lanteigne, eds. *The Chinese Party-State in the 21st Century.* New York, NY: Routledge, 2008.

Lanteigne, Marc. *Chinese Foreign Policy: An Introduction.* New York, NY: Routledge, 2009.

Layne, Christopher. *The Peace of Illusions: American Grand Strategy from 1940 to the Present.* Ithaca, NY: Cornell University Press, 2006.

Lee, Pak K. "China's Quest for Oil Security: Oil (Wars) in the Pipeline?" *The Pacific Review* 18, no. 2 (2005): 265–301.

Lesbirel, S. Hayden. "Diversification and Energy Security Risks: The Japanese Case." *Japanese Journal of Political Science* 5 (2004): 1–22.

Li, Nan. "The PLA's Evolving Warfighting Doctrine, Strategy, and Tactics, 1985–95: A Chinese Perspective." *China Quarterly* 146 (1996): 443–463.

Liangxiang, Jin. "Energy First: China and the Middle East." *Middle East Quarterly* 12, no. 2 (2005): 3–10.

Lieberthal, Kenneth, and Michel Oksenberg. *Policymaking in China: Leaders, Structures, and Processes.* Princeton, NJ: Princeton University Press, 1988.

Lijphart, Arend. "Comparative Politics and the Comparative Method." *The American Political Science Review* 65, no. 3 (1971): 682–693.

Lobell, Steven E., Jeffrey W. Taliaferro, and Norrin M. Ripsman, "Grand Strategy between the World Wars." In *The Challenge of Grand Strategy: The Great Powers and the Broken Balance between the World Wars*, edited by Jeffrey W. Taliaferro, Norrin M. Ripsman, and Steven E. Lobell, 1–36. New York, NY: Cambridge University Press, 2012.

Lobell, Steven E., Norrin M. Ripsman, Jeffrey W. Taliaferro. *Neoclassical Realism, The State, and Foreign Policy*. Cambridge, MA: Cambridge University Press, 2009.

Luttwak, Edward N. *Strategy: The Logic of War and Peace*. Cambridge, MA: Harvard University Press, 2003.

———. *The Grand Strategy of the Byzantine Empire*. Cambridge, MA: Harvard University Press, 2009.

———. *The Grand Strategy of the Roman Empire: From the First Century CE to the Third Revised and Updated Edition*. Baltimore, MD: Johns Hopkins University Press, 2016.

———. *The Rise of China vs. the Logic of Strategy*. Cambridge, MA: The Belknap Press of Harvard University Press, 2012.

Mann, James. *About Face: A History of America's Curious Relationship with China, from Nixon to Clinton*. New York: Alfred A. Knopf, Inc., 1998.

Marcell, Valérie. *Oil Titans: National Oil Companies in the Middle East*. Washington, D.C.: Brookings Institution Press, 2006.

Martel, William C. *Grand Strategy in Theory and Practice: The Need for an Effective American Foreign Policy*. New York, NY: Cambridge University Press, 2015.

May, Michael. "Energy and Security in East Asia." Report on America's Alliances with Japan and Korea in a Changing Northeast Asia, *Asia-Pacific Research Center* at Stanford University, 1998.

Mayer, Maximilian, and Jost Wübbeke. "Understanding China's International Energy Strategy." *Chinese Journal of International Politics* 6 (2013): 273–298.

McNally, Robert, and Michael Levi. "A Crude Predicament: The Era of Volatile Oil Prices." *Foreign Affairs* 90, no. 4 (2011): 99–111.

Meidan, Michal, Philip Andrews-Speed, and Xin Ma. "Shaping China's Energy Policy: Actors and Processes." In *China's Search for Energy Security: Domestic Sources and International Implications*. Edited by Suisheng Zhao, 46–71. New York, NY: Routledge, 2013.

Meisner, Maurice. *Mao's China and After: A History of the People's Republic*, Third Edition. New York, NY: The Free Press, 1999.

Miller, Richard G., and Steven R. Sorrell. "The Future of Oil Supply." *Philosophical Transactions of the Royal Society A* 372, no. 2006 (2014): 1–27.

Moran, Daniel. "The Battlefield and the Marketplace: Two Cautionary Tales." In *Energy Security and Global Politics: The Militarization of Resource Management*, edited by Daniel Moran and James A. Russell, 19–38. New York, NY: Routledge, 2009.

Moreira, Susana. "Learning from Failure: China's Overseas Oil Investments." *Journal of Current Chinese Affairs* 42, no. 1 (2013): 131–165.

Mufson, Steven, and Juliet Eilperin. "Trump Seeks to Revive Dakota Access, Keystone XL Oil Pipelines," *Washington Post*, January 24, 2017. https://www.wash

ingtonpost.com/news/energy-environment/wp/2017/01/24/trump-gives-green
-light-to-dakota-access-keystone-xl-oil-pipelines/?utm_term=.dfa96bf804e1.

Murphy, Martin. "Deepwater Oil Rigs as Strategic Weapons, Commentary." *Naval War College Review* 66, no. 2 (2013): 110–114.

Nagar, L., and Sudip R. Basu. "Infrastructure Development Index: An Analysis for 17 Major Indian States," *Journal of Combinatorics, Information and System Science* 27 (2002): 185–203.

———. "Weighting Socio-Economic Indicators of Human Development: A Latent Variable Approach." In *Handbook of Applied Econometrics and Statistical Inference*. Edited by Aman Ullah, Alan T. K. Wan, and Anoop Chaturvedi. New York: Marcel Dekker, Inc., 2002.

Nathan, Andrew J., and Andrew Scobell. *China's Search for Security*. New York, NY: Columbia University Press, 2013.

Naughton, Barry. *Growing Out of the Plan: Chinese Economic Reform, 1978–1993*. Cambridge, MA: Cambridge University Press.

———. *The Chinese Economy: Transitions and Growth*. Cambridge, MA: The MIT Press, 2007.

Navias, Martin S., and E. R. Hooton. *Tanker Wars: The Assault on Merchant Shipping During the Iran-Iraq Conflict, 1980–1988*. New York, NY: I.B. Tauris and Co., 1996.

Newmyer, Jacqueline. "Chinese Energy Security and the Chinese Regime." In *Energy Security and Global Politics: The Militarization of Resource Management*. Edited by Daniel Moran and James A. Russell, 188–210. New York, NY: Routledge, 2009.

Nixon, Richard: "Address to the Nation About National Energy Policy." November 25, 1973, edited by Gerhard Peters and John T. Woolley, The American Presidency Project, http://www.presidency.ucsb.edu/ws/?pid=4051.

Norris, William J. "Economic Statecraft with Chinese Characteristics: The Use of Commercial Actors in China's Grand Strategy." Doctoral Dissertation, Massachusetts Institute of Technology, November 12, 2010.

O'Brien, Kevin, and Rachel Stern. "Introduction: Studying Contention in Contemporary China." In *Popular Protests in China*. Edited by Kevin O'Brien, 11–25. Cambridge, MA: Harvard University Press, 2008.

Office of the Secretary of Defense. *Annual Report to Congress: Military and Security Developments Involving the People's Republic of China 2016*.

Olien, Roger M., and Diana D. Olien. *Oil and Ideology: The Cultural Creation of the American Petroleum Industry*. Chapel Hill, NC: The University of North Carolina Press, 2000.

Ong, Russell. *China's Security Interests in the Post–Cold War Era*. London, U.K.: Curzon Press, 2002.

Opsal, Ryan. "A Key Tool for Energy Investors." Oilprice.com, August 18, 2015, http://oilprice.com/Finance/investing-and-trading-reports/A-Key-Tool-For-Energy-Investors.html.

Opsal, Ryan C., and Remi B. Piet. "China and the Significance of Energy Security." In *Energy Security and Environmental Sustainability in the Western Hemisphere*. Edited by Remi B. Piet, Bruce M. Bagley, Marcelo R.S. Zorovich (Lanham, MD: Lexington Books, 2017).

Organization for Economic Cooperation and Development. *OECD Data*. https://data
.oecd.org/.

Orion, Assaf. "The Dragon's Tail at the Horn of Africa: Chinese Military Logistics
Facility in Djibouti," Institute for National Security Studies, Insight No. 791 (2016).

Owen, Nick A., Oliver R. Inderwildi, and David A. King. "The Status of Conventional World Oil Reserves—Hype or Cause for Concern?" *Energy Policy* 38, no.
8 (2010): 4743–4749.

Painter, David S. "Oil and the American Century." *Journal of American History* 99,
no. 1 (2012): 24–39.

———. *Oil and the American Century: The Political Economy of U.S. Foreign Oil
Policy, 1941–1954*. Baltimore, MD: Johns Hopkins University Press, 1986.

Pala, Christopher. "China Pays Dearly for Kazakhstan Oil." *New York Times*, March
17, 2006, http://www.nytimes.com/2006/03/17/business/worldbusiness/17kazakh
.html?_r=1&.

Pang, Anatole. "Chinese Overseas Oil and Gas M&A Strategy: Assessing the Finan-
cial and Strategic Performance of Foreign Upstream Acquisitions by the Chinese
National Oil Companies, 2005–2013." Master's Thesis, Tsinghua University,
Beijing, 2014.

Pantsov, Alexander V., and Steven I. Levine. *Deng Xiaoping: A Revolutionary Life*.
New York, NY: Oxford University Press, 2015.

Patey, Luke. *The New Kings of Crude: China, India, and the Global Struggle for Oil
in Sudan and South Sudan*. New York, NY: Oxford University Press, 2014.

Paton, James, and Aibing Guo. "Russia, China Add to $400 Billion Gas Deal With
Accord." *Bloomberg*, November 9, 2014. http://www.bloomberg.com/news/ar
ticles/2014-11-10/russia-china-add-to-400-billion-gas-deal-with-accord.

Pei, Minxin. *China's Trapped Transition: The Limits of Developmental Autocracy*.
Cambridge, MA: Harvard University Press, 2006.

People's Daily Online. "China's 'Iron Man' an Undying Legend." September 17,
2009. http://english.people.com.cn/90001/90776/90882/6760061.html.

Peters, Gerhard, and John T. Woolley, editors. "Jimmy Carter: 'The State of the Union
Address Delivered Before a Joint Session of the Congress,' January 23, 1980." The
American Presidency Project. http://www.presidency.ucsb.edu/ws/?pid=33079.

Pincus, Walter. "Secret Presidential Pledges Over Years Erected U.S. Shield for Saudis." *Washington Post*, February 9, 1992, https://www.washingtonpost.com/archive/
politics/1992/02/09/secret-presidential-pledges-over-years-erected-us-shield-for
-saudis/8252af1b-f6f6-43c1-985b-5385b59f90c2/.

Platts. "China's End-October Commercial Crude, Oil Product Stocks Fall on Month."
November 25, 2014. http://www.platts.com/latest-news/oil/singapore/chinas-end
-october-commercial-crude-oil-product-27868887.

Posen, Barry R. "Command of the Commons: The Military Foundation of U.S. Hegemony." *International Security* 28, no. 1 (2003): 5–46.

———. *The Sources of Military Doctrine: France, Britain, and Germany between the
World Wars*. Ithaca, NY: Cornell University Press, 1986.

Posen, Barry R., and Andrew L. Ross. "Competing Visions for U.S. Grand Strategy."
International Security 21, no. 3 (1996): 3–51.

Priest, Tyler. "The Dilemmas of Oil Empire." *Journal of American History* 99, no. 1 (2012): 236–251.

Princeton University Library. "Basic Factors in American Foreign Policy," Dartmouth College; 1949 February 14, George F. Kennan Papers, Box 299, Folder 23, Public Policy Papers, Department of Rare Books and Special Collections.

———. "Measures Short of War (Diplomatic)," National War College; 1946 September 16, George F. Kennan Papers, Box 298, Folder 12, Public Policy Papers, Department of Rare Books and Special Collections.

Ristuccia, Cristiano A. "1935 Sanctions in Italy: Would Coal and Crude Oil Have Made a Difference?" Discussion Papers in Economic and Social History, Oxford University, March 1997. http://www.nuffield.ox.ac.uk/economics/history/paper 14/14paper.pdf.

Rogers, John. editor. *Review of Maritime Transport 2014.* Geneva: UNCTAD, 2014.

Rose, Adam, and Aung Hla Tun. "Oil Pipeline through Myanmar to China Expected to Open in January." Reuters, January 20, 2015. http://www.reuters.com/article/petrochina-myanmar-oil-idUSL3N0U22PP20150120.

Rose, Adam, and Chen Aizhu, "UPDATE 1-China's Strategic Oil Reserves Double to 190 mln bbl–Stats Bureau," Reuters, December 11, 2015. http://www.reuters.com/article/china-oil-reserves-idUSL3N1402YL20151211.

Ross, Robert S. "China's Naval Nationalism: Sources, Prospects, and the U.S. Response." *International Security* 34, no. 2 (2009): 46–81.

Roubini Global Economics. "Oil Security Index." Securing America's Energy Future (SAFE) in partnership with Roubini Global Economics, Quarterly Update, 2014.

Roupas, Christos, Alexandros Flamos and John Psarras. "Comparative Analysis of EU Member Countries Vulnerability in Oil and Gas, Energy Sources." *Part B: Economics, Planning, and Policy* 6 no. 4 (2011): 348–356.

Salidjanova, Nargiza. "Going Out: An Overview of China's Outward Foreign Direct Investment." U.S.-China Economic and Security Review Commission, Staff Research Report, March 30, 2011. https://www.uscc.gov/sites/default/files/Research/GoingOut.pdf.

Sanger, David E. "China's Oil Needs Are High on U.S. Agenda." *New York Times*, April 19, 2006. http://www.nytimes.com/2006/04/19/world/asia/19china.html?ex=&_r=0.

Saul, Jonathan, and Renee Maltezou. "Somali Pirates Capture Oil Tanker Bound for US: Higher Oil Prices Ahead?" *Christian Science Monitor*, February 9, 2011. www.csmonitor.com/World/Latest-News-Wires/2011/0209/Somali-pirates-capture-oil-tanker-bound-for-US-Higher-oil-prices-ahead.

Scheyder, Ernest, and Terry Wade. "U.S. Shale Oil's Achilles Heel Shows Signs of Mending." Reuters, July 1, 2016. http://www.reuters.com/article/us-usa-shale-declinerates-idUSKCN0ZH3RQ.

Scobell, Andrew. *China's Use of Military Force Beyond the Great Wall and the Long March.* Cambridge, U.K.: Cambridge University Press, 2003.

Scott, David. *China Stands Up: The PRC and the International System.* New York, NY: Routledge, 2007.

Secretary of Defense, Department of Defense, Defense Strategy for the 1990s: The Regional Defense Strategy, Washington, D.C., 1993.

Segal, Robert A. "In Defense of the Comparative Method." *Numen* 48, no. 3 (2001): 339–373.

Shambaugh, David. *China Goes Global: The Partial Power*. New York, NY: Oxford University Press, 2013.

Shaofeng, Chen. "China's Self-Extrication from the 'Malacca Dilemma' and Implications." *International Journal of China Studies* 1, no. 1 (2010): 1–24.

———. "China's Self-Extrication from the 'Malacca Dilemma' and Implications." *International Journal of China Studies* 1, no. 1 (2010): 1–24.

Shift Project. "Energy Intensity of GDP." The Shift Project Data Portal. http://www.tsp-data-portal.org/Energy-Intensity-of-GDP#tspQvChart.

Shifter, Michael. "Crackdown in Caracas: Venezuela's Crisis Continues." *Foreign Affairs*, October 14, 2015. https://www.foreignaffairs.com/articles/south-america/2015-10-14/crackdown-caracas.

Shirk, Susan L. "Internationalization and China's Domestic Reforms." In *Internationalization and Domestic Politics*, edited by Robert O. Keohane and Helen V. Milner, 186–208. Cambridge, MA: Cambridge University Press, 1996.

———. *The Political Logic of Economic Reform in China*. Berkley, CA: University of California Press, 1993.

Sick, Gary. "The United States in the Persian Gulf: From Twin Pillars to Dual Containment." In *The Middle East and the United States: History, Politics, and Ideologies, Fifth Edition*. Edited by David W. Lesch and Mark L. Haas, 309–325. Boulder, CO: Westview Press, 2012.

Simoes, AJG and CA Hidalgo. "The Economic Complexity Observatory: An Analytical Tool for Understanding the Dynamics of Economic Development." Workshops at the Twenty-Fifth AAAI Conference on Artificial Intelligence (2011).

Singer, David J., and Melvin Small. "The Diplomatic Importance of States, 1816–1970: An Extension and Refinement of the Indicator." *World Politics* 24, no. 4 (1973): 577–599.

Singh, Mandip. "China's Strategic Petroleum Reserves: A Reality Check." *Institute for Defense Studies and Analysis Issue Brief*, May 21, 2012, http://www.idsa.in/system/files/IB_ChinasStrategicPetroleumReserves_MandipSingh_210512.pdf.

Stockholm International Peace Research Institute. SIPRI Military Expenditure Database. https://www.sipri.org/databases/milex.

Sutter, Robert G. *Chinese Foreign Relations: Power and Policy Since the Cold War*, Third Edition. Lanham, MD: Rowman & Littlefield, Inc., 2012.

Swaine, Michael D. "China's Assertive Behavior—Part 1: On 'Core Interests.'" *China Leadership Monitor* 34 (2011): 1–25.

Swaine, Michael D., and Ashley J. Tellis. *Interpreting China's Grand Strategy: Past, Present, and Future*. Santa Monica, CA: RAND, 2000.

Swann, Christopher, and Wei Gu. "With Oil Deals, Merger Advisors Rejoice." *New York Times*, April 15, 2010. http://www.nytimes.com/2010/04/15/business/15views.html?dbk&_r=0,.

Taipei Times. "MND Admits Strategic Value of Spratly Airstrip." January 6, 2006. http://www.taipeitimes.com/News/taiwan/archives/2006/01/06/2003287638.

Taliaferro, Jeffrey W., Steven E. Lobell, and Norrin M. Ripsman. "Introduction: Neoclassical Realism, the State, and Foreign Policy." In *Neoclassical Realism, the State, and Foreign Policy*. Edited by Steven E. Lobell, Norrin M. Ripsman, and Jeffrey W. Taliaferro, 1–41. New York, NY: Cambridge University Press, 2012.

Tang, Xu, Baosheng Zhang, Mikael Höök, and Lianyong Feng. "Forecast of Oil Reserves and Production in Daqing Oilfield of China." *Energy* 35, no. 7 (2010): 3097–3102.

Treverton, Gregory, and Seth G. Jones. "Measuring Power: How to Predict Future Balances." *Harvard International Review* 27, no. 2 (2005): 54–58.

Tyler, Patrick E. "No Chemical Arms Aboard China Ship." *New York Times*, September 6, 1993. http://www.nytimes.com/1993/09/06/world/no-chemical-arms-aboard-china-ship.html.

———. "U.S. Strategy Plan Calls for Insuring No Rivals Develop." *New York Times*, March 8, 1992. http://www.nytimes.com/1992/03/08/world/us-strategy-plan-calls-for-insuring-no-rivals-develop.html?pagewanted=all.

U.S. Department of State, Office of the Historian. Foreign Relations of the United States, 1977–1980, Volume XVIII, Middle East Region; Arabian Peninsula. https://history.state.gov/historicaldocuments/frus1977-80v18/ch1.

U.S.-China Economic and Security Review Commission. 2011 Report to Congress of the U.S.-China Economic and Security Review Commission, One Hundred Fourteenth Congress Second Session. Washington, D.C.: U.S. Government Publishing Office, 2011.

———. 2016 Report to Congress of the U.S.-China Economic and Security Review Commission, One Hundred Fourteenth Congress Second Session. Washington, D.C.: U.S. Government Publishing Office, 2016.

U.S. Energy Information Administration, China: International Energy Data and Analysis, May 14,2015, https://www.eia.gov/beta/international/analysis_includes/countries_long/China/china.pdf.

United Nations. UN Comtrade Database. https://comtrade.un.org/.

United Nations Development Program. Human Development Report 2013. http://hdr.undp.org/sites/default/files/hdr_2013_en_technotes.pdf.

United Nations Statistical Division. UN Data. http://data.un.org/.

United States Code. "43 U.S.C. 1651: Congressional Findings and Declaration, Chapter 34 Trans-Alaska Pipeline, Pub. L. 93–153, title II, §202, Nov. 16, 1973, 87 Stat. 584." http://uscode.house.gov/browse.xhtml.

United States Department of Justice. "Herfindahl-Hirschmann Index." https://www.justice.gov/atr/herfindahl-hirschman-index.

Vidal, John. "The End of Oil Is Closer than You Think." *The Guardian*, April 21, 2005, https://www.theguardian.com/science/2005/apr/21/oilandpetrol.news.

Vivoda, Vlado. "Diversification of Oil Import Sources and Energy Security: A Key Strategy or an Elusive Objective?" *Energy Policy* 37 (2009): 4615–4623.

Wachtmeister, Henrik, Linnea Lund, Kjell Aleklett, and Mikael Höök. "Production Decline Curves of Tight Oil Wells in Eagle Ford Shale." *Natural Resources Research* (2017): 1–15.

Waltz, Kenneth N. *Theory of International Politics*. Reading, MA: Addison-Wesley Publishing Company, 1979.

Wang, Yuan-kang. *Harmony and War: Confucian Culture and Chinese Power Politics*. New York, NY: Columbia University Press, 2011.

Ward, Andrew. "Saudi Aramco Warns Investment Cuts Risk Long-term Oil Crunch: Crude Producer Says Overall Demand for Fossil Fuels Will Continue to Rise." *Financial Times*, October 11, 2016. https://www.ft.com/content/14ec741a-8f94 -11e6-8df8-d3778b55a923.

Weatherley, Robert. *Mao's Forgotten Successor: The Political Career of Hua Guofeng*. New York, NY: Palgrave Macmillan, 2010.

Wei, Lim Tai. *Oil in China: From Self-reliance to Internationalization*. Singapore: World Scientific Publishing, 2010.

Wei, Zhang, translated by Shazeda Ahmed. "A General Review of the History of China's Sea-Power Theory Development." *Naval War College Review* 68, no. 4 (2015): 80–93.

Wenger, Andreas, Robert W. Orttung, and Jeronim Perovic. *Energy and the Transformation of International Relations: Toward and New Producer-Consumer Framework*. New York, NY: Oxford University Press, 2009.

White House, National Security Strategy, Washington, D.C.: The White House, 1995.

———, National Security Strategy, Washington, D.C.: The White House, 2002.

———, National Security Strategy, Washington, D.C.: The White House, 2006.

———, National Security Strategy, Washington, D.C.: The White House, 2010.

Williams, Justin. "Ghawar Oil Field: Saudi Arabia's Oil Future." *Energy and Capital*, Feb 19, 2013. http://www.energyandcapital.com/articles/ghawar-oil-field/3101.

Wilmot, Chester. *The Struggle for Europe*. Westport, CT: Greenwood Press, 1972.

Wolf, Wojtek M., and Brock F. Tessman. "China's Global Equity Oil Investments: Economic and Geopolitical Influences." *Journal of Strategic Studies* 35, no. 2 (2012): 175–196.

Woodard, Kim. *The International Energy Relations of China*. Stanford, CA: Stanford University Press, 1980.

World Bank. *World Bank Open Data*. https://data.worldbank.org/.

Wu, Gang, Lan-Cui Liu, and Yi-Ming Wei. "Comparison of China's Oil Import Risk: Results Based on Portfolio Theory and A Diversification Index Approach." *Energy Policy* 37 (2009): 3557–3565.

Xu, Jian, Jin-Suo Zhang, Qin Yao, and Wei Zhang. "Is It Feasible for China to Optimize Import Source Diversification." *Sustainability* 6 (2014): 8329–8341.

Xu, Tang, Zhang Baosheng, Feng Lianyong, Marwan Masri, Afshin Honarvar. "Economic Impacts and Challenges of China's Petroleum Industry: An Input-Output Analysis." *Energy* 36, no. 5 (2011): 2905–2911.

Yang, Jian. *The Pacific Islands in China's Grand Strategy: Small States, Big Games*. New York, NY: Palgrave Macmillan, 2011.

Yergin, Daniel. "Ensuring Energy Security." *Foreign Affairs* 82, no. 2 (2006): 69–82.

———. *The Prize: The Epic Quest for Oil, Money, and Power*. New York: Free Press, 2008.

————. *The Quest: Energy, Security, and the Remaking of the Modern World*. New York, NY: The Penguin Press, 2011.

Yoshihara, Toshi, and Richard Sokolsky. "The United States and China in the Persian Gulf: Challenges and Opportunities." *Fletcher Forum of World Affairs* 26, no. 1 (2002): 63–77.

Zhang, Shu G. *Economic Cold War: America's Embargo Against China and the Sino-Soviet Alliance, 1949–1963*. Stanford, CA: Stanford University Press, 2001.

Zhou, Hong, Jun Zhang, and Min Zhang. *Foreign Aid in China*. Berlin, DE: Springer-Verlag Berlin Heidelberg, 2015.

Index

About the Author

Dr. **Ryan Opsal** is currently an Energy Policy Manager for the State of Maryland and an Adjunct Professor in International Relations at Florida International University, where he teaches on issues ranging from security to political economy. His focus areas include energy, political economy, grand strategy, and political risk.